The Achievement of Literary Authority

The Achievement of Literary Authority

Gender, History, and the Waverley Novels

Ina Ferris

Cornell University Press

Ithaca and London

First published 1991 by Cornell University Press.

International Standard Book Number 0-8014-2630-8
Library of Congress Catalog Card Number 91-55076
Printed in the United States of America
Librarians: Library of Congress cataloging information appears on the last page of the book.

⊗The paper in this book meets the minimum requirements of the American National Standard for Information Sciences—Permanence of Paper for Printed Library Materials. ANSI Z39.48–1984.

for Stephen

Contents

Acknowledgments

This is a book about early nineteenth-century literary discourse and the institutions that helped shape that discourse. Its own completion would have been difficult without institutional sympathy and support, and I am especially grateful to the Social Sciences and Humanities Research Council of Canada for the grants that enabled me to do research and write and to the University of Ottawa and the English Department for their generosity in granting leaves from teaching.

I have been equally fortunate in having friends and colleagues who have not only endured but even encouraged my fascination with the phenomenon of the Waverley Novels. I thank in particular Robert Caserio and Steven Cohan for helpful comments and questions when the project was in its initial stages. To April London I owe a special debt. Her thoughtful reading of early versions of my argument helped to sharpen and develop the analysis, and her warm support has been much appreciated. Thanks also to Peter McCormick for timely intervention and encouragement. David Jeffrey, David Shore, and Keith Wilson have provided personal and intellectual support over the years, and I am grateful to them.

Like all books, this book owes a great deal to the work of others. I am indebted in particular to those who have worked on Walter Scott over the years, and some of my more prominent debts are recorded in the text. On a more personal note, I thank Ian Alexander, David Hewitt, and Gary Kelly for organizing the international conferences on Scott at which I tried out some of my ideas before sympathetic and knowledgeable audiences; Marilyn Orr for the pleasure and instruction of talking about Walter Scott with someone who knows him better than I; and

Jane Millgate, Jill Rubinstein, and Harry Shaw for their sympathetic responses to my work. My deepest debt as a student of the Waverley Novels and of nineteenth-century literary history remains to Alexander Welsh, who introduced me to Scott in graduate school, thereby not only reshaping my reading of the history of the novel (and of the novel as history) but presenting me with a puzzle to which this book is a belated response. He himself bears no direct responsibility for my book, but his own work on the Waverley Novels and on other fictions has been a constantly renewable resource through the years, so he cannot entirely escape blame.

The main argument of the book has its roots in a paper on the reception of *Waverley* delivered in 1986 at the first of a series of annual conferences arranged by the Society for the Study of Narrative Literature. These conferences have been the source of a lively and challenging exchange of ideas from which I have profited in many ways. A revised version of my conference paper was published as "Re-Positioning the Novel: *Waverley* and the Gender of Fiction" in *Studies in Romanticism* 28 (1989): 291–301. Copyright © 1989 the Trustees of Boston University. I am grateful to the editors for permission to draw on it in Part One. I am also grateful to the editors of *Journal of Narrative Technique* for permission to use material in Chapter 7 which appeared as "The Historical Novel and the Problem of Beginning: The Model of Scott," *JNT* 18 (1988): 73–82.

In appreciation of the support that has sustained me throughout my career, I dedicate this book to my husband, Stephen. He taught me how to use the computer and very much more.

INA FERRIS

Ottawa, Ontario

Bibliographic Note

A new critical edition of the Waverley Novels is being prepared by the University of Edinburgh Press. In the meantime, all my references to Scott's novels are to first editions with two exceptions: (1) references to *Waverley* are to the recent Oxford edition by Claire Lamont (Clarendon, 1981), which is based on the first edition; (2) references to the introductory matter and notes added by Scott for the "Magnum Opus" edition are to the Centenary Edition of *Waverley Novels*, 25 vols. (Edinburgh: Adam and Charles Black, 1870). For ease of reference, I follow the citation of the volume and page number of the first edition with the chapter as consecutively numbered in most modern editions (e.g., 3:23; chap. 36).

The following is a list of abbreviations used for nineteenth-century critical reviews:

AjR	*Antijacobin Review*
AR	*Annual Review*
BC	*British Critic*
BM	*Blackwood's Edinburgh Magazine*
BR	*British Review*
Champ	*Champion*
CR	*Critical Review*
DM	*Dublin Magazine*
EcR	*Eclectic Review*
EdCIn	*Edinburgh Christian Instructor*
EdM	*Edinburgh Magazine* (continuation of *Scots Magazine*)
EMR	*Edinburgh Monthly Review*

ER	Edinburgh Review
FM	Fraser's Magazine
GM	Gentleman's Magazine
LdM	Lady's Magazine
LM	London Magazine*
Gold's LM	London Magazine; and Monthly Critical and Dramatic Review
MM	Monthly Magazine
MR	Monthly Review
NAR	North American Review
NBR	North British Review
NMM	New Monthly Magazine
NUM	New Universal Magazine
QR	Quarterly Review
SM	Scots Magazine

*Two periodicals of the same name were founded in January 1820, and I follow John O. Hayden (*The Romantic Reviewers, 1802–1824* [London: Routledge, 1969]) in using *LM* to stand for the more famous of the two, the magazine published by Baldwin to which Hazlitt and others contributed. The lesser known magazine was published by Gold; hence the abbreviation Gold's *LM*.

The Achievement of Literary Authority

Introduction

The publication of *Waverley, or 'tis Sixty Years Since* in 1814 was a momentous event for the European novel, launching the series of Waverley Novels that in various and complex ways shaped the writing of fiction for the nineteenth century.[1] The impact of these novels was extraordinary, crossing cultures, genres, classes, and political parties. "To have been alive and literate in the nineteenth century," John H. Raleigh has justly remarked, "was to have been affected in some way by the Waverley novels."[2] A historically central and theoretically exemplary instance of generic innovation, the narratives of the Author of Waverley represent not simply the invention of a new novelistic form, the classical historical novel celebrated by Georg Lukács,[3] but also a (less analyzed) crucial alteration of the generic hierarchy in place at the turn of the nineteenth century.[4] The Waverley Novels moved the novel out of the subliterary margins of the culture into the literary hierarchy, and if the genre, arguably, did not achieve full literary status until the high modern-

1. For a subtle account of Scott's impact on the English novel, see Judith Wilt, "Steamboat Surfacing: Scott and the English Novelists," *Nineteenth-Century Fiction* 35 (1981): 459–86. On the wider, largely European, significance of Scott's fable of history, see Alexander Welsh, *Reflections on the Hero as Quixote* (Princeton: Princeton University Press, 1981), chap. 6.

2. "What Scott Meant to the Victorians," *Victorian Studies* 7 (1963): 10. See also Amy Cruse's chapter "The Waverley Novels and Their Readers," in *The Englishman and His Books in the Early Nineteenth Century* (London: Harrap, 1930).

3. *The Historical Novel*, trans. Hannah and Stanley Mitchell (1937; Harmondsworth: Penguin, 1962).

4. On generic innovation as the alteration of the interrelation of forms in place at a particular historical moment, see Ralph Cohen, "Innovation and Variation: Literary Change and Georgic Poetry," in Ralph Cohen and Murray Krieger, *Literature and History* (Los Angeles: William Andrews Clark Memorial Library, 1974), 3–42.

ism of the early twentieth century, the decisive move from literary outsider to literary insider was initiated by Scott's series of historical fictions. To understand something about their success is to understand something about the construction of literary authority in the very period when the modern literary field was being constituted.

Literary authority regulates generic hierarchy, and this book focuses on the generic implications of the authoritative event of the Waverley Novels. It draws on diverse strands of contemporary literary theory and history, and it makes three enabling assumptions. First, it assumes the existence of a social sphere that one can identify as a literary field. That is, I follow sociologists of literature like Pierre Bourdieu and Alain Viala in recognizing a relatively autonomous matrix of forces and institutions within a culture that counts as a literary field and that is in large part structured by struggles for literary legitimacy.[5] Further, I assume that concentration on the internal discursive relations of this field (as opposed to its various linkings with other fields and discourses) is historically useful. Recent new historicist and cultural materialist interest in the overlapping and homology of diverse cultural discourses has revealed important and suggestive conjunctions, but it has tended to discourage investigation of the internal mobility and productivity of the literary field itself. Literary historians, it seems to me, would do well to pay more direct attention to the contestatory workings of the complicated discourse that Mikhail Bakhtin (whose influence on my

5. In a special issue of *Critical Inquiry* titled "The Sociology of Literature," both Viala and Bourdieu draw out some implications of Bourdieu's notion of the literary field. Viala succinctly defines the field as "the relatively autonomous social space formed by the group of actors, works, and phenomena comprising literary praxis, a space whose structures are defined by the system of forces active within it and by the conflicts among these forces" ("Prismatic Effects," trans. Paula Wissing, *Critical Inquiry* 14 [1988]: 566). In his own contribution to this issue, Bourdieu argues that his concept of the literary field overcomes the opposition between "internal" readings and "external" analysis of literature ("Flaubert's Point of View," trans. Priscilla Parkhurst Ferguson, *Critical Inquiry* 14 [1988]: 539–62). For Bourdieu's early formulation of the concept of the literary field, see "Champs intellectuel et project créateur," *Temps modernes* 22, no. 246 (1966): 865–906. See also Viala's *Naissance de l'écrivain: Sociologie de la littérature à l'âge classique* (Paris: Éditions de minuit, 1985).

work is pervasive) has called "literary language."[6] This book, then, concentrates on the relationship between two forms of literary language—critical discourse and novelistic discourse—in the early decades of the nineteenth century in Britain.

Second, the volume assumes with Bakhtin and with the more formalized reception theory of Hans Robert Jauss that reception plays a formative role in literary history. More specifically, its interest is in the institutional "horizon of expectation," or, to use more Bakhtinian terminology, in the first accentuation that a text receives from those authorized to regulate the literary field.[7] In the early nineteenth century, the critical reviews, themselves performing an innovative role after the founding of the *Edinburgh Review* in 1802, functioned as the main site for the establishment of literary authority. Competing uneasily in the marketplace but modeling themselves on the gentlemanly ideal of the republic of letters, the reviews (like the novel that they regarded so warily) stood in a symbiotic relationship to the culture at large (the problematic "reading public") whose tastes they sought to direct and form. The reviews, frequently linked to but standing officially—even defiantly—apart from publishers, served as the mediating element in the triangular relationships that marked out the literariness (as opposed to the commercialism or politics) of the literary field: text-critic-public, text-critic-republic of letters. But the specter of the commercial and political triangles (text-publisher-market, text-critic-other critics, text-critic-party) shadowed the literary space they

6. See, for example, Bakhtin's classic essay "Discourse in the Novel," trans. Caryl Emerson and Michael Holquist, in *The Dialogic Imagination*, ed. Michael Holquist (Austin: University of Texas Press, 1981).

7. Bakhtin's whole theory of the dialogic assumes the centrality of response in the construction of discourse, and his sense of the continual "reaccentuation" of texts points to the role of response in shaping literary history. For Jauss, see *Toward an Aesthetic of Reception*, trans. Timothy Bahti (Minneapolis: University of Minnesota Press, 1982), especially the landmark essay "Literary History as a Challenge to Literary Theory." Critical interest in the institutional context of reception has been rather slow to develop, but some studies have begun to appear in recent years. See, for example, David H. Richter, "The Reception of the Gothic Novel in the 1790s," in *The Idea of the Novel in the Eighteenth Century*, ed. Robert W. Uphaus (East Lansing: Colleagues Press, 1988), 117–37.

sought to define, and this shadow accounts in part for the intensity of the struggle with the novel, the commercial sister and demeaning double of the gentlemanly reviewer.

My marking of gender in the preceding paragraph points to the third assumption in this book: that in the nineteenth century the history of men writing is entangled with the history of women writing, and that a key project for feminist literary history of any period is to understand the *relations* of gender that structure the literary field.[8] My concern in this book, then, is less with the representation than with the function of gender, specifically with the ways in which gender-constructs inform and maintain the distribution of genres (their status, territory, value, and so forth) at a given historical moment. The play of gender is never simple, even when only one genre is in view. So Lionel Gossman, looking at French Romantic historiography, argues that it draws on male and female signs in defining its project: return to a "maternal" past and construction of a "paternal" future.[9] Even under the male sign, early nineteenth-century history incorporates different modalities of masculinity, while the novel, routinely figured in critical discourse as a female field during the same period, not only is constituted under two different female signs (the female reading and feminine writing defined in Chapter 1) but moves ambiguously under a male sign with the advent of the Author of Waverley.

In using gender terms, I follow the practice of most feminist criticism in English in reserving "female" and "male" to denote that aspect of the code of sexual difference that stresses inherent and natural difference (hence the terms implicate the body and desire); "feminine" and "masculine," on the other hand, connote the codes of propriety that regulate "natural" sexual difference and construct the social roles of gender. These distinctions are not always clear or precise, but they remain useful for analyzing nineteenth-century discourses. The nineteenth-

8. On the importance of male-authored texts to feminist literary history, see Adrienne Munich, "Notorious Signs, Feminist Criticism and Literary Tradition," in *Making a Difference*, ed. Gayle Greene and Coppélia Kahn (London: Methuen, 1985), 238–59.

9. "History as Decipherment: Romantic Historiography and the Discovery of the Other," *New Literary History* 18 (1986): 23–57.

century term "manly," for example, which came to be applied routinely to Scott's novels, sits precisely on the border of "natural" maleness and "social" masculinity.

Following Elaine Showalter's pioneering work on the relations of gender and genre in her influential *A Literature of Their Own*,[10] feminist literary and cultural histories of the nineteenth century have tended to concentrate investigation of the novel, gender, and the politics of literary authority on the middle and late decades of the century. In her recent sociological study of novel writing and publishing, for example, Gaye Tuchman, aided by Nina Fortin, builds on Showalter's model to argue that after 1840 the novel (previously written mostly by women, she hypothesizes) began to be invaded by men, who then distributed the field into lowly popular fiction (female romance) and high-culture art (a male preserve).[11] As Tuchman herself recognizes, neither the play of gender in the regulation of the novelistic field nor the chronology of its change in gender was quite as straightforward as she wants to propose. Moreover, the rhetoric of gender and genre to which she rightly draws attention was set in place much earlier in the century with the founding of the new critical review and with the intervention of Scott's equally new historical novel into a dominantly female field. This is not to claim that no important changes in emphasis and inflection took place in the course of the century, nor that categories other than gender may have come to play an increasingly significant role, especially after the huge success of Charles Dickens.[12] But it is to argue that the early decades of the century produced the structure and main terms of the debate about fiction that would be carried on for the rest of the nineteenth century and, for that matter, well into our own time.

Central to the innovative impact of Scott's novels was their hybrid nature, the transgression of generic boundaries signaled

10. *A Literature of Their Own* (Princeton: Princeton University Press, 1977).

11. *Edging Women Out: Victorian Novelists, Publishers, and Social Change* (New Haven: Yale University Press, 1989).

12. I consider one kind of change in the discursive role of gender from early to midcentury, for instance, in a forthcoming article, "From Trope to Code: The Novel and the Rhetoric of Gender in Nineteenth-Century Critical Discourse," in *Theory, History and the Politics of Gender: Rewriting the Victorians*, ed. Linda Shires (London: Routledge, forthcoming).

in the very name "historical novel," for it allowed important openings in both the fictional and the historical genres dominant in Scott's time. "Genre," of course, is as unstable and fissured as "gender," and both terms may perhaps be understood most usefully as empty (but not meaningless) signifiers, marking out a particular position in a discourse or social formation.[13] They may be filled with different contents at different times, but their place in the structure remains relatively constant. Hence we have the struggle over high status terms like "history" by groups such as women and minorities who seek to establish their legitimacy in their culture: it is to the *place* of history in the hierarchy that they want access. But if it is imperative to recognize the more abstract, structural import of such terms, it is equally imperative to conduct the kind of concrete microanalysis for which Marilyn Butler has so ably argued.[14] Concentrating on three central moments in the career of the figure known as the Author of Waverley,[15] I offer a particularized analysis of the intersections of genre, gender, and literary authority in the establishment of a new form of, and a new place for, the novelistic genre with the invention of the classical historical novel.

Although the Waverley Novels participated in and helped effect the much-discussed transformation of European historical consciousness in the early nineteenth century, the present volume is motivated by a more particular question: how was it that for Scott's first readers the Waverley Novels appropriated so thoroughly the already existing category of historical novel,

13. Making a related point, the historian Joan Scott defines "man" and "woman" as "at once empty and overflowing categories," in "Gender as a Useful Category of Historical Analysis," *American Historical Review* 91, no. 5 (1986): 1074.

14. See, for example, Marilyn Butler, "Against Tradition: The Case for a Particularized Historical Method," in *Historical Studies and Literary Criticism*, ed. Jerome J. McGann (Madison: University of Wisconsin Press, 1985), 25–47.

15. The Author of Waverley is neither exactly the author of *Waverley* nor exactly the author of the collectivity known as the Waverley Novels. Rather, the phrase is itself a name, pointing to the authorial figure and role constructed by the reviews during the period of Scott's official anonymity, when the novels appeared under the rubric "By the Author of Waverley." For a similar use of the phrase, see, for example, Jane Millgate, *Scott's Last Edition: A Study in Publishing History* (Edinburgh: Edinburgh University Press, 1987).

becoming synonymous with it for the rest of the nineteenth century? T. H. Lister could claim in 1832, for example, that all "historical novels" before *Waverley* were "misnamed," and in 1847 *Fraser's Magazine* mistakenly but appropriately assumed that Scott's first critics had invented the term expressly for the Waverley Novels.[16] Scott's fictions, in other words, were as much a sign of the historical as of the literary, and the whole question of their cultural authority hinged on this double identification. The two terms are interdependent, but for analytic purposes, the book is divided into two parts, with each part placing in the foreground one of the two terms.

Part One, "Scott and the Status of the Novel," concentrates on the question of literary status. The issue of gender is central as I outline the assumptions about the novel circulating in the reviews at the time of the publication of *Waverley*. To be sure, neither the reviews nor their readers, as Jon Klancher has forcefully reminded us, were a homogeneous mass.[17] And singular terms like "middle class," it must be remembered, conveniently simplify a complex, highly stratified, and mobile social agency.[18] Nevertheless, it is striking how much the middle-class reviews of the early nineteenth century cohere in their response to the novel. The High Church *British Critic*, the Dissenting *Eclectic Review*, the Whiggish *Edinburgh Review*, and the Tory *Quarterly Review* all have their particular accents, party interests, and special targets, but they share a critical discourse that aligns itself with the hierarchic, male, and basically aristocratic model of the republic of letters. This discourse, as Chapter 1 illus-

16. [T. H. Lister], "The Waverley Novels," *ER* 55 (1832): 64; "Walter Scott—Has History Gained by His Writings?" *FM* 36 (1847): 346.

17. *The Making of the English Reading Audiences, 1790–1832* (Madison: University of Wisconsin Press, 1987). For a study that focuses on the quarterlies in particular, arguing that their audience was relatively homogeneous, see Joanne Shattock, "Spheres of Influence: The Quarterlies and Their Readers," *Yearbook of English Studies* 10 (1980): 94–104. See also her recent book, *Politics and Reviewers: The "Edinburgh" and the "Quarterly" in the Early Victorian Age* (London: Leicester University Press, 1989).

18. Although this is always the case, it is particularly so in the early nineteenth century when, as Leonore Davidoff and Catherine Hall have pointed out, the middle class was very much a loose and diversified configuration rather than a unified block; see their *Family Fortunes: Men and Women of the English Middle Class, 1780–1850* (Chicago: University of Chicago Press, 1987).

trates, responded uneasily to the novel—a form linked to the middle class, the product of the antihierarchical technology of print, and a genre whose long-standing association with women was intensified in the early years of the century when all the notable novelists were female. The two literary discourses (and the reading publics they mediated and constructed) stood in a symbiotic relationship. Popular and unofficial, the novel challenged the disciplinary authority of the reviews even as it sought to establish its credentials on the very grounds of taste, reason, and value controlled by the critical discourse. For its part, critical discourse confronted in the novel its own middle-class origins and anxieties about class, gender, reading, and value, striving to keep the novel outside the literary sphere but compelled finally by its own cultural mandate to begin to constitute the genre as an object of critical discourse, thereby granting it a measure of literary authority.

Around the turn of the century, the novel was beginning to make itself felt decisively as a significant cultural form—one that critical discourse could no longer afford simply to dismiss.[19] These years witnessed the first major and comprehensive collections of novels in English, notably the fifty-volume *British Novelists* edited by Anna Laetitia Barbauld in 1810 and prefaced by her lengthy essay "On the Origin and Progress of Novel-Writing." Scott himself was to be involved in the ten-volume *Ballantyne's Novelists's Library* (1821–24), writing the introductory essays (later collected as *Lives of the Novelists*) that constitute the first important review by a British novelist of his predecessors. In the same year as *Waverley*, a legal colleague of Scott's, John Dunlop, published the ambitious multivolume *History of Fiction*, a survey of fictional forms from Greek romance to the modern novel, and this relatively obscure publication attracted the notice of the two powerful quarterlies, the *Edinburgh*

---

19. For the sense that the novel was beginning to be taken more seriously by the reviews around this time, see John Tinnon Taylor, *Early Opposition to the English Novel: Popular Reaction from 1760 to 1830* (New York: King's Crown Press, 1943), 110; J. M. S. Tompkins, *The Popular Novel in England, 1770–1800* (1932; Lincoln: University of Nebraska Press, 1961), 330; Nancy Armstrong, *Desire and Domestic Fiction: A Political History of the Novel* (New York: Oxford University Press, 1987), 106.

Review and the *Quarterly Review*.[20] Increasingly, the literary reviews are peppered with general articles on novel writing, on
the history of the novel, and on the origins of fiction in general
(a characteristically romantic preoccupation). Reviews of individual novels are often prefaced by lengthy accounts of the
history of the English novel or attempts to establish a taxonomy
of fictional forms, as in William Hazlitt's rarely noticed review
of Fanny Burney's *Wanderer* for the *Edinburgh Review* in 1815.
Titled "Standard Novels and Romances," this review announces itself as an attempt "to contribute something towards
settling the standard of excellence, both as to degree and kind,"
in novel writing, arguing that the criticism of novels "deserves
more attention than we have ever yet bestowed on it."[21] John
Gibson Lockhart echoes Hazlitt's sentiments a few years later
when he notes in the *Quarterly* that the novel is "a department
of English literature, perhaps the most peculiar, certainly the
most popular, and yet, we cannot help thinking, among the
least studied of all that we possess."[22]

Suggestively, the attempts to construct histories and theories
of the novel in the early nineteenth century rely far less on
classical norms than do any such attempts in the eighteenth
century.[23] To be sure, classical roots and literary norms derived
from ancient drama or epic continued to play a prominent role
in authorizing the novel, but the early romantic critics were
turning more and more to the practices of fiction in postclassical

---

20. The full title of Dunlop's work is *The History of Fiction: Being a Critical
Account of the Most Celebrated Prose Works of Fiction, From the Earliest Greek Romances to the Novels of the Present Age*, 3 vols. (London, 1814). The reviews
appear in *ER* 24 (1814): 38–58 and *QR* 13 (1815): 384–408. Robert Colby discusses Dunlop briefly in his valuable survey of nineteenth-century attitudes
toward the novel, "'Rational Amusement': Fiction vs. Useful Knowledge in
the Nineteenth Century," in *Victorian Literature and Society: Essays Presented to
Richard D. Altick*, ed. James R. Kincaid and Albert J. Kuhn (Columbus: Ohio
State University Press, 1984), 46–73.

21. "Standard Novels and Romances," *ER* 24 (1815): 322. One of the few to
comment on Hazlitt's review is Michael Munday, "The Novel and Its Critics in
the Early Nineteenth Century," *Studies in Philology* 79 (1982): 205–26.

22. Review of Scott's *Lives of the Novelists*, *QR* 34 (1826): 350.

23. For a convenient sample of eighteenth-century comments on the novel,
see Ioan Williams, ed., *Novel and Romance, 1700–1800: A Documentary Record*
(New York: Barnes and Noble, 1970).

Europe to find the categories within which to understand this modern literary form. The novel itself, in other words, was becoming a critical category rather than being subsumed under earlier, more authoritative categories like the drama. *Waverley*, I argue, was precisely the text to accelerate this process of incorporation, assuaging critical anxieties so as to allow the novel definitive if still uneasy entry into the literary sphere. As the product of a noted member of the republic of letters (Scott's anonymity was never an obstacle to his first reviewers), this text worked in complex ways not only to legitimate novel writing as a literary activity but to validate novel reading as a male practice.

The validation effected by *Waverley* and its successors depended crucially on their appropriation of the authority of history. Part Two, "Defining the Historical Novel," considers some of the implications for both fiction and history of the kind of historical novel founded by Scott. Structured around the question of the relationship between fictional and historical discourse in this period, it takes as its central moment the publication of *Old Mortality*, an event that occasioned the sharpest critical controversy of Scott's career as the reviews debated the problem of the historical novel. With the shift to this problem in Part Two, the argument about gender and the literary field that dominated Part One gives way to an argument about the contest of genres within the field, for the scene of literary conflict moves from one between masculine and feminine to one within the masculine zone. The problem of masculinity, already introduced in the analysis of *Waverley* and its reception, now comes into sharper if not always explicit focus, as Part Two considers the struggle over cultural power highlighted by the debate in both critical and novelistic discourse over *Old Mortality*. At issue was the question of what counts as history (that is, as the authoritative discourse of the past), a question posed largely in terms of territory, legitimacy, and allegiance to the father. Where the critical reviews of *Old Mortality* (Chapter 5) activated notions of territory and legitimacy in making their case, the counterfictions by John Galt and James Hogg discussed in Chapter 6 invoked an appeal to the father and to the notion of fidelity. Developing a point made earlier in the book when Scott's first novel was placed in relation to alternative fictions of cultural difference by Maria Edgeworth and Lady Morgan (Chapter 4), Chapter 6 argues for the importance of Scott's handling of narrative distance in accounting for the specifically historical authority granted to his, rather than to competing, fictions. Where the Covenanter novels of Galt and Hogg deployed models of the past as presence and repetition of the father, *Old Mortality* assumed its distance and difference, and herein lies the key to its definitive recognition under the sign of history.

But here, as elsewhere, the Waverley Novels exhibit their much-noted duality and doubleness, for distance and difference yield the particularity and vividness that make the past "present." It is in negotiating their relationship to official history that the novels of Scott generated this doubleness and had, in their turn, their effect on history writing. Accordingly, Chapter 7 generalizes the project of the classical historical novel by placing it in relation to the historical genre, arguing that the form of the classical historical novel depends on an oblique relationship to official history. The argument sets up two different points of entry into the problem. First, it considers the particular form of intertextual anxiety symptomatic of historical fiction (that is, its problematic relationship to the authoritative discourse of history) by focusing on the special pressure created by the act of beginning for the historical novelist. Reversing the angle, the second part of the chapter traces the pressure of Scott's historical novel on historiography, taking as a focal point two key nineteenth-century reflections on history writing that invoke the Waverley Novels as exemplary for the practice of history. Both Augustin Thierry and Thomas Babington Macaulay responded to the historical novel as an ancillary form whose insights history had to absorb. But the direction of implication for historical narrative in each differs markedly, underlining Stephen Bann's point about the ambivalence of the muse of history for the nineteenth century: "History as the Law, inscribed on tablets of stone, contrasts and combines with history as a sustaining Otherness."[24] Whereas Thierry derived from the

24. *The Clothing of Clio: A Study of the Representation of History in Nineteenth-Century Britain and France* (Cambridge: Cambridge University Press, 1984), 177.

rich ambivalence of Scott's example a recognition of history as "sustaining Otherness," Macaulay found, by contrast, motive for the expansion of history as "the Law."

The final chapter, focusing on the publication of *Ivanhoe* in 1820 as the culminating moment in the critical process of legitimation that began with *Waverley*, returns more directly to the question of literariness and gender with which the book opened. In canonizing the Author of Waverley, it suggests, the reviews figured his literary power largely through motifs that turn out to be attached to the notion of female reading, but these are now inflected with a positive as opposed to negative value. As a result, Scott comes to occupy a potentially ambiguous discursive space: a "manly" sign that depends in important ways on the trope of female reading. Thomas Carlyle's famous essay of 1838, intensifying the male/female binaries of earlier critics, is exemplary in defining the Author of Waverley as at once "healthy" masculine writer and "diseased" female reader. Thus the Waverley Novels, now located precariously on the very border (inside/outside) of the literary sphere, stand poised for expulsion from the literary space for fiction that they themselves had so decisively helped to create. That expulsion, set in motion by Carlyle, gained momentum by the end of the nineteenth century and was completed in the twentieth century, as Scott's fiction increasingly became identified with children's classics and Hollywood romances.

Largely under the impetus of feminist research and its narrative turn, critical awareness of the variegated fictional practices of the late eighteenth and early nineteenth centuries has been growing rapidly. Neglected women writers like Amelia Opie and Mary Brunton are coming back into print (if not always for very long), and novels like theirs and those of Maria Edgeworth and Lady Morgan have complicated and enriched the fictional field that was regarded for most of the twentieth century as dominated by the solitary and rather anomalous figure of Jane Austen.[25] But the Waverley Novels have profited little from this

25. For the sense of an enlarged field, see, for instance, Ann H. Jones, *Ideas and Innovations: Best Sellers of Jane Austen's Age* (New York: AMS Press, 1986); Terry Lovell, *Consuming Fiction* (London: Verso, 1987); Judith Lowder Newton, *Women, Power, and Subversion: Social Strategies in British Fiction, 1778–1860* (1981;

narrative turn, and they continue to be erased from literary history.[26] Banished first by the modernist paradigms of E. M. Forster and F. R. Leavis,[27] they have proved equally uncongenial (though for different reasons) to poststructuralist and feminist critical paradigms. Clifford Siskin's recent generic history of romanticism, for example, cites Jane Austen (who was rarely noticed in her own time) as central to the reordering of the generic hierarchy effected by the romantic discourse of development. In addition, Nancy Armstrong's influential study of domestic fiction (whose subtitle designates it as history of "the novel") suggestively designates as a "gap" for novel history the period of the dominance of the Waverley Novels.[28]

It is therefore important to remind ourselves of the way in which Scott's contemporaries registered his innovative achievement, and two passages (both connected with the *Edinburgh Review*) will serve to illustrate. The first is from the general article "The Waverley Novels" written by T. H. Lister for the *Edinburgh Review* shortly before Scott's death in 1832. In the course of his article, Lister reminds his readers of the impact of the publication of *Waverley* less than twenty years before:

> In 1813, before the appearance of Waverley, if any one should have ventured to predict that a writer would arise, who, when every conceivable form of composition seemed not only to have been

---

New York: Methuen, 1985); Mary Poovey, *The Proper Lady and the Woman Writer* (Chicago: University of Chicago Press, 1984). Austen still remains the dominant figure, but she is no longer quite so solitary.

Interest in gender is also beginning to redefine the category of "romantic," posing questions about the masculinity of the concepts of poetry inherited from the male poets and critics of the period and about male negotiations of female forms. See, for example, the useful collection of Anne K. Mellor, ed., *Romanticism and Feminism* (Bloomington: Indiana University Press, 1988).

26. A noteworthy exception is Marilyn Butler's *Romantics, Rebels and Reactionaries: English Literature and Its Background, 1760–1830* (New York: Oxford University Press, 1981).

27. E. M. Forster, *Aspects of the Novel* (New York: Harcourt, 1927); F. R. Leavis, *The Great Tradition* (London: Chatto & Windus, 1948). Ian Watt's landmark book, *The Rise of the Novel* (London: Chatto & Windus, 1957), has no place for Scott in its final chapter, "Realism and the Later Tradition: a Note."

28. Clifford Siskin, *The Historicity of Romantic Discourse* (New York: Oxford University Press, 1988) 125–47; Armstrong, *Desire and Domestic Fiction*, 161–62.

tried, but exhausted, should be the creator of one hitherto unknown, and which, in its immediate popularity, should exceed all others—who, when we fancied we had drained to its last drop the cup of intellectual excitement, should open a spring, not only new and untasted, but apparently deep and inexhaustible—that he should exhibit his marvels in a form of composition the least respected in the whole circle of literature, and raise the Novel to a place among the highest productions of human intellect—his prediction would have been received, not only with incredulity, but with ridicule . . . [29]

The rhetoric of exhaustion/renewal centered on the image of a new and abundant spring is typical of the idiom through which Scott's first readers articulated their experience of *Waverley* as an unexpected incursion of energy into a stale form: water in a dry season. Equally typical is Lister's vertical argument, combining the motifs of height and depth, to make the point of a double innovation: the "deep" spring of invention raises the novel from "the least respected in the whole circle of literature" to "a place among the highest productions of human intellect." New form creates a new place.

A similar claim, figured even more intensely and in a rather different rhetoric, structures the recollection of the rise of the novel by the aged first editor of the *Edinburgh Review*. Writing in the 1840s, Francis Jeffrey asserts that the fictional field at the turn of the century was dominated by the "trash and rubbish" of "ordinary Novels." There were, he admits, some notable exceptions like the novels of Maria Edgeworth, but "the staple of our Novel market was, beyond imagination, despicable: and had consequently sunk and degraded the whole department of literature, of which it had usurped the name." Entering this "sunk and degraded" field, the Waverley Novels effected a radical change:

All this, however, has since been signally, and happily, changed; and that rabble rout of abominations driven from our confines for

29. *ER* 55 (1832): 64. Lister's article is reprinted in *A Victorian Art of Fiction: Essays on the Novel in British Periodicals, 1830–1850*, ed. John Charles Olmstead (New York: Garland, 1979), 105–23. Thomas Henry Lister (1800–1842) was a minor novelist allied by marriage with the powerful Whig family of the Edens. His best-known fiction was the society novel *Granby* (1826).

ever. The *Novels* of Sir Walter Scott are, beyond all question, the most remarkable productions of the present age; and have made a sensation, and produced an effect, all over Europe, to which nothing parallel can be mentioned since the days of Rousseau and Voltaire; while, in our own country, they have attained a place, inferior only to that which must be filled for ever by the unapproachable glory of Shakespeare.[30]

Cast now with the supremely canonical Shakespeare ("the unapproachable glory"), Scott is characterized as purifying the novelistic field of the "rabble rout of abominations" that dominated before his intervention. In such terms Jeffrey marks the entrance of the novel into the properly literary sphere, for if novels can achieve "sensation" and "effect" by appealing to readers in the marketplace, they can achieve "a place" in the canon only through recognition by the institutions granted the powers of inclusion and exclusion.

In such a passage, we encounter the distinctive accent of early nineteenth-century literary authority, an accent of particular note given the power of the *Edinburgh Review* in the first two decades of the century.[31] Of special interest is Jeffrey's linguistic excessiveness, an excessiveness that agitates the passage, generating (despite the marks of order and control) a sense of struggle in the literary field. Thus the fondness for exclusive generalization ("All this," "for ever," "nothing parallel") and the puritan rhetoric of condemnation ("that rabble rout of abominations") is not simply an exercise in discipline but the registering of a great drama of pressures and counterpressures, extraordinary heights of achievement and immense depths of depravity. Admittedly, Jeffrey has his calmer moments, but the passage is representative in this: whenever the ordinary or common novel comes into view in the reviews of this period, critical discourse tends to move toward excess. The relationship between these two genres is fraught with a complex tension, and the Waverley Novels as literary-historical event cannot be understood outside the literary discourse that received them.

30. *Contributions to the Edinburgh Review*, 4 vols. (London, 1844). These unpaginated remarks appear in the preface to the collection of novel reviews in volume 3.

31. John Clive argues that the *ER* was at the height of its power around 1814; see his *Scotch Reviewers: The Edinburgh Review, 1802–1815* (London: Faber, 1957).

Part One

Scott and the Status of the Novel

In short, to the largest part of the reading public, including, perhaps, the worthiest portion of it, it must be confessed that the novel, like the pole-cat, was known only by name and a reputation for bad odour.

This state of things was completely changed in less than two years by the irresistible popularity of Scott.

—*Fraser's Magazine* (1847)

1

Critical Tropes:
The Republic of Letters, Female
Reading, and Feminine Writing

We have heard of the republic of letters, till we almost
believe it to exist.

—*Edinburgh Review* (1803)

The founding of the *Edinburgh Review* in 1802 by four under-
employed young Whigs in Tory-controlled Edinburgh was a
definitive moment in the formation of nineteenth-century critical discourse.[1] In his *Life of Lord Jeffrey*, Lord Cockburn recalls
the "electrical" impact of the first issue: "It was an entire and
instant change of every thing that the public had been accustomed to in that sort of composition. The old periodical opiates
were extinguished at once."[2] In his own later assessment of the
impact of the *Edinburgh*, Francis Jeffrey himself argues that the
review succeeded "in permanently raising the standard, and
encreasing the influence of all such Occasional writings; not
only in this country, but over the greater part of Europe, and the
free States of America."[3] Sparking imitators and making itself

1. On the significance of the *ER*, see John Clive, *Scotch Reviewers: The Edin-
burgh Review, 1802–1815* (London: Faber, 1957); John O. Hayden, *The Romantic
Reviewers, 1802–1824* (London: Routledge, 1969), especially chap. 1; Peter F.
Morgan, *Literary Critics and Reviewers in Early 19th-Century Britain* (London:
Croom Helm, 1983). See also the important early study by A. S. Collins, *The
Profession of Letters, 1780–1832* (1928; Clifton, N.J.: Kelley, 1973) and Walter
Bagehot's classic Victorian essay, "The First Edinburgh Reviewers" (1855), reprinted in his *Literary Studies*, ed. Richard Holt Hutton, 2 vols. (London, 1879),
1:1–40.
2. *Life of Lord Jeffrey with a Selection from His Correspondence*, 2 vols. (Edinburgh, 1852), 1:131.
3. Preface to *Contributions to the Edinburgh Review*, 4 vols. (London, 1844),
1:ix.

the subject of critical discussion, the *Edinburgh Review* altered the practice and cultural status of reviewing.

By the end of the eighteenth century, the literary reviews and their editors had come to be regarded widely (if not always fairly) as the hacks and drudges of booksellers, servile toilers in the trade of "puffery" rather than liberal practitioners of the art of criticism.[4] Earlier in the century, when writers like Samuel Johnson and journals like the *Monthly Review* (under Ralph Griffiths) had been engaged in the practice of criticism, it had come to occupy a prominent place in the literary sphere. As noted by Elizabeth Eisenstein, in the course of the eighteenth century, the leadership of the republic of letters shifted from merchant publishers and scholar-printers to the editors of literary reviews.[5] But neither the leadership nor the status was established once and for all, and by 1802 in Britain the whole practice had lost caste. The reviews generally had been moved out of the literary into the commercial sphere, which stood in antithetical relation to it in the culture.[6]

Precisely this identification with trade and commerce caused Francis Jeffrey profound anxiety when he was offered the editorship of the *Edinburgh*, for to commit himself to the review, he feared, was to place at risk his status as a member of the genteel profession of law (and hence potential member of the republic of letters). In May 1803, for example, he wrote to Francis Horner, cofounder of the *Edinburgh* and a fellow lawyer, that assumption of the editorship should not impede his legal career: "It will be known that my connection with the Review is not for life, and that I will renounce it as soon as I can do without it. The risk of sinking in the general estimation, and

4. Derek Roper reviews the negative "legend" of the eighteenth-century review, in *Reviewing before the Edinburgh, 1788–1802* (London: Methuen, 1978), chap. 1. On the centrality of the distinction between "servile" (or "mechanic") trade and "liberal" art in structuring the discourse of civic humanism that generated the trope of the republic of letters in the eighteenth century, see John Barrell, *The Political Theory of Painting from Reynolds to Hazlitt: "The Body of the Public"* (New Haven: Yale University Press, 1986).

5. *The Printing Press as an Agent of Change*, 2 vols. (Cambridge: Cambridge University Press, 1979), 1:xv. See also Alvin Kernan, *Printing Technology, Letters & Samuel Johnson* (Princeton: Princeton University Press, 1987).

6. Barrell emphasizes the antithetical relation of the two spheres in his *Political Theory of Painting*.

being considered as fairly articled to a trade that is not perhaps the most respectable, has staggered me more, I will acknowledge, than any other consideration."[7] A few months later, he wrote again to Horner: "I hope you do not imagine that I have made a *trade* of this editorship" (2:83). Repeatedly, Jeffrey keeps assuring his correspondents in the early days of the review that the *Edinburgh* will be a different kind—and class—of journal, having "none but gentlemen" connected with it (2:74). For the first few numbers, indeed, the journal did not pay its contributors. "It was to be all gentlemen, and no pay," wryly comments Cockburn (1:133). As it turned out, the policy was quickly reversed: not only did the *Edinburgh* pay (very highly); it also forced all contributors to accept payment, thereby ensuring that the gentlemanly distinction between amateur and professional was collapsed in such a way that all contributors could be at once gentlemen and professionals but emphatically not tradesmen or commercial hacks. "If it ever sink into the state of an ordinary bookseller's journal," Jeffrey declared, "I have done with it" (2:74).

Jeffrey's anxiety underlines the degree to which the *Edinburgh Review* had to reclaim a space for criticism in the literary field. It also points to the general instability of the literary field at the end of the eighteenth century. By that time various social, economic, and ideological pressures following the French Revolution and industrialization had fragmented the model of the consensual public sphere, which had been central to the maintenance of literary discourse earlier in the century.[8] This was, in Jon Klancher's phrase, an "inchoate cultural moment";[9] the literary field was being reformed, realigned, and repowered. Of

7. Cockburn, *Life*, 1: 145. Additional quotations by Jeffrey that appear in this paragraph are taken from Cockburn's work, with volume and page numbers cited in the text.

8. The notion of the public sphere (variously termed classical, liberal, bourgeois) has entered the literary-critical vocabulary through the work of Jürgen Habermas, *Strukturwandel der Öffentlichkeit: Untersuchungen zu eine Kategorie der bürgerlichen Gesellschaft* (Darmstadt: Luchterhand, 1962). For relevant studies drawing on Habermas, see Peter Uwe Hohendahl, *The Institution of Criticism* (Ithaca: Cornell University Press, 1982) and Terry Eagleton, *The Function of Criticism: From "The Spectator" to Post-Structuralism* (London: Verso, 1984).

9. *The Making of the English Reading Audiences, 1790–1832* (Madison: University of Wisconsin Press, 1987), 3.

special pertinence to the shape of the new literary review in this process is that the fragmentation of the public sphere was linked, as Peter Hohendahl has argued, to the spread of literacy.[10] The period is filled with signs of an urgent, widespread sense that large numbers of new and diverse readers had appeared on the scene. Whatever the empirical data on literacy (and they are notoriously problematic), the *perception* in the reviews was of a huge, recent increase in readers. Jeffrey, for instance, describes the audience for the reviews as "the growing multitudes," and Walter Bagehot (looking back at the emergence of the *Edinburgh*) interprets its invention of the review essay as symptomatic of the new need to "instruct so many persons."[11]

These "multitudes" and "persons" formed the frequently invoked trope of "the reading public."[12] Neither the actual composition of this public nor its semantic value as a cultural category was fixed or clear, but in general the term seems to have been directed at two primary readership formations. The first is the small, almost exclusively male group that Walter Houghton, drawing on G. M. Young, has called "the articulate classes."[13] Houghton locates these "articulate classes" in diverse sites of social power such as the ministries, industry, the town council, the universities, and parliament. This group, though a much enlarged and less secure readership in comparison to its equivalent in the eighteenth century, constituted "a small minority even of the literate; small, but important—and confused."[14] Also at stake was a second, much larger read-

10. Hohendahl, *Institution of Criticism*, 53–54.
11. Jeffrey, *Contributions*, 1:ix; Bagehot, "The First Edinburgh Reviewers," 3.
12. The classic work on the actual nineteenth-century reading public remains Richard D. Altick, *The English Common Reader: A Social History of the Mass Reading Public, 1800–1900* (Chicago: University of Chicago Press, 1957). For a recent attempt to reconstruct more specifically the readership of the early novel, see J. Paul Hunter, "'The Young, the Ignorant, and the Idle': Some Notes on Readers and the Beginnings of the English Novel," in *Anticipations of the Enlightenment in England, France, and Germany*, ed. Paul J. Korshin and Alan C. Kors (Philadelphia: University of Pennsylvania Press, 1987), 259–82.
13. "Periodical Literature and the Articulate Classes," in *The Victorian Periodical Press: Samplings and Soundings*, ed. Joanne Shattock and Michael Wolff (Toronto: University of Toronto Press, 1982), 3–27. For the phrase "the articulate classes," see G. M. Young, *Victorian England: Portrait of an Age*, 2d ed. (London: Oxford University Press, 1953), 6.
14. Houghton, "Periodical Literature," 7.

ership that included both genders. This was the less institu-
tionally defined, more stratified and unpredictable readership
that the pioneer of cheap literature, Charles Knight, had in
mind when he described the "reading public" as divided into
"almost endless subdivisions, arising out of station, or age, or
average intelligence, or prevailing taste."[15] Knight is writing in
the 1850s after technological advances in printing had made
possible a much more diversified literary market, but his sense
of "the reading public" as a shifting and elusive mass was present in the reviews at the turn of the century as well, especially
when the question of novel readers came into play.

The point is that in neither form did this "reading public"
represent the commonality and consensus (the clubbiness) that
the liberal public sphere ideally embodied. Hence the space of
criticism became less the social space of conversation and exchange among equals (its ideal figuration in the early eighteenth century) than a juridical space of judgment and discipline.[16] If the *Edinburgh Review*, arising as it did out of the clubs
and debating societies central to intellectual life in turn-of-the-
century Edinburgh, was rooted in the classic sites associated
with the liberal public sphere, its notorious motto, *Judex damnatur cum nocens absolvitur* (the judge is condemned when the
guilty go free), signaled at the same time its breakdown.[17]

Critical Discourse, the Novel, and the Republic of Letters

In establishing a new generic model for the literary review,
the *Edinburgh* shaped the potent, anonymous discourse that
would count as legitimate critical discourse for most of the nine-

15. *The Old Printer and the Modern Press* (London, 1854), 185–86.
16. The notion of discourse as discipline has become virtually synonymous
with the name of Michel Foucault, and I draw generally on his work throughout this book.
17. The motto was the subject of much contemporary comment. Witness,
for example, the *New Monthly Magazine*'s acid comment in 1820: "Their very
motto, 'Judex damnatur cum nocens absolvitur,' applied to works offending
only by their want of genius, asserted a fictitious crime to be punished by a
voluntary tribunal. It implied that the author of a dull book was a criminal,
whose sensibilities justice required to be stretched on the rack, and whose
inmost soul it was a sacred duty to lacerate!" ("Modern Periodical Literature,"
NMM 14 [1820]: 305).

teenth century. As Jon Klancher has noted: "No discourse was so immediately identified with power in the nineteenth century as that of the great party quarterlies, the *Edinburgh Review* and the *Quarterly Review.*"[18] Attempting to shape and control reading practices so as to counter the disseminative force of the entry of new groups of readers, the new critical discourse sought to forge a unity that would replace the disintegrated public sphere. Jeffrey was not alone in his sense of "growing multitudes" of readers (and books); reviews of the period are filled with the rhetoric of "the multitude," "the mass," and "the many" who are now entering the culture of literacy. Shortly before the turn of the century (in the resonant year 1789 in fact), the *Lady's Magazine* marvels that just over two centuries ago very few were literate, but now it is "difficult to find any, unless among the very lowest classes, who cannot read and write." Commending in particular the admission of women into literacy, the journal terms it "a happy revolution," for the "charms" thereby added to conversation outlast those of "mere beauty."[19]

Where reading in this article appears as the complacent adjunct of the "conversation" that ensures the proper relation of the sexes, other journals are more concerned with the destabilizing potential of "multitudes" rapidly entering the field. So the *Edinburgh Review* notes with some awe in 1804 that "there are in these kingdoms at least *eighty thousand* readers," an estimate common in the period and generally invoked to underline the enormous number of readers who now were, so to speak, loose in the kingdom.[20] Largely drawn from "the middling classes" that formed the particular target audience of quarterlies like the *Edinburgh*, these readers were imaged as undiscriminating but predisposed to be placed under authority because of a class willingness to grant to texts a special privilege. Jeffrey

18. Klancher, *Making of the English Reading Audiences*, 69.

19. "Hints on Reading," *LdM* 20 (1789): 79.

20. Review of Maria Edgeworth's *Popular Tales, ER* 4 (1804): 329. The source for this common estimate of eighty thousand readers is obscure. A. S. Collins cites Burke in the 1790s in support of the figure but does not name a particular text (*Profession of Letters*, 29). Historians of the novel (e.g., Ian Watt, *Rise of the Novel* [London: Chatto & Windus, 1957], 37) have generally accepted Collins's attribution, but Altick reports that all efforts to locate the statement in Burke's writings have failed (*English Common Reader*, 49n).

argues in 1809, for instance, that "the middling classes" (in contrast to "the fashionable classes") take books seriously; for them, a book "is still a thing of consequence" and is granted "considerable authority among the regulators of their lives and opinions."[21] Jeffrey himself took very seriously the project of turning this inexperienced and vulnerable readership into a responsible "public," a public distinct from the mass readership of whose existence the quarterlies were also well aware.[22]

The formal innovations of the *Edinburgh* were thus specifically aimed at the reformation of readers, that is, at evaluating the reception as much as the production of texts. As frequently noted, the definitive generic change instituted by the *Edinburgh* was the exchange of the eighteenth-century Enlightenment model of encyclopedic coverage (which had governed the monthly reviews of the previous century) for a model of selective evaluation.[23] Announcing the project of the new journal, the editorial statement prefacing the first issue notes that the editors have declined "any attempt at exhibiting a complete view of modern literature," proposing instead "to confine their notice, in a great degree, to works that either have attained, or deserve, a certain portion of celebrity." The key point is the *social* ground ("celebrity"—either attained or deserved) of the selection. The interest of the early *Edinburgh* reviewers, in other words, explicitly lay less in what was being written than in what was—or should be—read. This orientation meant that the purpose and interest of the review did not, as the editors put it, "depend very materially upon the earliness of its intelligence." It chose therefore to publish on a quarterly rather than monthly basis, and in this choice the *Edinburgh* established from the outset the independence of its discourse from the merely temporal: the timeliness that had governed earlier types of re-

21. Review of Maria Edgeworth's *Tales of Fashionable Life*, ER 14 (1809): 376–77.

22. The *Quarterly* review of James Montgomery, *The World before the Flood*, for instance, comments on publishers "whose market lies among that portion of the people who are below what is called the public, but form a far more numerous class" (QR 11 [1814]: 78). On the different readerships of different periodicals in this period, see Klancher, *Making of the English Reading Audience*.

23. For the model that informed the earlier monthlies, see Roper, *Reviewing Before the Edinburgh*, chap. 1.

views. If its discourse was generated by a timely problem (the new literacy), its authority did not derive from being up-to-date. On the contrary. By locating itself in a critical, reflective space organized by general rules and laws that lay outside time, the discourse shaped by the *Edinburgh* could identify itself with the enduring republic of letters. "Poetry has this much, at least, in common with religion," declared Jeffrey in opening his slashing review of Robert Southey's *Thalaba* in the first issue, "that its standards were fixed long ago, by certain inspired writers, whose authority it is no longer lawful to call in question."[24]

If neither Jeffrey's claim nor his juridical tones remained outside question, his journal achieved remarkably rapid and firm authority in the literary field. "There is more of mind in this Review," wrote John Scott (shortly before assuming editorship of the important liberal *London Magazine*), "than ever appeared in any periodical journal of this country."[25] Others, equally persuaded of the preeminence of the early *Edinburgh*, were nevertheless suspicious of its extraordinary success.[26] As early as 1811, Josiah Conder (himself soon to become editor of the nonconformist *Eclectic Review*) registered with alarm the "fearful ascendancy" of the critical reviews. Conder saw in innovations like the *Edinburgh* (whose "great superiority to any existing critical work" he concedes) a sinister extension of critical power: "Criticism has of late years been gradually assuming a new character. It is no longer the study or the pastime of a few. Its dominion is no longer confined to the speculative regions of

24. *ER* 1 (1802): 63.

25. "Comparison of the Edinburgh and Quarterly Reviewers: Chiefly as to Their Intellectual Characters," *Champ* (3 April 1814): 110. John Scott's political hostility to the *QR* is apparent throughout this piece and helps account for his favorable analysis of the *ER*, but similar positive responses to the advent of the *ER* marked the reaction of those of various political ideologies. The Tory Walter Scott, for example, was pleased to write for Jeffrey's journal in the early years, though a violent political dispute did end the connection and lead directly to the founding of the rival *QR* in 1809 by Scott and his political allies.

26. The actual number of readers of the *ER*, as in other nineteenth-century cases, is impossible to determine, for circulation figures tell only part of the story. John Clive records that from 1802 to 1814, the printing of copies of the *ER* increased twenty-fold, i.e., from 750 copies per issue to 13,000 copies. Clive estimates that each copy was probably read by about three people (*Scotch Reviewers*, 135).

taste, and scholastic learning: but *a new power has sprung up under this name*, whose pretensions embrace all the various subjects of human opinion, and whose influence is felt in a greater or less degree through all the orders of society [italics added]."[27] Conder's evocation of a criticism that was "the study or the pastime of a few" allows him to mark a profound and troubling generic change: the extension of discursive control through the new critical discourse, that "new power" which has appropriated the idealized name of Criticism and pervaded "all the orders of society." There is more at work here than a conservative resistance to an opening up and professionalizing of critical discourse, for what troubles Conder, it becomes clear, is an almost Foucauldian sense of the sinister, invisible power of discourse. Summing up his uneasiness in a telling phrase, Conder identifies the power of the new reviews with "the spell of a mysterious anonymous agency" (26).[28]

This anonymous critical discourse regulated entrance into the literary sphere, commonly figured in the period through the traditional metaphor of the republic of letters. By now rather routine and tired, the metaphor was nevertheless central to the notion that criticism employed its juridical power of distinguishing and discriminating in order to maintain the unified—and unifying—space of freely circulating words and ideas that constituted the discourse of civilization. In an age of nationalism and revolution, the republic of letters affirmed internationalism and the harmony of minds in spite of divisions of nation, geography, war, and so forth.

Referring to the common reliance on this image in literary discourse, Thomas Brown comments rather sardonically in 1803 that "we have heard of the republic of letters, till we almost believe it to exist." He identifies this fiction as an "innocent cosmopolitanism" that "atones in some degree the violence of

27. *Reviewers Reviewed* (Oxford, 1811), 2. This pamphlet was published under the pseudonym John Charles O'Reid. Further references will be included in the text. Conder will appear again in Chapter 5 when I discuss the debate over *Old Mortality*.

28. Cf. Klancher's comment that from the time of the *ER*, "the journal represented itself as an institution blending writer, editor, and publisher in what could only appear to be an essentially authorless text" (*Making of the English Reading Audiences*, 51).

national animosity." But he also points out its dependence on a kind of willful blindness: "we willingly forget that the great Republic, one and indivisible, has in truth almost as many divisions, with mutual jealousies and mutual ignorance, as the political relations which it comprehends."[29] Where Brown draws attention to the fragility of the metaphor (and of the political model on which it depends), another Edinburgh reviewer, writing in 1832, prefers to see the metaphor as literally realized in his time. In his article on the Waverley Novels, T. H. Lister recharges the originally classical and aristocratic notion of the literary republic by transforming it into modern, technological space, claiming that until the mid-eighteenth century, "the 'Republic of Letters' existed only in name." It became an actual sign only in "the present period, when the transmission of knowledge is rapid and easy, and no work of unquestionable genius can excite much interest in any country, without the vibration being quickly felt to the uttermost limits of the civilized world."[30] Thus, for Lister, technology allows the republic of letters, whose boundaries are identical with "the uttermost limits of the civilized world," to realize its ideal homogeneity: texts move without resistance across national, linguistic, geographical, and temporal boundaries.

But the flow is purely horizontal, that is, it moves along one band of the social hierarchy. Those below may not participate, for the literary republic is emphatically a space for gentlemen. Given the class anxieties we witnessed on the part of Jeffrey and the question of the editorship, it is hardly surprising to find an insistence on gentility by the discourse seeking to reinstate itself as guardian of the republic. Of greater interest is the way in which that insistence, like the juridical form of the review itself, testifies to the pressure exerted on the literary sphere by the extension of literacy. By the end of the eighteenth century, those outside the traditional sites of certification (like the universities) were writing and publishing more easily, and reviews like the *Edinburgh* complain repeatedly that the lazy and the vain among

29. Review of Charles Villers's *Philosophie du Kant*, ER 1 (1803): 253.
30. "The Waverley Novels," ER 55 (1832): 63.

the uneducated take to literature under the delusion that writing provides an easy route to social and financial success.

Jeffrey's 1803 review of a volume of poetry by John Thelwall, the well-known radical charged in the treason trials of 1794, offers a striking example. Jeffrey opens with the generalization that to those without advantage of birth and fortune, literature seems "so pleasant a way to distinction" that large numbers of the untalented seek entry. Thelwall, son of a silk mercer, turns out to be one of these, and the passage in which Jeffrey castigates Thelwall's "unlucky ambition" suggestively juxtaposes gender, class, criminality, and writing. Thelwall's writing, Jeffrey claims, reveals "traces of that impatience of honest industry, that presumptuous vanity, and precarious principle, that have thrown so many adventurers upon the world, and drawn so many females from their plain work and their embroidery, to delight the public by their beauty in the streets, and their novels in the circulating library."[31] If the writing of lower-class men is a form of roguery, that of women of any class is a type of prostitution. Jeffrey's linking here of female text and female body is standard in the reviews (as we will see in the next section), but the immediate point is the vehemence of the rhetoric of exclusion from the genteel space of the literary sphere. And Thelwall himself accepted both the metaphor of the republic of letters and the norm of gentility when, in his turn, he rebuked Jeffrey for disregarding the rules of "the republic of Letters" and implied that the editor had encouraged the "ungentlemanlike effrontery" of the hecklers encountered by Thelwall when he attempted to give a lecture in Edinburgh.[32]

The vehemence with which a reviewer like Jeffrey sought to exclude outsiders and to establish his own discourse as sign of membership in the republic of letters testifies to a more general anxiety in the reviews about that very membership. Despite the

31. Review of John Thelwall's *Poems Written Chiefly in Retirement*, ER 2 (1803): 200.

32. *A Letter to Francis Jeffray, Esq. on Certain Calumnies and Misrepresentations in the Edinburgh Review* (Edinburgh, 1804), v, x. Cockburn discusses the Jeffrey-Thelwall affair in *Life*, 1:154–55.

university, professional, and club background of many of the reviews, they fit as uneasily into the republic as did the novel that they so often derided as vulgar, commercial, and superficial. Walter Bagehot was to see the review as symptomatic of the temporary, fragmentary character of modern culture ("People take their literature in morsels, as they take sandwiches on a journey").[33] Much earlier in the century Josiah Conder sounded a familiar charge when he lamented that the reviews themselves were undermining "the republic of taste and letters" (27). Identifying the golden age of that republic with the previous century, Conder images the new reviews as usurpers assuming "the chair of Addison and Johnson" (27). Their ascent marks a grievous degeneration of the whole enterprise of criticism: "The mighty critic died," Conder laments, "and has divided his empire among the Reviewers" (28). Such canonization of the eighteenth century was symptomatic of the early decades of the nineteenth century, and it was not confined to the genre of criticism. Indeed the canonical move that allows Conder to define the contemporary practice of criticism as degenerate was used by the same reviews (as the next chapter will illustrate) to degrade contemporary practices of fiction as a decline from the truly novelistic.

The two discourses—novelistic and critical—stood in peculiarly close and tangled relationship in this period, for each was a borderline discourse, neither fully literary nor fully commercial, and each was a response to the expansion of print culture and of the literary marketplace. Even as the reviews sought to define the novel as commercial outsider, not only were the reviews themselves commercial ventures but a significant portion of their targeted audience depended on manufacture and commerce. The cultural signification of the two as signs of modernity overlapped, as did the rhetoric of condemnation that these genres aroused.

Thus Conder argues that the reviews have become "a substitute for all other kinds of reading," attracting "the indolent and the superficial." Their proliferation signals "an encreasing passion for novelty," encourages "superficialness," and de-

33. Bagehot, "The First Edinburgh Reviewers," 2.

mands "the least expense of intellect" (7–12). Less hostile but equally insistent on the way in which the reviews encouraged easy, affective reading was the *New Monthly Magazine*. In 1820 it observed that Joseph Addison and Richard Steele could not have anticipated the "strange era" of writing and reading which they helped to produce: "Little did they know that they were preparing the way for this strange era in the world of letters, when Reviews and Magazines supersede the necessity of research or thought—when each month they become more spirited, more poignant, and more exciting—and on every appearance awaken a pleasing crowd of turbulent sensations in authors, contributors, and the few who belong to neither of these classes, unknown to our laborious ancestors."[34] In awakening "a pleasing crowd of turbulent sensations," the reviews are allied with the sensuous pleasures of romance rather than with the intellectual rigours of "research or thought." And again it is Conder who makes most explicit the buried analogy at work in such representations of the reviews, declaring plainly that the reviews are "hardly less pernicious" than are "novels and works of the same nature." Both genres, he feels, have undermined the authority of the text, and, in discussing the impact of the reviews, he makes this point in a striking erotic metaphor: "[Books] are rather considered as mistresses, than companions and instructors: and hence it is upon their novelty, their external attractions, and transient fame, that they must rest their hope of gaining the regards [sic] of this dissipated age" (8). Those producing such texts are accordingly oddly feminine, and Conder goes on to dismiss the essays of the *Edinburgh Review* as resembling "the brilliant prattle of an accomplished woman, much more than the sober and dignified disquisitions of a moralist" (70).

In light of such charges, the masculine accent of authority exploited by the language of critics like Jeffrey takes on a special charge, and it is not surprising that readers of novels assumed a particular, equivocal significance for writers of reviews. On the one hand, the lowly readers of novels (commonly but not exclusively figured as female) stood disturbingly close to the supe-

34. "Modern Periodical Literature," *NMM* 14 (1820): 304.

rior readers of reviews and had to be distinguished from them—hence they had to be kept outside. On the other hand, the increasing popularity of the novel meant that if the reviews were to establish any control over this clearly potent cultural form, they had to move it into critical discourse—hence, they had to allow it inside. As Nina Baym puts it: "If an educated elite was to reassert its role as arbiter of taste, then it had to establish some control over novels."[35] Suggestively, when a novel is the subject of a review at this time, questions of audience come into explicit focus, as they do not when works of history, theology, or science are at issue. The *Edinburgh* review of Maria Edgeworth's *Popular Tales* (1804), for example, begins by noting the large number of readers "in these kingdoms" and goes on to distinguish Edgeworth's audience from the "millinery misses and aspiring apprentices of our country towns." Her audience, the reviewer explains, is "the great and respectable multitude of English tradesmen, yeomen, and manufacturers . . . the well-educated in the lower and middling orders of the people."[36]

For its part, the rival *Quarterly*, reviewing another Edgeworth novel (*Tales of Fashionable Life*) in 1809, opens its review by using the large size of the audience for novels to justify the notice of novels in the first place: "If the importance of a literary work is to be estimated by the number of readers which it attracts, and the effect which it produces upon character and moral taste, a novel or a tale cannot be deemed a trifling production." But it is less the number than the kind of readers that justifies critical attention, for the novel as a genre "finds readers of a more ductile cast whose feelings are more easily interested, and with

35. *Novels, Readers, and Reviewers: Responses to Fiction in Antebellum America* (Ithaca: Cornell University Press, 1984), 30. Baym's fine study concentrates on the United States and on a later period, but many of the responses she outlines are analogous to those in Britain earlier in the century, even though there are important differences in the way in which culture (the literary republic) was placed in America versus Britain.

36. *ER* 4 (1804): 329–30. The Wellesley Index is unsure of the authorship of this review, though it regards Jeffrey as possible; see *The Wellesley Index to Victorian Periodicals*, ed. Walter E. Houghton, 5 vols. (Toronto: University of Toronto Press, 1966–88). In light of Jeffrey's other reviews of Edgeworth, this identification seems to me doubtful.

whom every impression is deeper, because more new."[37] The comparatives ("more ductile," "feelings . . . more easily interested," "impression . . . more new") invoke two main codes: those of age and gender. The two combine, in fact, to produce the generic young female reader of novels who must be protected by the disciplinary authority of the reviewer. Readers of novels, the reviewer concludes, are "so numerous, and so easily imposed upon, that it is of the utmost importance to the public that its weights and measures should be subject to the inspection of a strict literary police."[38] In the following year a writer signing himself Criticus in the *Scots Magazine* draws on a more ancient and violent model of disciplinary power in order to figure the role of the critic vis-à-vis the novel. Modern novels, Criticus complains, are "useless and absurd productions," which have "bewildered the brains of our young misses, and even engaged the attention of their wise mothers, who ought to be very differently occupied." Because such novels are "pernicious consumers of time, and corrupters of good taste and rational amusement," they must be violently expelled: "it is incumbent on every conductor of a Scottish Review to lash nonsense out of the circle, in order that something better may be substituted in its place."[39]

Part of the problem was that the novel itself was seeking to be "that something better," and the reviews register a degree of resentment and alarm at the way in which novels have begun to encroach on the territory of more serious discourses. Novels are no longer content, one reviewer remarks in 1808, "to make old women sleep, and to keep young women awake." In the past, they had not "interfered . . . with the serious affairs of the world, but dwelt in a region of their own. . . . Now, however, they are frequently made the vehicles of the most marked and serious instruction."[40] A similar sense informs the claim in the Unitarian *Annual Review* that the "importance" that novels

37. *QR* 2 (1809): 146. The reviewers are H. J. Stephen and W. Gifford.
38. Ibid.
39. "On Modern Tales or Novels," *SM* 72 (1810): 418–19. The *SM* had its roots in the urban and cosmopolitan tradition of the Scottish Enlightenment, and it prided itself on maintaining that tradition.
40. Review of Sydney Owenson's *Wild Irish Girl*, *MR*, n.s., 57 (1808): 378.

"have lately been allowed to usurp in the republic of letters, is at once a curious and an alarming symptom of the age." Novels have begun to assume intellectual pretensions, this reviewer finds, offering lessons in history, demonstrating new schemes of education or ethics, and otherwise moving beyond their generic station.[41] What especially alarmed the reviews was less that many of these novels were written by women (though this played its part) than that they were addressed to readers assumed to be "ductile," unable to distinguish between truth and fiction. The High Church *British Critic* is particularly severe on this point, asserting that novels have an insidious power over the minds of "the idle" and "the dissipated," for novels relax their mental guard (such as it is) and so are able to make a deeper impression. Novelists, having recognized the enormous power of their discourse, now "interweave history, morality, and religion into the text of a novel," attempting in effect to change the role of the genre. They seek "to render what was intended only as a refuge for the indolent, a vehicle of instruction and a means of improvement." For all these reasons, then, the *British Critic* calls for "a strict examination of the principles of those works which have so powerful, though imperceptible, an influence on the public mind, lest popularity should be mistaken for truth, and what was written for the purpose of amusement or instruction should become the fruitful source of false notions and erroneous ideas."[42]

Such passages exemplify the uneasy recognition in the reviews that the novelistic field was changing and that its power in the culture at large was something that had to be taken into account. William Hazlitt summed up the case clearly in the *Edinburgh* in 1815 when he urged that novel writing was "a department of criticism, which deserves more attention than we have ever yet bestowed on it."[43] What the novel brought into view for reviews like the *Edinburgh* (themselves innovations in response to the spread of literacy) was a whole field of writing and reading outside critical order and literary control. This field had to be brought within critical discourse (no matter how reluctantly) if the reviews were to maintain their cultural authority.

41. Review of Amelia Opie's *Adeline Mowbray*, AR 4 (1805): 653.
42. Review of Edgeworth's *Patronage*, BC, n.s., 1 (1814): 160.
43. "Standard Novels and Romances," ER 24 (1815): 321–22.

Female Reading, the Ordinary Novel, and Lady Morgan

The strategy of critical appropriation of the novelistic genre was complex and variegated, but the manipulation of gender was always central. Indeed, as argued in the rest of this chapter and the one following, the reviews tend to cohere in beginning their organization of novelistic discourse by dividing contemporary fictional practice into two kinds of novels under two different female signs: that of female reading, which is identified as the origin of the worthless "ordinary novel"; and that of feminine writing, which is credited with generating the superior, morally edifying mode of the "proper novel." These signs, however, are engaged in a closed dialectic, so that both serve to mark confinement and limitation as the general condition of the practice of fiction in the period. They thus open up a space for the construction of another kind of novel under another kind of sign, as the reviews counter present practice with past greatness and begin to set up the male canon that coincides with the "highest" form of novel.

Women, novels, and reading had formed a cluster of critical concern since the eighteenth century, and by the end of that century the perception that the novel was a female field was well entrenched.[44] It is not a question of the actual distribution of women reading or writing novels—the figures are elusive, as Gaye Tuchman discovered in conducting her recent sociological analysis of gender distribution.[45] Rather, the point is the establishment in the culture of what Robert Uphaus has called "the consensus view of female reading": female reading as a practice

44. On the novel as female field by the end of the eighteenth century, see the pioneering surveys of John Tinnon Taylor, *Early Opposition to the English Novel: Popular Reaction from 1760 to 1830* (New York: King's Crown Press, 1943) and J. M. S. Tompkins, *The Popular Novel in England, 1770–1800* (London: Methuen, 1932). For more recent discussions, see Nancy Armstrong, *Desire and Domestic Fiction: A Political History of the Novel* (New York: Oxford University Press, 1987) and Jane Spencer, *The Rise of the Woman Novelist: From Aphra Behn to Jane Austen* (Oxford: Blackwell, 1986).

45. *Edging Women Out: Victorian Novelists, Publishers, and Social Change* (New Haven: Yale University Press, 1989). Tuchman relies on quantitative analysis, and she has to content herself with a heavily qualified statement of probability about the period with which I am concerned: "it seems likely that from the late eighteenth century through the mid-nineteenth century at least half of the published novelists were women" (45).

marked by passion, sentiment, and delusion.[46] This consensus view was restricted neither to critical discourse nor to men. The attack on female reading, as Uphaus points out, was in fact promulgated largely by women who sought to enact an alternative program of reading for women. The negative trope of female reading, for example, informs both the criticism and the fiction of a figure like Mary Wollstonecraft, who was committed to moving women (stigmatized as irrational and hence outside serious discourse) under the sign of rationality.[47] And it underlies the important novelistic subgenre of the anti-romance, which took as its subject the reformation of a foolish female romance reader.[48] The trope of female reading, then, entered into several discourses and was constructed by both genders (including some of the most thoughtful and progressive among them), but my focus is on its role in male critical discourse in the early years of the century.[49]

Through the trope of female reading, the reviews articulate a whole cluster of literary anxieties about technology, the market,

46. "Jane Austen and Female Reading," *Studies in the Novel* 19 (1987): 334–45. The trope of female reading is well illustrated in the surveys of Tinnon Taylor and Tompkins, and analyses appear in Armstrong (*Desire and Domestic Fiction*, 96–108), Spencer (*Rise of the Woman Novelist*, chap. 3), and Mary Poovey, *The Proper Lady and the Woman Writer* (Chicago: University of Chicago Press, 1984). See also the introduction to Carla L. Peterson, *The Determined Reader: Gender and Culture in the Novel from Napoleon to Victoria* (New Brunswick, N.J.: Rutgers University Press, 1987).

47. For a convenient collection of Wollstonecraft's criticism for the *Analytical Review*, see *A Wollstonecraft Anthology*, ed. Janet Todd (Bloomington: Indiana University Press, 1977). Wollstonecraft assumes a female audience for the novel and a mainly female authorship. For an argument that intellectual women like Wollstonecraft perpetuated the social bias against women, see Lynn Agress, *The Feminine Irony: Women on Women in Early-Nineteenth-Century English Literature* (Rutherford, N.J.: Farleigh Dickinson University Press, 1978).

48. Robert A. Colby discusses the anti-romance at the turn of the century in *Fiction with a Purpose: Major and Minor Nineteenth-Century Novels* (Bloomington: Indiana University Press, 1967), chap. 2.

49. Despite the participation of a few women (Anna Laetitia Barbauld is one example), the critical sphere at the turn of the century was a male sphere. Women did not have even the kind of prominence they had achieved at certain moments in the eighteenth century or were to achieve later in the nineteenth. My discussion also assumes an implied male reader for the most part (witness the male "we" and references to women as "the other sex" in cited passages), though I do occasionally refer to journals like *Lady's Magazine* that assumed a female readership. The question of the historical construction of women read-

sexuality, the body—in short, about that which was defined as outside the literary sphere yet obscurely threatened to erupt from within. It is not simply that women writers threatened male dominance of public writing, as in the jocular warning delivered by the *New Monthly Magazine* in 1820: "By the bye, the ladies, if we don't take care, will get the mastery over us, for they are making most rapid inroads into those long-guarded territories of knowledge and learning, in which we had so valiantly entrenched ourselves. . . . Apollo must beware of his bays, or some of the goddesses will be snatching them."[50] This writer clearly does not feel much alarm at the incursion of "the ladies" into the "territories of knowledge and learning" that "we" have dominated, and the reviews in general bear out his attitude. The danger is less displacement than corruption. What emerges as most disturbing about novels and women is that they represent the potential for chaos *within* the nonfictional and male discourse that was central to social, moral, intellectual, political, and—not so incidentally—psychic order for those in charge of the culture.

The striking thing about the characterization of female reading is that it makes reading an act of the body rather than the mind. More specifically, it typifies it as a form of eating, hence as part of the material realm repudiated by the republic of letters as low and unliterary. So ordinary novels are cooked and served up to be "devoured" by eager readers, recalling Pierre Bourdieu's point that the language of gastronomy and the language of aesthetics converge in exploiting similar oppositions (e.g., coarse/delicate, flavorful/insipid) in order to set up the hierarchy of taste (high/low, pure/impure) governing each field.[51] Low and impure, the texts and readers figured in the trope of female reading become the subject of satirical "recipes"

---

ers through the periodical press has not received much attention, but some investigation has begun. See, for example, Kathryn Shevelow, *Women and Print Culture: Constructing Femininity in the Early Periodical* (New York: Routledge, 1989).

50. "On Reading and Readers," *NMM* 14 (1820): 536–37.

51. *Distinction: A Social Critique of the Judgement of Taste,* trans. Richard Nice (Cambridge, Mass.: Harvard University Press, 1984).

in the reviews. The Gothic novel is a favorite target, as in the following example from the turn of the century:

> In the mean time, should any of your female readers be desirous of catching the season of terrors, she may compose two or three very pretty volumes from the following recipe:
> *Take*—An old castle, half of it ruinous.
>> A long gallery, with a great many doors, some secret ones.
>> Three murdered bodies, quite fresh.
>> As many skeletons, in chests and presses.
>> An old woman hanging by the neck, with her throat cut.
>> Assassins and desperadoes, *quant. suff.*
>> Noises, whispers, and groans, threescore at least.
> Mix them together, in the form of three volumes, to be taken at any of the watering-places before going to bed.[52]

Craving (predictable) sensation, the female reader characteristically ingests the text, and she does so in the vaguely erotic posture/space signaled by "before going to bed."

Reading as ingestion and as eroticism function as two key motifs of the trope of female reading. As Nina Baym has observed, the rhetoric of eating and drinking associated with fiction defines the novel as a substance taken into the *body* where it has effects beyond the reader's control.[53] So the *Lady's Magazine* declares in the 1812 article "On Novel-Reading, and the Mischief Which Arises from Its Indiscriminate Practice": "Books, merely entertaining, produce the same effect upon the mental faculties, which a luxurious diet does upon the corporeal

52. "Terrorist Novel Writing," *The Spirit of the Public Journals for 1797*, 1 (1802): 229. The satirical motif of the recipe is not limited to fiction. One finds it used for nonfictional genres like history when the reviewer finds the conventions of the genre to have lost their explanatory power, but the other "recipes" are neither as physical nor as gendered as the ones for fiction. J. A. Murray affords an example in his review of a history by Alexander Stephens in the *ER* 3 (1804): 488–91. Murray damns the work by giving a "receipt" for the writing of history, noting that in order to produce the required "philosophical disquisition," the historian "has nothing to do but to take some authors who have written on the progress of civilization from the savage to the hunting state, and to add a few remarks upon the feudal system, serfs, villains, vassalage—the progress of commerce, and the distinction of ranks" (491). This has the great advantage, he adds, of doing as well for almost any one modern history as for another.

53. Baym, *Novels, Readers, and Reviewers*, 58.

frame: they render it incapable of relishing those pure instructive writings, which possess all the intrinsic qualities of wholesome, unseasoned food."[54] Aside from clearly placing the novel with impure writing, a passage like this dissolves the distinction between "mental faculties" and "the corporeal frame" in such a way that reading becomes literally a form of eating. From here it is but a short step to the frequent charge in the period that novel reading led to disease, breakdown, and other maladies in women that straddled the border between the physical and the psychological. The *Scots Magazine* is entirely conventional in its 1802 article "On Novels and Romances," which cites a medical treatise claiming that "young females" may be "precipitated" into the disorder of "an extravagant degree of love" merely by "reading improper novels."[55] The Society of Friends banned novels, and Thomas Clarkson's account of the movement in 1806 records that "a physician of the first eminence" found that "music and novels have done more to produce the sickly countenances and nervous habits of our highly educated females, than any other cause that can be assigned." The problem with novels, it appears, is that "excess of stimulus on the mind from the interesting and melting tales, that are peculiar to novels, affects the organs of the body, and relaxes the tone of the nerves."[56]

"Melting tales," like the "melting tones" of music, are linked to sedentary habits and to a relaxed body. Novel reading in particular seems literally to affect the backbone; certainly, the posture of the novel reader is rarely upright. The most common image is that of the reader on the sofa, an image whose lux-

54. *LdM* 43 (1812): 222.

55. *SM* 64 (1802): 471–72. The notion that reading novels produced disease is not restricted to the Anglo-American tradition. Foucault, for example, cites similar charges in eighteenth-century France, including the following one in 1768: "The existence of so many authors has produced a host of readers, and continued reading generates every nervous complaint; perhaps of all the causes that have harmed women's health, the principal one has been the infinite multiplication of novels in the last hundred years . . . [sic] a girl who at ten reads instead of running will, at twenty, be a woman with the vapors and not a good nurse" (*Madness and Civilization*, trans. Richard Howard [New York: Vintage, 1965], 219).

56. *Portraiture of Quakerism*, 3 vols. (New York, 1806), 1:135n. I am indebted to Anthony Harding for drawing special attention to this work.

uriousness and languor Charles Knight nicely crystallizes in his description of the archetypal novel reader as "the luxurious fair one, who lolled upon the sofa through a long summer's day."[57] Associated with sofas and softness, novel reading is located outside the sites of legitimate, upright reading: the study and the library.[58] In dubious spots like watering places, hairdressing shops, and bedrooms, novel readers typically pursue a kind of horizontal reading—supine, erotic, luxurious, and vaguely Oriental. Suggestively, one of the stock references in the period was Thomas Gray's remark on reading fiction: "Now as the paradisiacal pleasure of the Mahometans consists in playing upon the flute and lying with Houris, be mine to read eternal new romances of Marivaux and Crébillon."[59]

Constructed in this way, reading becomes a form of sensuality. It is not simply the romantic *content* of the ordinary novel that is seductive and inflaming; the act of reading itself becomes identified with pleasuring the body, even with the working of sexual desire. A notable example is afforded by the article "On Novels and Romances" in the *Scots Magazine* cited above. In the standard rhetoric of the period, the writer worries that women, who form the bulk of the novel audience, are more vulnerable to fiction because they are "circumscribed" by society and have "flexible" minds, along with "quickness and delicacy of sensation." Absorbed by endless love stories, women readers sacrifice sleep and develop a "false estimate" of life. While such charges were routine, the highly sexual language used to describe the experience of female reading is rather less so:

They return with palled senses, to the world's concerns, after revelling in the luxurious and voluptuous descriptions, which appear in

57. Knight, *Old Printer and the Modern Press*, 230.
58. On this point, see Tinnon Taylor, *Early Opposition to the English Novel*, 8.
59. *Correspondence of Thomas Gray*, ed. Paget Toynbee and Leonard Whibley, 3 vols. (Oxford: Clarendon, 1935), 1:192. The passage appears in a letter to West in April 1742. Charles Knight concludes his image of the fair one on the sofa with the comparison, "as Gray did when he was deep in Crébillon" (*Old Printer and the Modern Press*, 230). Walter Scott was also fond of Gray's remark, invoking it, for example, in his article on Alain Le Sage and in his review of *Frankenstein*. Both are reprinted in the useful collection *Sir Walter Scott on Novelists and Fiction*, ed. Ioan Williams (New York: Barnes and Noble, 1968).

the pages of a novel—scenes on which their readers' enraptured fancy is ever found to dwell with inexpressible delight; but which, at last, irresistibly impel the tender and too susceptible heart, to yield to the delusive sensations of bliss, with which the bosom is filled.[60]

Reading a story, the orgasmic language suggests, provides the sexual satisfaction that real life (and men) do not.[61] Some such suspicion may help account for the resentment of female reading that surfaces so often in the reviews, most often in the conventional charge that novel reading takes wives and daughters away from their domestic duties and diverts their emotional energies from their families.[62]

Like its readers, the novel in the trope of female reading is all body. The ordinary novel stocked by the circulating library is emphatically a thing, a product of paper and print, and its physical existence is constantly foregrounded, as in the comment by a writer for the *Gentleman's Magazine* that the events in novels are "inflicted with a beautiful type, and upon paper wire-wove and hot-pressed."[63] In a similar vein, Sydney Smith observes in the *Edinburgh Review* that the Minerva Press has always on hand a "ready composed" stock of type to produce its novels of adultery.[64] The point of such comments is to draw attention to the artificiality of novels, to their divergence from real life, but the effect is more ambiguous, for there is something oddly sexual about print and paper in this discourse. The

60. "On Novels and Romances," *SM* 64 (1802): 471.

61. Ruth Perry, arguing that the eroticism of novels functioned to enclose women in bourgeois ideology, makes the point that the intoxication of reading novels resembled the intoxication of romantic love (*Women, Letters, and the Novel* [New York: AMS Press, 1980], chap. 6).

62. David H. Richter notes that the chief complaint against fiction at the end of the eighteenth century was that it seduced women from the actual world and from their social duties ("The Reception of the Gothic Novel in the 1790s," in *The Idea of the Novel in the Eighteenth Century*, ed. Robert W. Uphaus [East Lansing: Colleagues Press, 1988], 123–25). The fear that fiction encouraged women to neglect the domestic realm persisted well into the nineteenth century. See, for example, Kate Flint, "The Woman Reader and the Opiate of Fiction: 1855–1879," in *The Nineteenth-Century British Novel*, ed. Jeremy Hawthorn, Stratford-upon-Avon Studies, 2nd series (London: Edward Arnold, 1986), 47–62.

63. "The Projector, No XLIX," *GM* 75 (1805): 912.

64. Review of Mme de Stael's *Delphine*, *ER* 2 (1803): 176.

book itself becomes a source of pleasure, as in the comment in the *New Monthly Magazine* that "we know of no pleasure like that of getting a new and well-written novel into our possession, and after commencing the attack by assaulting its yet untouched leaves with our long, smooth, white paper-knife, sitting down where one knows one shall not be disturbed, and becoming acquainted with a dozen or two of people of different characters . . . without the slightest danger of their ever doing any thing but entertain one."[65] While various pleasures mingle here, the physical, quasi-sexual pleasure of penetration is the one on which the writing dwells.

If the man stands outside the body of the text whereas the woman inhabits it, both forms of pleasure cohere in transforming the text into female body. Repeatedly, the reviews present a curious collapsing of text, writing, and reading into female body. And that collapse serves to underline the way in which the novels incorporated under the sign of female reading exemplified an unliterary allegiance to the "low" taste of the senses. John Wilson Croker's review of *The Wanderer* by Fanny Burney is exemplary. Croker begins by turning Burney's text into the body of her famous early heroine: "The Wanderer has the identical features of Evelina—but of Evelina grown old; the vivacity, the bloom, the elegance, 'the purple light of love' are vanished; the eyes are there, but they are dim; the cheek, but it is furrowed; the lips, but they are withered." Behind the identification with Evelina, of course, is the identification of both heroine and text with Burney herself, and it is this identification that motivates the entire elaboration of the image. Burney and her text become the same body, and that body does not grow up or mature: it simply grows old. Croker concludes the image by characterizing Burney-*The Wanderer* as "an old coquette who endeavours, by the wild tawdriness and laborious gaiety of her attire, to compensate for the loss of the natural charms of freshness, novelty, and youth."[66]

In the same review Croker draws on a second theme that enters into the matrix of female reading and materiality when

65. "On Reading and Readers," *NMM* 14 (1820): 538.
66. *QR* 11 (1814): 125–26.

he scorns "the thousand-and-one volumes with which the Minerva press inundates the shelves of circulating libraries."[67] For all its self-indulgence, female reading is oddly impersonal in that predictability is its condition. It both is and seeks sameness, demanding "repetition of the same adventures, the same language, and the same sentiments" in an endless loop.[68] Demand stimulates a supply of equally impersonal texts, and here the trope of female reading incorporates the motif of print. Over and over again, the ordinary novel is depicted as stamped out by machines, produced not by authors but by printing presses. It thus appears as a discourse outside the author-function identified by Foucault as fundamental to the category of the literary as it was developed by the eighteenth and early nineteenth centuries.[69] Ordinary novels appear in "hordes," "swarms," and "shoals"—always plural and undifferentiated. So the *Lady's Magazine* registers its sense that books are "heaped upon the world . . . in multitudes," while Anna Barbauld deplores the "trash" that is "poured out upon the public from the English presses."[70] Summing up the critical consensus, the *Gentleman's Magazine* mockingly elaborates a commercial metaphor of "manufactories" of novels established to ensure "a regular supply of sameness," thereby underlining the general critical perception that the ordinary novel participated in an economic system of manufacture and consumption rather than in the literary reciprocity of writing and reading.[71]

Relegated to the servile sphere of trade and commerce, the ordinary novel nevertheless marked a discursive promiscuity and fertility that threatened to overwhelm the literary sphere.

67. Ibid., 124.

68. "The Projector, No XLIX," GM 75 (1805): 911–12.

69. "What Is an Author?" in *Language, Counter-Memory, Practice*, trans. Donald F. Bouchard and Sherry Simon, ed. Donald F. Bouchard (Ithaca: Cornell University Press, 1977), 113–38. See also Martha Woodmansee, "The Genius and the Copyright: Economic and Legal Conditions of the Emergence of the 'Author'," *Eighteenth-Century Studies* 17 (1984): 425–48.

70. "Hints on Reading," LdM 20 (1789): 79; Barbauld, "On the Origin and Progress of Novel-Writing," in *The British Novelists*, 50 vols. (London, 1810), 1:58.

71. "The Projector, No LXXXVIII," GM 78 (1808): 882–85. On the novel as commodity, see Terry Lovell, *Consuming Fiction* (London: Verso, 1987), chap. 3.

As the satiric imagery of hordes and swarms suggests, critical discourse responded to the ordinary novel as a signifier of a potentially uncontrollable, destructive energy. The dark side of the reproductive power of printing and writing, it threatened to smother and fragment civil society, more specifically the quasi-aristocratic hierarchy on which the literary sphere depended. Print, as Walter Benjamin has noted, withers the "aura" of the work of art, and Elizabeth Eisenstein has drawn attention to the antihierarchical implications of print culture in relation to the scribal culture that it displaced.[72] Nineteenth-century writers were well aware of such implications, and Thomas Carlyle makes the point with characteristic firmness and alarm in his essay on Walter Scott, an essay that is especially careful to keep "Book-publishing and Book-selling" apart from "Literature": "For if once Printing have grown to be as Talk, then DEMOCRACY (if we look into the roots of things) is not a bugbear and probability, but a certainty, and event as good as come!"[73]

Reinforcing the political anxiety was a related temporal anxiety that assumes special pertinence for the problem of the regulation of novelistic discourse. Print culture yields a paradoxical temporality in that it at once transcends and surrenders to linear flow. If print makes books permanent, it also makes them ephemeral, a contradictory effect of print culture that Alvin Kernan has termed its "library" effect in contrast to its "remainder-house" effect.[74] For the critical reviews, themselves more clearly a product of the multiplying rather than the canonizing power of print, the ordinary novel opened up an anxiety about their own status that the anonymous authority of critical discourse was designed to overcome and disguise. It was not only novels that were characterized in terms of inundation, fragmentation, and transience. Josiah Conder sounded a familiar note when, in commenting on the state of periodical literature, he drew attention to "the number and talents of rival

72. Benjamin, "The Work of Art in the Age of Mechanical Reproduction," in *Illuminations*, trans. Harry Zohn, ed. Hannah Arendt (1955; New York: Schocken, 1969), 217–51. Eisenstein stresses the antihierarchical implications of print throughout *The Printing Press as an Agent of Change*.

73. *Critical and Miscellaneous Essays*, 5 vols. (London, 1899), 4:82.

74. Kernan, *Printing Technology*, 54–55.

hosts, of every dimension and character, pouring from the press" (7).

This "deluge" of periodicals, Klancher has argued, was registered by the middle-class audience as a sign of the dissolution of cultural duration into "mere random impulses, smudging past and future into an endlessly repetitive, disorganized present."[75] Critical discourse organized itself precisely to shape such fluidity and randomness into meaningful pattern—into signs. But its own involvement in "the times" implicated it in that which it sought to order. Walter Bagehot recognized this implication when he read the genre of the review as a sign of "the casual character of modern literature" because "everything about it is temporary and fragmentary." For confirmation of his point, Bagehot looked to a railway stall, appropriately placing the modern scene of reading in the space of transit: "People take their literature in morsels, as they take sandwiches on a journey. The volumes at least, you can see clearly, are not intended to be everlasting. It may be all very well for a pure essence like poetry to be immortal in a perishable world; it has no feeling; but paper cannot endure it, paste cannot bear it, string has no heart for it."[76] In its very playfulness, the passage is a measure of the confidence of critical discourse by midcentury, for Bagehot readily highlights a dependence on matter and time— the "perishable world" scorned by "pure" essences like poetry. But the reviewers attempting to establish that discourse earlier in the century could not afford his levity. Exploiting gender codes, they constructed the fugitive writing and reading of modernity into a female trope and rescued for themselves a certain ungendered seriousness.

The case of Sydney Owenson, better known by her married name, Lady Morgan, provides a particularly interesting gloss on the generalizations about the reviews and female reading made above. Neither anonymous scribbler nor producer of potboilers, Morgan achieved a reputation with the great success of her third novel, *The Wild Irish Girl*, in 1806, a novel widely regarded as the first "National Tale" (see Chapter 4). Its harp-

75. Klancher, *Making of the English Reading Audiences*, 73.
76. Bagehot, "The First Edinburgh Reviewers," 2–3.

playing Gaelic heroine, Glorvina, sparked a whole set of commercial Glorvina products from bodkins to cloaks, and Morgan herself (following the cultural tendency to conflate female text and female body) adopted something of her heroine's style.[77] Dependent on her own resources, Morgan wrote prolifically and in several genres: poetry, biography, travelogue, cultural commentary, literary essay. When the *Monthly Review* reviewed *The Wild Irish Girl* two years after its publication, for example, it also reviewed in the same issue her recent publications in two other genres: a collection of poems called *The Lay of an Irish Harp* and a volume of essays titled *Patriotic Sketches of Ireland*.[78] Morgan was a social and literary success, making her way despite low family connections (her father was an itinerant Irish actor), an ardent Irish nationalism, frequently unpopular liberal politics, and the drawbacks of gender. In 1837 she was awarded by the prime minister the first literary pension ever offered to a woman by the British government.[79]

Morgan, then, was an unusually successful literary woman, but the critical terms in which she was cast locate her within the negative paradigm of female reading. To be sure, the reviews acknowledge in her writing a certain mimetic power, generally commending Morgan for her delineation of Irish scenery and Irish manners. Her patriotism, as well, is often noted with approval even as her Irishness is assumed to account (along with her gender) for her failings.[80] But two characteristics emerge as most insistent—her sensibility and her ambition. The three re-

77. Morgan thus encouraged the kind of conflation that we witness in these verses addressed to her by J. Atkinson of Dublin: "For sure Glorvina lives reviv'd in you; / And to complete the moral story told, / May you another Mortimer behold!" (*MM* 22 [1806]: 154). Compare the more famous conflation in Kipling's "Jane's Marriage" (appended to his 1926 story "The Janeites"), which also wishes for "Jane" a hero from her novels (Captain Wentworth of *Persuasion*).

78. *MR*, n.s., 57 (1808): 374–84.

79. For a recent account of her life, see Mary Campbell, *Lady Morgan: The Life and Times of Sydney Owenson* (London: Pandora, 1988). See also the chapter on Morgan in Ann H. Jones, *Ideas and Innovations: Best Sellers of Jane Austen's Age* (New York: AMS Press, 1986).

80. See, for example, "On the Living Novelists" (Gold's) *LM* 1 (1820): 606. The reviewer praises Morgan's "intense love" for Ireland and defines her as "a true epitome of Irish talent." Her "Irish talent," it turns out, means that she has "its wonderful powers of imagination; its eloquence, and its feeling, with no inconsiderable share of its puerilities and its bombast."

views gathered in the issue of the *Monthly Review* mentioned earlier are exemplary. The reviewer describes Morgan as "gifted with an ardent mind, and an active imagination," but these "gifts" produce a linguistic excess that is in effect a sign of emptiness: *The Wild Irish Girl* abounds in "high-coloured terms"; the *Patriotic Sketches of Ireland* is full of "swelling diction and high-sounding sensibility"; and *The Lay of an Irish Harp* illustrates "the language of feeling carried to excess."[81] Morgan's excessive sensibility, typically signaled as it is here through metaphors of high color and high sound, hollows out her language, creating a "swelling diction" that is a matter of words rather than of meaning. Such language generates an agitated, neurasthenic text, as becomes clear when the reviewer exploits the text-body analogy of the trope of female reading to lament of Morgan's poetry that "instead of presenting us with a figure that is beautiful and engaging,—which is surely the office of the poet,—this fair writer often drags into our presence a being that is all nerve and agitation, well fitted to torture and offend, but altogether incapable of affording delight."[82] Eschewing the beauty and charm proper to (feminine) poetry, Morgan's text becomes an instance of the female grotesque.

This sense of a high-strung, overwrought writing—and the recoil from it—is symptomatic not only of the male critical reviews but of the response of Morgan's more feminine contemporaries. Jane Austen, for example, drew on the standard text-body analogy but inflected it with her own dryness when she observed of Morgan's writing: "if the warmth of her Language could affect the Body, it might be worth reading in this weather."[83] Maria Edgeworth, on the other hand, disturbed by the tendency to link her name with that of Morgan, flatly declared: "God forbid as my dear father said I should ever be such a thing as that—."[84] It is thus not surprising to find the writer of the 1820 article "On the Female Literature of the Present Age" turn-

81. *MR*, n.s., 57 (1808): 382, 380, 383, 375.

82. Ibid., 375.

83. *Jane Austen's Letters to Her Sister Casssandra and Others*, ed. R. W. Chapman, 2nd ed. (London: Oxford University Press, 1952), 64. The occasion of Austen's remark (17 January 1809) was her having received Morgan's *Ida of Athens*.

84. Quoted by Marilyn Butler, *Maria Edgeworth: A Literary Biography* (Oxford: Clarendon, 1972) 448.

ing with relief from Morgan's "dazzling brilliancy" to "repose on the soft green of Miss Austen's sweet and unambitious creations."[85]

If Morgan's high-colored sensibility threatened the decorum of femininity through a female excessiveness, her ambition challenged it through an assumption of masculine power. So the critic in the *Monthly Review*, commenting on *Patriotic Sketches*, records his disappointment in finding that Morgan here "assumes the office of a philosopher, despises novel writing as an employment much beneath her newly assumed dignity, and sets up for an essayist." Once again, he characterizes her discourse in terms of swelling and emptiness: Morgan fills out each "slender" thought, he remarks, "with ornamental finery, to the size and dignity of a Falstaff." He advises "our fair moralizer" to lay down Rousseau and Volney and "to lead us once again into the appropriate regions of fancy and of poesy."[86] The problem of propriety in gender and genre is articulated even more explicitly by the *Critical Review* a few years later in its review of Morgan's novel *O'Donnel*. After commending Morgan as a "national writer" and as a "descriptive writer," this reviewer stops to deplore "the frequent occasions taken by the fair author to shew [sic] us, that her reading is far beyond the usual studies of her sex; and that she prefers the boldness of masculine reasoning to the softer claims of feminine opinions."[87]

Such motifs structure John Wilson Croker's notorious attack on Morgan in the *Quarterly*, an attack that was decisive in setting her reputation and in making her an object of critical attention in the most powerful sites of critical discourse. Remembered today primarily as the writer of the notorious slashing review of Keats's *Endymion*, Croker was a compatriot but a political opponent of Morgan. A successful Tory politician (member of Parliament and first secretary of the Admiralty), he was also a fellow of the Royal Society, a founder of the Athenaeum Club, and a man of letters, who, aside from his prolific

85. *NMM* 13 (1820): 637.
86. *MR*, n.s., 57 (1808): 382, 384.
87. *CR*, 4th ser., vol. 6 (1814): 277.

reviewing, was a respected editor and authority on the French Revolution.[88] Croker's enmity to Morgan appears to have begun early when he was a young barrister in Dublin and she responded critically to some anonymous satires of which he was widely believed to be the author.[89] Whatever the cause, Croker's attack on Morgan gained her attention and sympathy in the reviews as the victim of an "unmanly attack."[90]

Croker's attack, launched in the first issue of the *Quarterly* in a review of Morgan's novel *Woman: Or Ida of Athens*, replays the familiar motifs—excessive sensibility, overwrought style, pretension—but it exhibits a special sexual and political charge that firmly places Morgan within the syndrome of female reading. Where her story in *Ida of Athens* is "merely foolish" and her language "an inflated jargon," her "sentiments" are much more dangerous: "mischievous in tendency, and profligate in principle; licentious and irreverent in the highest degree."[91] Promiscuous and irreligious, the novel is the product of an unchristian author who substitutes for God a power "that she dignifies with the name of Nature, which . . . as we gather from her creed, is to be honoured by libertinism in the women, disloyalty in the men, and atheism in both." For Croker, Morgan's is a transgressive text, crossing the bounds of purity and propriety and wallowing in sexual and political anarchy. What makes Morgan's writing especially offensive is that it is writing by a woman, and at the end of the review Croker moves gender into the foreground as he dismisses Morgan from the literary sphere:

She has evidently written more than she has read, and read more than she has thought. But this is beginning at the wrong end. If we

88. For Croker's career, see Morgan, *Literary Critics and Reviewers in Early 19th-Century Britain* and Hayden, *Romantic Reviewers*.

89. On the Croker affair, see Campbell, *Lady Morgan*, 56, 71–75, 96. For a nineteenth-century account, see the early and entertaining (if not always reliable) biography by William J. Fitzpatrick, *The Friends, Foes, and Adventures of Lady Morgan* (Dublin, 1859).

90. Commenting on Morgan in 1820, for example, the *New Monthly* survey of women writers refers to "the gross and unmanly attack on her feelings and her fame by the Quarterly Reviewers" ("On the Female Literature of the Present Age," *NMM* 13 [1820]: 637).

91. *QR* 1 (1809): 52.

were happy enough to be in her confidence, we should advise the immediate purchase of a spelling book, of which she stands in great need; to this, in due process of time, might be added a pocket dictionary; she might then take a few easy lessons in 'joined-hand,' in order to become *legible*: if, after this, she could be persuaded to exchange her idle raptures for common sense, practise a little self-denial, and gather a few precepts of humility, from an old-fashioned book, which, although it does not seem to have lately fallen in her way, may yet, we think, be found in some corner of her study; she might then hope to prove, not indeed a good writer of novels, but a useful friend, a faithful wife, a tender mother, and a respectable and happy mistress of a family.[92]

The special cut here ("not indeed a good writer of novels") depends on excluding Morgan from writing defined in any sense other than the technical. Practice in spelling and inscription, combined with the exercise of the virtues of self-denial and humility, might make possible the transformation of "idle raptures" into real-life productivity. The literary sphere is closed, but the domestic sphere may still be open.

Croker continued his attacks on Morgan in the *Quarterly*, notably in a long article on her *France* in 1817, but the terms of his critique were established by this first review.[93] What his persistence generated was not so much a development of his own argument as a defense of Morgan in rival journals. Defense, however, tended to duplicate rather than displace the critique, as in the *Edinburgh*, which was motivated less to defend Morgan than to protest the Tory attack. Reviewing Morgan's *Life and Times of Salvator Rosa* was William Hazlitt, ideologically opposed to Croker and a much finer literary intelligence but as prone as his Tory rival to wield the well-established tropes of gender in order to dismiss women writers. "We are not among the devoted admirers of Lady Morgan," Hazlitt declares in opening his review, observing that Morgan is "not very judicious, and not very natural." What has prompted the attention of the *Edin-*

---

92. Ibid.

93. Morgan had responded to Croker's attack in her preface to *France* (1817), and this preface in turn inspired the slashing review of that volume in *QR* 17 (1817): 260–86. Campbell discusses the controversy generated by this review and by Morgan's comments on France, in *Lady Morgan*, 149–55.

burgh, he explains, is that "we have never seen anything more utterly unjust, or more disgusting and disgraceful, than the abuse she has had to encounter from some of our Tory journals."[94] Politics and honor satisfied, Hazlitt then goes on to make much the same points as other reviewers: "On the meagre thread of biography, in short, Lady Morgan has been ambitious to string the flowers of literature and the pearls of philosophy, and to strew over the obscure and half-forgotten origin of poor Salvator the colours of a sanguine enthusiasm and a florid imagination!"[95]

The regularity with which Morgan's writing is characterized in terms of the painterly image of color (it is routinely described as "high coloured," "coloured too highly," or, "florid") underlines the degree to which her language was perceived not only as out of proportion but as somehow aggressive—assaulting the eye and calling attention to itself. Certainly, as in Croker's review, she is often advised literally to watch her language (as well as her sentiments). Morgan's own habit of claiming in her prefaces that she had had no opportunity to correct her manuscript invited such advice; moreover, her high sentimental style not only works uneasily in English prose at the best of times but was old-fashioned even when she began writing.[96] The important point, however, is the way in which the literary argument about "natural" versus "artificial" style is inflected for gender in the criticism of Morgan. Invoking gender, the reviews can control, defuse, and dismiss the kind of excess that Morgan represents, and a passage in Hazlitt's review in the *Edinburgh* nicely underlines the code that informs critical indignation at the "pre-

94. *ER* 40 (1824): 316.
95. Ibid., 317.
96. Morgan commented on the limitations of English as a language of sentiment in an article on the novel; she argued that the progress of the novel in England had been less rapid because the language itself "affords a less appropriate medium for the development of refined sentiment, for the minute analysis of tender emotion, for those varieties of manner, those shades of character, which are exhibited in the intimate intercourse of social life, and to which the delicate *nuance* of the French, the most artificial of European languages is so exquisitely adapted" ("On the Origin and Progress of Fictitious History," *NMM* 14 [1820]; 27–28). For a useful introduction to the novels of sentiment and sensibility, see Janet Todd, *Sensibility* (London: Methuen, 1986).

tension" of Morgan's writing. "Women write well, only when they write naturally," Hazlitt declares. "And therefore we could dispense with their inditing prize-essays or solving *academic questions;*—and should be far better pleased with Lady Morgan if she would condescend to a more ordinary style, and not insist continually on playing the diplomatist in petticoats, and strutting the little Gibbon of her age!"[97]

The reviews merge the unfeminine ambition of Sydney Morgan with the unfeminine fantasies of female reading by identifying both with an improper relationship to language and genre. Confusion, imbalance, and excess mark desire in both cases, and both involve a loosening and crossing of culturally fundamental boundaries: between reality and fiction, public and private, masculine and feminine. Both are defined in terms of the vulgar body, as the rhetoric of criticism conflates reading, writing, and text, materializing them as female body. In their materiality, women contaminate and invade the abstract and intellectual realm of signification conventionally opposed to material and animal being. Inappropriately strutting in petticoats, Morgan demeans the sphere of significant public action and discourse guarded by the reviews.

Feminine Writing, the Proper Novel, and Amelia Opie

In light of the disturbing energies of female reading, it is not surprising that Sydney Smith urged as one argument in favor of female education in 1810 the degree to which serious knowledge would eradicate the taste for the "horrid trash of novels" and promote "a calm and steady temperament of mind."[98] But a fictional form was already in place to do precisely that. Standing against the ordinary novel, ready to harness the asocial energies of female reading, was feminine writing, specifically the proper novel that directly functioned as a corrective counterfiction. This pattern of contesting versions of womanhood in the fic-

---

97. *ER* 40 (1824): 318.
98. Review of Thomas Broadhurst's *Advice to Young Ladies on the Improvement of the Mind, ER* 15 (1810): 312.

tional field was by no means new. Popular fiction in the eighteenth century, as John Richetti notes, witnessed the countering
of the disreputable tradition of women novelists like Delarivière
Manley and Elizabeth Haywood by "a counter-tradition of the
moral lady novelist." At her most exemplary in Mrs. Aubin, the
lady novelist developed a formative public image as "moral
censor of the age," an image that not only became increasingly
powerful in the course of the eighteenth century but moved
firmly into the nineteeth.[99] In the wake of the popularity of
Gothic romance and a new interest in educational reform, the
turn of the century produced a whole series of women like
Maria Edgeworth, Hannah More, and Jane West who developed the fictional form that we know as the proper novel.[100]

The function of the proper novel as corrective to female reading was quite explicit and was explicitly recognized in the reviews. The *Monthly Review*, for example, published the following notice of Hannah More's *Coelebs in Search of a Wife* in 1809:

> By the usual furniture of circulating libraries, deceptive views of
> life, a false taste, and pernicious principles, have been dissemi-
> nated; and it is the commendable object of the writer of these vol-
> umes before us to counteract the poison of novels by something
> which assumes the form of a novel; to read a lecture to the fair sex
> on "their being, end, and aim;" to repel the tyranny of fashion and
> the fascination of example; to shew them what they ought to pur-
> sue, in order to qualify themselves for wives; and to inculcate those
> religious and moral principles by which they ought to be gov-
> erned.[101]

As an antidote to the "poison of novels," the proper novel
"assumes the form of a novel" but only in order to reform the
practice of reading novels and to direct its readers to "what they
ought to pursue, in order to qualify themselves for wives." The
proper novel has proper names; that is, individual novelists
(and not generic types) are credited with its functioning. So
John Scott includes a note on the late Mary Brunton in an article

---

99. *Popular Fiction before Richardson* (Oxford: Clarendon, 1969), 229–40.
100. On the proper novel, see Poovey, *Proper Lady and the Woman Writer*.
101. *MR*, n.s., 58 (1809): 128.

on the Author of Waverley, lamenting her death because novels like hers kept readers "safe from seduction."[102] In the same year, a review of Amelia Opie's *Tales of the Heart* commends Opie as a novelist whose works "confine the imagination within due bounds, direct it to proper objects, inculcate sound and approved principles, and tend altogether, in rational and practical points of view, to improve the head and the heart."[103] In contrast to the language of languor, seduction, irresponsibility, and desire that characterized female reading, feminine writing is constructed in the language of enclosure and decorum: "confine . . . within due bounds," "direct . . . to proper objects," "sound and approved principles," "rational and practical," and so on. Where the ordinary novel sprawls and proliferates, the "well-conducted" proper novel regulates and controls; it replaces body with virtue, as it promulgates—and itself enacts— the restrained values of propriety. It is no accident that the Mary Brunton lauded by John Scott should write novels with titles like *Self-Control* and *Discipline*.

What critical reputation the contemporary novel had in the first decades of the nineteenth century derived from the proper novel, which was widely perceived as possessing a kind of realism and a social utility that the ordinary novel so conspicuously lacked. Remarking on the lessening of prejudice against novels in 1814, the *Quarterly* attributed it in part to their recent moral improvement, an improvement owing in large measure to the fact that novels had "fallen very much into the hands of the other sex, who are restrained by education, disposition, and custom within those bounds which have been too frequently passed by the celebrated writers [i.e., Richardson, Rousseau, Fielding] of whom we have just ventured to complain."[104]

The "restrained" form of the proper novel seems to have been practiced almost exclusively by women. Certainly, the novelists consistently cited as exemplary by the reviews were all women, and the *Antijacobin Review* is representative, at least in this one

102. "The Author of the Scotch Novels," *LM* 1 (1820): 11.
103. Gold's *LM* 2 (1820); 178.
104. [John Ward], review of Edgeworth's *Patronage*, *QR* 10 (1814): 303.

respect, in declaring in its review of *Waverley* in 1814 that "among the novellists [sic] of the present day, the female writers have borne away the palm."[105] Its own honor roll includes Jane West, Maria Edgeworth, Ann Radcliffe, Elizabeth Hamilton, and Mary Brunton. Other reviews added other names (Elizabeth Inchbald, for instance), but none in 1814 included Jane Austen, whose first important notice did not appear until the 1815 review of *Emma* in the *Quarterly* by Walter Scott.[106] Austen, however, produced the novel that remains the best-known example of the way in which the proper novel functioned self-consciously as antidote to female reading, *Northanger Abbey*. Catherine Morland, heroine of the novel, is the foolish female reader who cannot distinguish between forms of fiction and forms of experience, and through her Austen makes clear the distrust of sensibility and of absorbed reading that she shared with Wollstonecraft and others interested in the project of making women more rational.

But in the male literary reviews the proper novel typically functioned less as a sign of rationality than as a sign of the feminine virtues, virtues whose conservative appeal may have made sense but which had little to do with Enlightenment values like rationality. What relieved the reviewers was the prospect of feminine writing—of which the proper novel was only one (if privileged) example—whose central characteristic was restraint. A memorable articulation of the theme of restraint appeared in a review of Felicia Hemans's *The Sceptic; a Poem* in the *Edinburgh Monthly Review* in 1820. Peppered with terms like "elegance," "delicacy," and "gentleness," the review commends Hemans for staying within the proper bounds of gender: "With more than the force of many of her masculine competitors, she never ceases to be strictly *feminine* in the whole current of her thought and feeling, nor approaches by any chance, the verge of that free and intrepid course of speculation, of which

---

105. *AJR* 47 (1814): 217. Stuart Curran draws attention to the number of now mostly forgotten women active in various genres at this time in "The I Altered," *Romanticism and Feminism*, ed. Anne K. Mellor (Bloomington: Indiana University Press, 1988) 185–207.

106. *QR* 14 (1815): 188–201. Although dated October 1815, this issue did not in fact appear until March 1816.

the boldness is more conspicuous than the wisdom, but into which some of the most remarkable among the female literati of our times have freely and fearlessly plunged." Where "female literati" are marked by recklessness, expending energy unwisely, the "feminine" Hemans operates within an economy of prudence. And the reviewer stresses (as will reviewers of Edgeworth) that this economy of prudence depends not simply on working within certain bounds but on placing bounds on one's own talents and imagination. "Nothing surely can be more beautiful and attractive than such a character as this,—richly endowed with every gift which is calculated to win regard or to command esteem, yet despising all false brilliancy, and keeping every talent in sweet and modest subordination to the dignity of womanhood."[107] Where Sydney Morgan's "gifts" were nullified by being defined in terms of the "false brilliancy" alluded to here, Hemans' "gifts" are full and real but equally defused, this time by an ethics of containment.

The appeal of femininity tended to override specific political differences and agendas in the reviews. Thus Amelia Opie, a former actress linked to the Godwin-Wollstonecraft circle, was praised for her pure and charming writing by both a cultural arbiter of whiggish cast like the *Edinburgh* and a vigilant guardian of Anglican orthodoxy and Tory principle like the *British Critic*.[108] Certainly, Opie was no radical despite her links to radical circles, and hers was a quietist temperament (she later joined the Society of Friends and turned to religious and moral writing); nevertheless, she was poised—socially and politically—for sharp critique by the literary republic. Instead, the reviews foregrounded her as exemplar of femininity, finding her writings touched by "simple and unaffected, yet deep feeling" (Gold's *London Magazine*) and "so strictly pure, that they do not present a single thought, or expression, which can excite any improper idea" (*British Critic*).[109]

107. *EMR*, n.s., 3 (1820): 374, 375.

108. Opie is beginning to receive some critical attention. Pandora has republished *Adeline Mowbray* (1804), the novel to which Dale Spender drew attention in *Mothers of the Novel* (London: Pandora, 1986), 315–23. See also the chapter on Opie in Jones, *Ideas and Innovations*.

109. Review of *Tales of the Heart*, Gold's *LM* 2 (1820): 180; review of *Tales of Real Life*, *BC*, n.s., 2 (1814): 654.

Two early reviews of Opie's work in two different genres (poetry and fiction) in the *Edinburgh* serve to outline the trope of feminine writing. The very first issue of the *Edinburgh* contained a routine and condescending review of her *Poems* by Thomas Brown that strikes two keynotes: Opie's strength lies in simplicity of feeling, her weakness in a concomitant failure of formal construction. Over and over again, the reviews construct feminine writing in terms of an opposition between feeling and form, allowing feminine writing special access to certain kinds of feeling but at the cost of formal control. Thus Opie's power for Brown lies in smaller verses, those of "simple tenderness, or simple grief" and, notably, those of "solitary pathos." She is unable to connect isolated emotions or scenes into a meaningful structure, and she is "unfit" for a poetry that attempts "to reason, while it pleases." Lacking architectonic and intellectual power, she can produce only affecting but disconnected fragments of emotion. Brown includes in the review a paragraph consisting of a series of parallel sentences recording Opie's attempts—and failure—at high literary verse forms (the Ovidian epistle, blank verse, the anacreontic), each sentence opening with "She has *attempted* . . ."[110]

Feminine writing is thus placed outside the properly literary sphere; its place is inside the ethical. But the ethical and the literary are always related in this critical discourse, so that feminine writing in effect stands on the border of the literary sphere and not outside it as does female reading. Insofar as feminine writing has literary value, that value depends, paradoxically, on its unliterariness. The *Edinburgh* review of Opie's *Simple Tales* makes the point when it calls her art a "happy art" and explains: "There is something delightfully feminine in all Mrs Opie's writings; an apparent artlessness in the composition of her narrative, and something which looks like want of skill or of practice in writing for the public, that gives a powerful effect to the occasional beauties and success of her genius." Where Morgan's "want of skill" invalidated her art, Opie's validates hers, functioning as testimony to a modesty and innocence in "writing for the public." The "delightfully feminine," then, creates an intimacy that is neither invasive nor scandalous. Operating in the

110. *ER* 1 (1802): 115–16.

space of intimacy and privacy, this writing operates outside an aesthetic of representation and allies itself with an ethics of expression: Opie's texts present "virtuous emotions under a graceful aspect." With its emphasis on simplicity, purity, and spontaneity, the "artlessness" central to the trope of feminine writing marks the critical desire to find an innocent and transparent language that would make possible immediate communication, understanding, and community. "She does not reason well," the reviewer notes, "but she has, like most accomplished women, the talent of perceiving truth, without the process of reasoning, and of bringing it out with the facility and the effect of an obvious and natural sentiment."[111]

As with the texts of female reading, Opie's text merges with authorial body and becomes "amiable" and "beautiful." Its keynote is grace. So Opie's language may be "often inaccurate," but it is "almost always graceful and harmonious." Underlying such representation is the figure of the lady, a figure that explicitly emerges when the reviewer notes that Opie's writing "would do very well to form a woman that a gentleman should fall in love with" (471). As romantic object, the lady is not asexual; on the contrary, the review casts Opie and her writing in delicately sensuous terms. At one point, for example, the reviewer commends her writings for containing "nothing like an ambitious or even a sustained tone in her stories; we often think she is going to be tedious or silly; and immediately, without effort or apparent consciousness of improvement, she slides into some graceful and interesting dialogue, or charms us with some fine and delicate analysis of the subtler feelings, which would have done honour to the genius of Marivaux" (467). Sliding gracefully out of silliness and charming the male reader, Opie's text performs seductively, but it is a seductiveness far removed from the overwrought aggression of "female literati" like Morgan. Moreover, where the sexuality of the texts of female reading generally repelled male critics and attracted female readers, that of the texts of feminine writing, aimed at female readers, clearly charmed gentleman reviewers. Charm, however, was not

111. *ER* 8 (1806): 467. The Wellesley Index speculates that this review may be by Francis Jeffrey. Further references will be included in the text.

enough for the republic of letters, and the review of Opie's *Simple Tales* concludes with an invocation of the intellectual and moral superiority of Maria Edgeworth. In the first years of the century Edgeworth stood in the reviews as normative novelist, and it is to her role in critical discourse about the genre that I want now to turn.

2

Utility, Gender, and the Canon:
The Example of Maria Edgeworth

So far as utility constitutes merit in a novel, we have no
hesitation in preferring the moderns to their predecessors.
—John Wilson Croker, *Quarterly Review* (1814)

Croker's remark is symptomatic, pointing to the centrality of
utility as a critical criterion in the reviews even as it suggests
that utility may not, after all, constitute the supreme merit of a
novel: how far is "so far as"?[1] Both the affirmation and qualifica-
tion of utility as a literary value evoke the figure of Maria Edgeworth in this period (Croker in fact goes on to refer to Edgeworth), for she functioned almost exclusively in the reviews
under its sign.[2] "Utility is her object," wrote John Ward in the
same journal, "reason and experience her means."[3] Standing
against the flamboyant Sydney Morgan and the graceful Amelia
Opie was the earnest Maria Edgeworth for whom novels were
less fictions than didactic tools, part of the rational program of
education that she and her father, Richard Lovell Edgeworth,

1. [John Wilson Croker], review of *Waverley*, QR 11 (1814): 355.
2. Susan M. Gilbert and Susan Gubar argue that women writers themselves
in this period tended to define their writing in terms of utility in order to justify
their presumptuous turn to the male domain of writing in the first place; see
*The Madwoman in the Attic: The Woman Writer and the Nineteenth-Century Literary
Imagination* (New Haven: Yale University Press, 1979), especially chap. 5. By
contrast, the studies of Nancy Armstrong (*Desire and Domestic Fiction: A Political
History of the Novel* [New York: Oxford University Press, 1987]) and Jane
Spencer (*The Rise of the Woman Novelist: From Aphra Benn to Jane Austen* [Oxford:
Blackwell, 1987]) find that by the late eighteenth century certain forms of
writing were linked to the code of femininity, and the case of Maria Edgeworth
bears out their claim.
3. Review of *Patronage*, QR 10 (1814): 305. Further references will be included
in the text.

had devised in their *Practical Education* (1798). Cautioning in that work against "immoderate novel reading" and advising "scrupulous caution" in books chosen for girls, Maria Edgeworth produced in her own novels a kind of writing quickly hailed by the reviews as contributing to the education and discipline of the newly literate.[4]

The *Edinburgh* review of her *Popular Tales* (1804), for instance, opens by drawing attention to the large number of readers ("at least *eighty thousand* readers") now in Great Britain, and it goes on to commend Edgeworth for writing tales of "common life" directed at "that great multitude who are neither high-born nor high-bred." These tales teach the positive value of "industry, perseverance, prudence, good humour, and all that train of vulgar and homely virtues that have hitherto made the happiness of the world, without obtaining any great share of its admiration."[5] Edgeworth's efforts, which are placed in contrast to the "pernicious absurdities" encouraged by Thomas Paine on the one hand and "Messrs Wordsworth & Co" on the other, are credited with creating in the "lower and middling orders of the people" a taste for realism: "a relish for the images of those things which must make the happiness of their actual existence" (330).[6] Herein lies her innovative power, and in this respect the reviewer likens Edgeworth to "those patriotic worthies" of the Renaissance who first ventured to write outside ancient authority and in the vernacular, writers "who spoke of love without allusion to Ovid, constructed dramas altogether independent of the Scriptures, and published tales that were not to be found in the Book of Troy." For Edgeworth, writing in a genre that favored aristocratic romance and scandal, the

---

4. *Practical Education*, 2 vols. (1798; New York: Garland, 1974). The first phrase appears in vol. 1, chap. 12, 333; the second in vol. 2, chap. 20, 550.

5. *ER* 4 (1804): 329–30. The Wellesley Index speculates that the reviewer may be Francis Jeffrey. Further references will be included in the text.

6. Cf. a contemporary American comment on the impact of feminine writing in Great Britain: "We ascribe no small part of the generally improved state of morals among the labouring classes in the mother country, to the condescending exertions of Miss Edgeworth and Miss More. The Cheap Repository Tracts, especially . . . by their influence in promoting habits of economy and industry, did as much, we apprehend, towards stemming the revolutionary torrent . . . as all the precautions of Pitt, and terrours [sic] of the king's attorney-general" ([Rev. J. G. Palfrey], review of *Tales of My Landlord*, *NAR* 5 [1817]: 261).

choice of common life and ordinary characters was a bold one: "It required almost the same courage to get rid of the jargon of fashionable life, and the swarms of peers, foundlings and seducers, that infested our modern fables, as it did in those days to sweep away the mythological personages of antiquity, and to introduce characters who spoke and acted like those who were to peruse their adventures" (330).

Such passages cast Edgeworth as significant innovator, and they highlight her status in the reviews from the publication of *Castle Rackrent* in 1800 to that of *Waverley* in 1814. During these years, as Marilyn Butler has pointed out, Edgeworth "was easily the most celebrated and successful of practising English novelists."[7] Moreover, as Butler also notes, she was the first novelist of any stature to be "regularly and intelligently reviewed."[8] Taken seriously and endorsed by both powerful quarterlies, Edgeworth was the exemplary novelist of the day, and the reviews are always careful to separate her from what the *Quarterly* calls "the ordinary class of manufacturers of novels."[9] Francis Jeffrey, whose promotion of Edgeworth in the *Edinburgh* was vital to her reputation, makes the point even more forcefully. He announces that her combination of "sober sense and inexhaustible invention" is so "singular" that "it cannot be thought wonderful that we should separate her from the ordinary manufacturers of novels, and speak of her Tales as works of more serious importance than much of the true history and solemn philosophy that comes daily under our inspection."[10] If Edgeworth's tales were not, in the end, as serious as history and philosophy, Jeffrey's critical move underlines the degree to which her narratives were linked by her first official readers to "true" and "solemn" discourses.

Here was no high-colored romance but "sober sense," and that sober sense was signaled for the reviewers by Edgeworth's decentering of romantic love in her fiction. As H. J. Stephen approvingly notes in the *Quarterly*, she "knows how to assign to

7. *Maria Edgeworth: A Literary Biography* (Oxford: Clarendon, 1972), 1.
8. Ibid., 338.
9. [H. J. Stephen with W. Gifford], review of *Tales of Fashionable Life*, QR 2 (1809): 146.
10. Review of *Tales of Fashionable Life*, ER 20 (1812): 100–101.

it its just limits."[11] The displacement of love not only validated Edgeworth's good sense but also enabled her to open up the mimetic space of fiction. John Wilson Croker sums up the critical consensus when, reviewing the later volumes of *Tales of Fashionable Life* in 1812, he praises Edgeworth's "accurate discrimination of the various classes of Irish society." Other writers, he argues, depend on received and crude generalizations, so that in their work "every thing that is Irish is pretty much alike." By contrast, Edgeworth depends on the experiential specificity of "keen observation," and Croker accordingly finds in her writings "the most accurate and yet the most diversified views that have ever been drawn of a national character."[12] Over and over again, the reviews sound the note of Edgeworth's power of cultural representation, and the motif of accuracy-and-observation becomes so well established that a *New Monthly Magazine* survey of contemporary women writers in 1820 can simply declare: "In extent and accuracy of observation Miss Edgeworth has no rival."[13]

But even as Edgeworth was praised for her intelligence and discriminating representation of the Irish, she figured in the reviews primarily as a moral force, and her narratives are typically termed "moral tales," "moral medicine," or "moral fictions." Jeffrey is especially strong on this point, maintaining in 1809 that Edgeworth has "done more good than any other writer, male or female, of her generation." Her writings, he avows, are "the most useful of any that have come before us since the commencement of our critical career."[14] All the reviews agree that Edgeworth has done much to encourage the prudential virtues and to provide a "sober" (a favorite critical term) alternative to extravagant romance. Her own plots contain improbabilities, to be sure, but these represent technical rather than imaginative or moral failure. Characterized by accuracy, humor, and good sense, her narratives combat "disorder" at all levels of society, urging the control of passion and the necessity of exertion.

11. Review of *Tales of Fashionable Life*, QR 2 (1809): 146.
12. QR 7 (1812): 336.
13. "On the Female Literature of the Present Age," NMM 13 (1820): 274.
14. Review of *Tales of Fashionable Life*, ER 14 (1809): 376, 388.

The narratives achieve their social utility at a certain price, however. Enacting the moderation and control that they preach, Edgeworth's tales depend on a deliberate renunciation and channeling of fictional energy. Jeffrey makes the point directly when he applauds Edgeworth for a "singular force of judgment and self-denial, which has enabled her to resist the temptation of being the most brilliant and fashionable writer of her day, in order to be the most useful and instructive."[15] A few years later John Ward is more explicit and rather less tactful in his review of *Patronage* for the *Quarterly*, which lays out the negative effects of Edgeworth's "uniform systematic preference of what is *useful* to what is *splendid*" (306). Although he treats Edgeworth with respect and praises her for her good sense, humor, and so on, Ward clearly finds her didacticism something of a trial, and he initiates his discussion of the problems it creates by (like Jeffrey) constructing her narrative as self-denial. In his account, Edgeworth has "voluntarily renounced" various sources of narrative power; she has made "sacrifices" of fictional effect. "Her pictures," he explains, "are all drawn in the soberest colours. She scarcely makes use of a single tint that is warmer than real life" (304). To complete the model of a cautious and cold narrative, Ward notes that Edgeworth not only avoids "the stronger and more impetuous feelings of our nature" but makes less allowance than has been usual in novels for "amiable" weaknesses and "sudden" impulses.

Ward's review points to the restiveness and resentment that tend to underlie official critical approval of Edgeworth's commitment to rational virtue and social utility. Especially striking in this regard is his comment on her handling of "the minor passions" when, after drawing attention to her "cure" of characters who suffer love, he writes: "Having mastered love, of course she treats the minor passions with very little ceremony, and indeed she brings them out so curbed, watched, and circumscribed, that those who have been accustomed to see them range at large would hardly know them in their new trammels" (304). Curbing, watching, and circumscribing, Edgeworth enacts a disciplinary force that not only constrains and imprisons

15. Review of *Tales of Fashionable Life, ER* 20 (1812): 103.

but deforms: one hardly knows the minor passions in their new trammels. The very observation and prudence that rendered Edgeworth's cultural representations so "accurate" now undercut her mimetic power, introducing a dissonance between ethical intent and the representation of feeling that will become increasingly significant as the century unfolds. More immediately, however, Ward's comment makes apparent what is implied in the critical characterization of Edgeworth's writing as an act of self-denial. Literally the product of limitation, such writing can easily come to seem itself limited and limiting. The positive values that it initially represented for reviews like the *Edinburgh*—values of containment and control vis-à-vis female reading, dangerous male texts, social anarchy—can readily be redefined negatively as constriction and narrowness.

And such charges are soon explicit, as reviewers begin to chafe more openly at her fiction and to confirm Ward's remark that the reader of Edgeworth "sees too plainly that he is under discipline" (307). By 1817 even Jeffrey finds Edgeworth too obsessively "a *Moral Teacher*," her every page making the reader feel that it was "intended to do good." He now sees her didactic dedication as alienating readers by infantilizing them: "Persons of full age revolt from instruction presented in too direct and officious a form,—and take it amiss to have a plain lesson, however much needed, driven into them in so persevering and unrelenting a manner."[16] For Jeffrey, as for most of Edgeworth's critics, the limitation of her narrative stems from two main sources: her didacticism and her gender. In Jeffrey's 1817 analysis, both "her system" and "her sex" locate Edgeworth's writing on the inferior side of a series of culturally central binaries. Where her "system" limits her range in terms of height and depth, her "sex" vitiates her attempts to move out of the private into the public sphere. On the first point, Jeffrey argues that Edgeworth's "excessive care for the moral utility of her works" has "injured" her narrative by encouraging her to exclude "the higher passions" and "the deeper and more tumultuous emotions." Her "rigid rejection of everything that does not teach a

16. Review of *Harrington* and *Ormond*, ER 28 (1817): 391, 392. Further references will be included in the text.

safe and practical moral lesson" means that her narrative takes no risks, offers no "attractive" feelings. She has restricted herself to a safe, middle course, to "well-behaved, considerate, good-natured people, who are never in any very terrible danger, either from within or from without." As a result, she has "sacrificed" much of the "freedom," "grace," and "boldness" of her invention (392–95).

Moreover, the virtues highlighted by Edgeworth come to seem increasingly "selfish" to Jeffrey, and his 1817 review repeatedly invokes the term: "selfish feeling," "selfish enjoyments," "selfish considerations." Surely, he urges, there is a "nobler" and "higher" use of life than "vulgar prosperity." In Edgeworth, however, "we meet with little that can be called heroic—and nothing that is romantic or poetical. She is so much afraid of seducing her pupils from the practical duties of social life, that she will not even borrow a grace from the loveliness of nature" (394, 395). In Jeffrey's characterization of Edgeworth's moral code as "safe" and "selfish," he voices a common concern of the period that the private and domestic virtues, no matter how necessary and useful, smacked too much of self-interest to count as genuine social virtues. Certainly, as Alexander Welsh has observed, this was an age of high prudence;[17] at the same time, for those attempting to construct the public space of letters, prudence carried an ambiguous inflection, at once essential and yet inimical to the values the literary republic sought to affirm. Compounding the problem in the case of Edgeworth was her careful avoidance of any appeal to the religious sphere, as is clear in the complaint of the *New Monthly Magazine* that her virtues "have no root in feelings or in principles that cannot be shaken. Their fibres are not inherently entwined in the living rock which no mortal changes can alter. They are planted in the shifting sands of earthly utility and expedience."[18] Edgeworth's ethical values, unsustained by "the living rock" of religious faith, drift in "shifting sands," subject to transience and to mere utility.

Edgeworth's lack of "principles" and her eschewal of "feel-

---

17. *The Hero of the Waverley Novels* (1963; New York: Atheneum, 1968), 25–27.
18. "On the Female Literature of the Present Age," *NMM* 13 (1820): 274.

ings" locate her outside the sublime space of height and depth where the early nineteenth-century reviewers (prudence and rationality notwithstanding) tended to locate imaginative truth and value. For all the differences among individual reviewers and individual reviews, there was a consensus on behalf of the expansive and the generous virtues (generally coded as "heart" and "feeling") that was to prove crucial for the reception of the novels of Scott. Suggestively, Jeffrey's 1817 review of *Harrington* and *Ormond* cites the recently arrived Author of Waverley in explicit and exemplary contrast to the cautious and mundane Edgeworth.[19] Increasingly, she comes to figure in the reviews as deficient in the key signs of heart and feeling—sources of "depth" in writing. For John Ward, her morality ascribes too large a part "to the head and too little to the heart" (308). (Gold's) *London Magazine* finds, more generally, that her "genius" springs "from the head, unaccompanied with any redeeming qualities of the heart."[20] The "fire" of her talent, this reviewer elaborates, "is the cold vapid flame of lightning that plays round the beetling rocks, but never penetrates them; it is the moon beam that gleams along the surface of the waters, pleasant to the eye, but chilling to the heart."[21] As cold fire, chilling light, and distanced eye, Edgeworth's imagination lacks warmth and penetration, failing to provide either feminine comfort and nurture or masculine passion and depth.

If Edgeworth's rational "system" deprives her writing of vertical range, her gender limits its horizontal scope by undermining her attempts to represent the public world to which her rational interests attract her. This second charge in the critical indictment of Edgeworth becomes especially pronounced with the publication in 1814 of *Patronage*, a long novel that indicts the evils of patronage and prominently features male characters involved in politics, law, medicine, and the military. So the *British Critic*, which had not made an issue of gender in its earlier

19. Jeffrey here notes that there is more "sympathy with rural beauty" and "sense of the expression of the great or majestic features of the universe" in one speech by Edie Ochiltree of *The Antiquary* than in "all the works" of Edgeworth (*ER* 28 [1817]: 395).

20. "On Novel Reading; With Observations on the Living Novelists," Gold's *LM* 1 (1820): 495.

21. Ibid., 496.

reviews of Edgeworth, now insists on gender boundaries. Granting her skill in tracing "the mazes of female intrigue" and in delineating "the Irish character," the reviewer draws the line at politics: "But where Diplomacy is brought upon the stage, she has evidently been but a spectatress of the drama; she has not been admitted behind the curtain."[22] After one reads *Patronage*, one's understanding of government will be "narrowed" much as is one's sense of the magnificence of a place when one exchanges a "comprehensive" external view for the confinement of the servants' hall or the inferior apartments. Matters are no better when Edgeworth moves to the professional discourses of law or medicine where she produces "palpable absurdities." But her failure in "the representation of public intrigue" is matched by "her success in the portrait of private manoeuvring," and Edgeworth is advised to cease her transgressions and stay in her place. Or, rather, Richard Lovell Edgeworth is advised to monitor his daughter in the review's final lines: "it is not upon our ingenious and lively authoress that our censures rest so heavily, as upon that Father, who could give his paternal imprimatur, as the preface informs us, to such palpable and dangerous misrepresentations of public character and public principle."[23]

As the self-conscious organ of orthodoxy, the *British Critic* may be especially insistent on upholding existing boundaries and hierarchies, but the other reviews exhibit a similar vigilance in patrolling the borders of masculine discourse. In his review of *Patronage*, John Ward (former member of Parliament and future foreign secretary) corrects Edgeworth's law and questions the propriety of her introduction into her "romance" of the figures of the king and certain ministers of state (312–14). The *Monthly Review* finds the medical cures represented in the novel "trifling and improbable" and its legal scenes "inaccurately conceived."[24] Francis Jeffrey sums up the point in his 1817 review of *Harrington* when he traces the "faults" in Edgeworth attribu-

22. *BC*, n.s., 1 (1814): 164.
23. Ibid., 173. Interestingly, Gilbert and Gubar make a similar move, if for very different reasons, in identifying the father as the source of the daughter's writing (*Madwoman in the Attic*, 146–54).
24. *MR*, n.s., 74 (1814): 109.

table to "her sex": "With all her sound sense and intelligence, it is plain that she is not at all at home in the representation of public transactions, or the actual business of men." The problem is that Edgeworth has only "a derivative and conjectural knowledge" of how political intrigues and business matters are "actually" managed, so that her representations of public transactions depend purely (and unconvincingly) on "conjecture" (395). The novelist praised in an earlier *Edinburgh* review for her "*manly* understanding"[25] turns out to be a woman after all, her social and moral utility limited to the feminine field that lies outside—even as it supports—the "actual business of men."

The reception of Edgeworth points to the way in which critical discourse about the novel at once granted women centrality in the history of the genre and moved them out to the periphery. Changes in the role of women were generally regarded as crucial to the emergence of the modern novel, as in the brief generic history prefaced to Ward's 1814 review of *Patronage* in the *Quarterly Review*. Ward argues that the invention of the novel depended on the development of the social "influence" of women, which transformed private life and made it a source of "interest and variety." The ancient world, rooted in slavery and the exclusion of women, spread "a gloomy uniformity" over most of Greece and Rome; not until Christianity combined with chivalry to purify and soften "the manners of men" did private life develop sufficient interest to make it a subject of fiction (301–2). The model linking women to the origins of the novel was so pervasive that John Dunlop's sprawling *History of Fiction* (1814), which does not privilege either the novel or women, comments in relation to ancient Greek romance that the "seclusion" of women in that culture "gave a certain uniformity to existence, and prevented the novelist from painting those minute and almost imperceptible traits of feeling and character; all those developments, which render a well-written modern novel so agreeable and interesting."[26] Moreover, as an index to the private life of a culture, the novel was seen as peculiarly suited to women not simply as readers and subjects of the fiction but

25. Review of *Patronage*, ER 22 (1814): 417.
26. *The History of Fiction*, 3 vols. (London, 1814), 1:97.

as writers. "Private life is everything to them," Ward comments in making this case in his 1814 review, and his argument highlights the degree to which the writerly fitness of women was perceived as a function of their enclosure: "The laws of society confine them within its sphere, and they are therefore likely to observe it with care and to describe it with precision." Enclosure is equally crucial to the moral "improvement" of the novel in recent years, an improvement that for Ward owes a great deal to the novel's "having fallen very much into the hands of the other sex, who are restrained by education, disposition, and custom within those bounds which have been too frequently passed by the celebrated writers [i.e., Le Sage, Richardson, Rousseau, Fielding] of whom we have just ventured to complain" (303).

Confinement empowers women to write in certain ways—precisely, subtly, morally—and implicitly rules out their writing in other kinds of ways. So the *British Review*, commenting on Hemans's *Poems* in 1820, notes that neither the education nor "the mind of woman" is generally favorable to "that deep-toned emotion which constitutes the very essence of the higher kinds of poetry."[27] Similar comments appear repeatedly, and the height-and-depth binary becomes so entrenched in (though not exclusive to) critical discourse about women's writing that it dominates R. H. Hutton's important article on masculine and feminine novelists in the *North British Review* almost forty years later. To note only one instance in relation to the feminine pole itself, Hutton considers the "deeper feminine school of modern fiction" typified by Charlotte Brontë, and he finds that, in general, it is less successful than the earlier, less deep feminine school of Austen and Edgeworth. "In many ways," he argues, "the natural limitations of feminine power are admirably adapted to the standard of fiction held up as the true model of a feminine novelist in the last century" when it was thought sufficient "to present finished sketches of character, just as it appeared under the ordinary restraints of society; while the deeper passions and spiritual impulses, which are the springs of all the higher drama of real life, were, at most, only allowed so far

27. *BR* 15 (1820): 300.

to suffuse the narrative as to tinge it with the excitement necessary for a novel." And these earlier feminine novelists, he believes, "gained by the restriction thus laid upon their aims," for
they produced more complete and harmonious works than a
writer like Charlotte Brontë who seeks "to sound the depths
and analyze the secret roots of individual character."[28] In either
case, women writers lack the fullness of masculine writing,
which Hutton identifies with breadth and width and freedom.
The Victorian Hutton makes explicit what is often implicit in the
early romantic reviewers: if the novel is to achieve the height,
depth, and breadth that mark literary value, it cannot be a
female genre.

The early nineteenth-century reviews thus constitute the contemporary novelistic field under female signs of confinement
(female reading, feminine writing) in such a way as to clear a
discursive space for another, less confined kind of fiction: the
eighteenth-century canon that was being set in place during
these years. The reviews consistently situate the contemporary
novel in a context of generic decline from the great and male
tradition of the eighteenth century as represented mainly by
four novelists: Henry Fielding, Samuel Richardson, Tobias
Smollett, and Laurence Sterne. The canon is not yet firmly established, and other novelists (including women) appear from
time to time in honorific lists. But these four are the core of the
canon, and their names are routinely invoked. "The days of
Richardson and Fielding" becomes a stock phrase of the period,
and the mideighteenth century comes to represent a time
when, in the words of the *Antijacobin* in 1814, novel writing
stood high "in the estimation of the rational and well-informed
part of the world."[29] A cursory glance at the response of rational
and well-informed eighteenth-century readers may cast some
doubt on the statement,[30] but this is less a historical than critical
statement enabling the *Antijacobin* to validate a position from
which to castigate the "shoals of compositions" of recent years.

28. "Novels by the Authoress of 'John Halifax,'" *NBR* 29 (1858): 472–73.
29. Review of *Waverley*, *AjR* 47 (1814): 217.
30. For a convenient collection of eighteenth-century responses to the novel,
see Ioan Williams, ed., *Novel and Romance, 1700–1800: A Documentary Record*
(New York: Barnes and Noble, 1970).

More precisely, setting up the canon allows appropriation of the novel as a genuinely male form that has become feminized and so has lost the centrality it supposedly once enjoyed, and it provides a ground from which current practice of the genre can be designated as either degenerate (the ordinary novel) or narrow (the proper novel).

Significantly, the turn of the century witnessed a rise in the reputation of Fielding and a waning of that of Richardson.[31] The debate between Fielding and Richardson, as Jane Spencer has pointed out, not only divided the novelistic field into two strands but also gendered the division, producing the "masculine" mode of Fielding and the "feminine" mode of Richardson.[32] In these terms, the early nineteenth century saw a distinct turn to the masculine, as Fielding increasingly came to occupy the place of founder and to achieve the status of supreme novelist. For Sydney Owenson, the "immortal Fielding" stood at the "head" of English novelists; for Walter Scott, he was "the first of British novelists." [33] Indeed, in Scott's account, Richardson (whose reputation Scott notes is experiencing "a temporary shade") emerges as very like a proper novelist, his "miniature painting" standing in contrast to Fielding's "free, bold, and true sketches."[34] Richardson remains canonical, but it is noteworthy that he is often omitted from honorific lists in the first decades of the century. In 1819, for example, *Blackwood's Magazine* includes in "the highest class" of realist novels in the past the names of Cervantes, Lesage, Fielding, and Smollett— but not that of Richardson.[35] And Gold's *London Magazine* offers a striking instance of the tendency to shed the feminine in the following year when it celebrates "the Augustan age . . . of novels," providing a roll call of novel characters "eminently conspicuous in the republic of letters." The list includes neither Richardson's fiction nor a female name: "Tom Jones, and Joseph

31. On the rise in Fielding's reputation, see J. M. S. Tompkins, *The Popular Novel in England, 1770–1800* (London: Methuen, 1932), 330.

32. Spencer, *Rise of the Woman Novelist*, 90.

33. Owenson, "On the Origin and Progress of Fictitious History," NMM 14 (1820): 27; Scott, "Henry Fielding," in *Sir Walter Scott on Novelists and Fiction*, ed. Ioan Williams (New York: Barnes and Noble, 1968), 47.

34. "Samuel Richardson," in *Scott on Novelists*, 45, 41.

35. "Thoughts on Novel Writing," BM 4 (1819): 394.

Andrews, My Uncle Toby, and Parson Adams, Roderic [sic] Random, and Humphry Clinker."[36]

Behind such canonical lists lie particular critical strategies and informing narratives, and the narrative of the canon in the early nineteenth-century reviews is typically placed within a narrative of literary decline. For example, the *Blackwood's* article cited above shapes its canon in order to make the point that "English literature is running waste, and sinking into degradation, from the want of a philosophy to guide its combinations."[37] Canons at once confirm current literary decline and affirm a perennial literary power, and through their narrative of cultural decline the early nineteenth-century reviews appropriated the novel for the literary republic. Of special pertinence is William Hazlitt's review of Fanny Burney's *Wanderer* for the *Edinburgh* in 1815.[38] Entitled "Standard Novels and Romances," the review defines itself as an attempt to contribute something to the settling of "the standard of excellence" in novel writing, and it combines politics, nationalism, literature, and gender in a characteristic mix as it tells the story of the genre founded by Cervantes.

Character is central to Hazlitt's evaluation of fiction, and he seeks in character a combination of the "ideal" and the "true to nature." Together these engender a sense of the deep and the essential in human existence in contrast to the merely external and accidental. Novels tend to fall in one or the other camp, beginning with *Don Quixote*, Hazlitt's exemplary fiction. His impassioned encomium makes this the first and best of novels, and Hazlitt constructs Cervantes's text under the signs of aspiration ("the longing after something more than we possess") and liberty, marking it as having kept alive "the spark of generous sentiment and romantic enterprise" which may yet kindle "the flame of Spanish liberty" (322–23). Next stands Lesage's *Gil Blas*, the "head" of a "class" very different from and inferior to the class represented by *Don Quixote*: "The author is a describer

36. Review of *Ivanhoe*, Gold's *LM* 1 (1820): 80.
37. "Thoughts on Novel Writing," 396.
38. "Standard Novels and Romances, *ER* 24 (1815): 320–38. Further references will be included in the text. On the significance of this review, see Michael Munday, "The Novel and Its Critics in the Early Nineteenth Century," *Studies in Philology* 79 (1982): 205–26.

of manners, and not of character" (325). Quickly dispensing with Lesage, Hazlitt moves to "our four best novel-writers," the familiar canonical four of English fiction. He ranks Fielding first on account of his skill with character, the important point being that even though his representations are "local and individual," they are "not the less profound and natural" (326). Smollett occupies the same position in relation to Fielding that Lesage occupied in relation to Cervantes, for he "exhibits only the external accidents and reverses to which human life is liable—not 'the stuff' of which it is composed" (328–29). Up to this point, Hazlitt's binary model has produced a coherent story, but when he turns to Richardson and Sterne, he encounters types of novels that he cannot easily accommodate to his model. In different ways neither Richardson nor Sterne is for Hazlitt "true to nature"; both are "artificial." And with them, he pretty much abandons his attempt at a systematic account of "the standard of excellence" in novel writing, settling for readerly impressions and random remarks. Hazlitt thus underlines the degree to which Richardson and Sterne were by this time so clearly canonical that no account of "excellence" could exclude them even if their inclusion undermined critical coherence.

Hazlitt then merges the story of the novelistic canon with a specifically political story, as he turns the canonical period of novel writing into something of a golden age of English comedy. He remarks that the period of the canonical four saw also the appearance of the "inimitable" Hogarth and of some of the "best" writers of the middle style of comedy. In accounting for why these modes should all have flowered at the same period, Hazlitt explicitly refuses to operate at the high level of generality represented by the standard stages-of-society argument, which posited "that imagination naturally descends with the progress of civilization" (334). Instead, the radical Hazlitt, writing in a counterrevolutionary age, turns to a more concrete and political explanation of literary activity, claiming that the establishment of the Protestant ascendancy and the Hanoverian succession gave "a more popular turn to our literature and genius, as well as to our Government. It was found high time that the people should be represented in books as well as in parliament" (334). The people so represented are quintessentially English, and here Hazlitt activates the old radical trope of the democratic English spirit. After obligatory swipes at the aristocratic French, Hazlitt celebrates the period of George II as a time when "there was a general spirit of sturdiness and independence, which made the English character more truly English than perhaps at any other period—that is, more tenacious of its own opinions and purposes" (335).

But the reign of George III undermined individual sturdiness and independence by plunging the nation into wars that concentrated energy and imagination, producing turmoil and confusion. "It is not to be wondered," Hazlitt remarks, "if, amidst the tumult of events crowded into this period, our literature has partaken of the disorder of the time; if our prose has run mad, and our poetry grown childish" (335). Suggestively, the examples now cited by Hazlitt are all female, as he goes on to define the particular appeal of Radcliffe, Inchbald, and Edgeworth. It is not that these writers are necessarily defined as childish— Edgeworth, for example, offers a "common sense" that contests "audacious paradox and insane philosophy" (336)—but that in the context of cultural decline, the literary field seems to have changed its gender. And the implications of this become quite explicit when Hazlitt finally turns to the subject of his review, Fanny Burney.

For Hazlitt, Burney stands apart from the madness of contemporaneity: he places her in "the old school" that simply observed manners instead of succumbing to the "prejudice of the moment" (like Inchbald) or attempting to counteract the workings of unreason (like Edgeworth). She is also "a very woman," and it is this, he says, that "forms the peculiarity of her writings, and distinguishes them from those masterpieces [Fielding et al.] which we have before mentioned" (336). The way in which Burney's gender "distinguishes" her becomes clear when Hazlitt, allowing Burney the female privilege of keen observation, adds that she "always" observes person and things "with a consciousness of her sex, and in that point of view in which it is the particular business and interest of women to observe them. We thus get a kind of supplement and gloss to our original text, which we could not otherwise have obtained" (336). As "supplement" and "gloss," Burney's narrative can only circle in and around the "original text," those male "masterpieces" whose structures contain and define value and significance.[39] Women for Hazlitt have no power of initiation or insight. Their characterization tends to caricature because women have "a quicker perception of any oddity or singularity of character than men," in part because social restraint makes them more observant of such matters and in part because "the surface of their minds, like that of their bodies, seems of a finer texture than ours; more soft, and susceptible of immediate impression" (337). So located on the outside of this discourse through Hazlitt's pronominal tactic ("than ours"), women are cast as secondary and reflective, rather than primary and constructive, beings. Female susceptibility to "immediate impression" means that women tend to be "more alive to every absurdity which arises from a violation of the rules of society, or a deviation from established custom" (336). The absurdities that strike women are social, not logical and metaphysical, and their propensity to note such absurdities signals their inherently superficial and conservative nature as creatures ruled by convention and custom. Hazlitt underlines this point as he elaborates his mind/body analogy: "They have less muscular power,—less power of continued voluntary attention,—of reason—passion and imagination. But they are more easily impressed with whatever appeals to their senses and habitual prejudices" (337). Women's observation is not, he concedes, "less accurate on that account, as far as it goes; for it has been well said, that 'there is nothing so true as habit'" (337).

39. Compare Hazlitt's remarks with those of a more recent commentator: "But it is not fair to expect too much of the good Fanny Burney. The best examples before her of unquestionable *excellence* in the English novel were the novels of Fielding, and Fielding's virtues are entirely masculine. Her outlook and her gifts were a woman's, and in opening up a woman's world (no doubt in the main for women readers) she had to find her own way, confining herself to that world as a woman was then permitted to know it . . . under the disadvantages of limited contacts and the continuing overweening and unarguable assumptions of male superiority" (Harrison R. Steeves, *Before Jane Austen: The Shaping of the English Novel in the Eighteenth Century* [London: Allen and Unwin, 1966], 233). Steeves's parenthetical remark that Burney no doubt wrote mainly for women recalls Terry Lovell's argument that a condition of literary canonization in the Victorian period was less the gender of the author than the gender of the addressee: "the work must be addressed to men and read by them, and not addressed exclusively to women" (*Consuming Fiction* [London: Verso, 1987], 83).

A similar, if less explicit, recourse to gender and to qualified concession ("as far as it goes") appears in the much briefer excursus into the history and hierarchy of novel writing that John Wilson Croker prefaces to his review of *Waverley* in the *Quarterly*. Unlike Hazlitt, Croker adapts the general stages-of-society argument in order to construct a downward-sloping curve of three distinct, chronological phases of novel writing: the idealist phase, the generic phase (exemplified by Fielding), and the current particularist phase (represented by Edgeworth and Elizabeth Hamilton). This last phase is characterized by "a copying not of man in general, but of men of a peculiar nation, profession, or temper, or, to go a step further—of *individuals*."[40] Invoking a painterly comparison whose terms a Victorian realist like George Eliot will later invert, Croker states that novels of the particularist class may be compared to Dutch paintings, which delight in their "vivid and minute details of common life" and testify to "the accuracy, observation and humour of the painter." But such painting excites "none of those more exalted feelings, giv[es] none of those higher views of the human soul which delight and exalt the mind of the spectator of Raphael, Correggio, or Murillo" (355).[41] In providing observation rather than exaltation, "minute details" instead of "higher views," the contemporary novel is for Croker "less comprehensive and less sublime" than that of the eighteenth century. This does not, he stresses, mean that it is either less entertaining or less useful: "On the contrary, so far as utility constitutes merit in a novel, we have no hesitation in preferring the moderns to their predecessors. We do not believe that any man or woman was every improved in morals or manners by the reading of Tom Jones or Peregrine Pickle, though we are confident that many have profited by the Tales of Fashionable Life, and [Elizabeth Hamilton's] the Cottagers of Glenburnie" (355). The concessive "so far as utility constitutes merit" recalls Hazlitt's "as far as it goes," and there is little doubt that for Croker *Tom Jones* is the better, if less useful, novel.

Confined by such constructions, women's writing must appear marginal and thin, outside the height and breadth where

40. *QR* 11 (1814): 355. Further references will be included in the text.
41. George Eliot's classic realist inversion of Renaissance versus Dutch painting appears in chapter 17 of *Adam Bede*.

literary value is located. Women are by definition excluded from
the representation of what Hazlitt calls manners "in the most
extended sense of the word, as implying the sum-total of our
habit and pursuits." Instead, he says, women have narrowed
the concept to *"the manners of people in company"* (336–37). Reinforcing his point, the *New Monthly Magazine* considers the
"great fault" of Burney's novels to be the fact that their "dis-
tresses" often arise "from mere inattentions to the forms of
society, from provoking combinations of petty circumstances,
or from some finely attenuated delicacy out of place and reason.
These things fret and vex the reader, who feels that the whole is
'much ado about nothing,' and instead of sympathizing only
longs to explain."[42] To underline his argument, the reviewer
contrasts the effect on the feelings of the reader aroused by
Caleb Williams ("where the interest arises from the irreversible
error of a noble nature, and the struggle and conflict of two high
characters") with the effect generated by *Camilla* (where "paltry
misconceptions" move the plot). Consider this contrast, he advises, and the reader "will feel how more deep, yet more calm
and tranquillizing, the first is, than the last."[43] Making a similar
point about Burney, Hazlitt is more blunt in his assessment of her
fiction. Playing on the full title of the particular novel under his
review, *The Wanderer; or, Female Difficulties*: "The difficulties in which
she involves her heroines are indeed 'Female Difficulties;'—
they are difficulties created out of nothing" (337).

By activating the canonical move, the reviews thus open up a
space—higher, deeper, broader than that of women's writing—
for the critic and for the male reader and writer of novels. And
into this space, answering certain key male anxieties, came the
not-so-anonymous Waverley Novels, products of a noted man
of letters and hailed from the outset as restoring to the novel
fact, variety, sublimity—in short, all the breadth, depth, and
centrality that the contemporary novelistic field was defined as
lacking.

42. "On the Female Literature of the Present Age," *NMM* 13 (1820): 635.
43. Ibid.

3

A Manly Intervention: *Waverley*, the Female Field, and Male Romance

Your manner of narrating is so different from the slipshod sauntering verbiage of common novels and from the stiff, precise, and prim sententiousness of some of our female novelists, that I think it can't fail to strike any body who knows what style means; but, amongst the gentle class, who swallow every blue-backed book in the circulating library for the sake of the story, I should fear half the knowledge of nature it contains, and all the real humour, may be thrown away.

—John Morritt to Scott on reading *Waverley* (1814)

Morritt's comment nicely underlines not only the degree to which the critical tropes outlined in the last two chapters were internalized by gentlemanly readers but also the way in which the reception of *Waverley* itself was conditioned by those tropes.[1] To register his sense of the innovative force of Scott's text, we note, Morritt immediately places it as different from both the common novel and the proper novel, a difference that he identifies with the literary and gentlemanly quality of "style." Exhibiting neither the slipshod verbiage of the one mode nor the prim sententiousness of the other, Scott's writing cannot fail to impress "any body who knows what style means." Moreover, it encourages a mode of reading quite dis-

1. For Morritt's comment, see John Gibson Lockhart, *Memoirs of the Life of Sir Walter Scott, Bart*, 7 vols. (Edinburgh, 1837–38), 3:298. John Morritt of Rokeby was Scott's close friend and one of the very few to whom he revealed his authorship of *Waverley*. A wealthy Yorkshire landowner, he was something of a classical scholar. On Morritt, see Edgar Johnson, *Sir Walter Scott: The Great Unknown*, 2 vols. (New York: Macmillan, 1970), 1:295–296.

tinct from the mindless swallowing that marks female reading. Indeed, such readers will miss half of its "knowledge of nature" and all of its "real humour," unable to respond fully to the expansion of fiction that *Waverley* clearly marks for Morritt. Morritt is responding privately and immediately to a novel that he has not yet finished reading, but his response points more generally to the way in which the Waverley Novels opened up the novel to the male gender as both writing and reading, establishing novel writing as a literary activity and legitimating novel reading as a manly practice.

The implications of the publication of *Waverley* for the literary status of the novel were not immediately recognized or trumpeted in the reviews.[2] John Wilson Croker of the *Quarterly* wished that the author had written a history; the crusty *Critical Review* (on its last legs after its great success in the eighteenth century) disliked it enormously; and John Scott, soon to be editor of the important liberal *London Magazine*, did not think that it ranked with "our best novels."[3] Certainly, the novel was widely and well reviewed, but its critical success was not as extraordinary as would soon be believed. Looking back in 1820, for example, Gold's *London Magazine* affirms that "the Author of the Scotch Novels" was greeted with "reiterated huzzas by the band of critics, who were drawn up as a guard of honor [sic] to receive him; for whatever were their ideas on less important literary topics, on this occasion, at least, there seemed but one undivided opinion."[4] What matters is not so much that the 1814 reviews did not form quite the "guard of honor" claimed by Gold's as that within six years the Waverley Novels had achieved such authority and prestige that the moment of their

2. For an account of the nineteenth-century reception of the Waverley Novels, see James T. Hillhouse, *The Waverley Novels and Their Critics* (Minneapolis: University of Minnesota Press, 1936). For a sampling of reviews, see John O. Hayden's useful collection in *Scott: The Critical Heritage* (New York: Barnes and Noble, 1970).

3. [John Wilson Croker], *QR* 11 (1814): 354–77; *CR* 5th ser. 1 (1815): 288–97; [John Scott], *Champ* (24 July 1814): 238–39. For the reviews of *Waverley* in this chapter, I will provide a full citation only once; thereafter all references will be included in the text. For a list of the reviews, see Claire Lamont's edition of *Waverley* (Oxford: Clarendon, 1981), xli.

4. "On the Living Novelists," Gold's *LM* 2 (1820): 265.

entrance into the literary field was already legendary. Suggestively, the same article images the appearance of the Author of Waverley as the incursion of newly awakened male energy into a fictional field enervated by female practices: "The Luximas, the Wanderers, and the innumerable spawn of the Mysteries of Udolpho, were gradually sinking into the tomb of all the Capulets, when the author of the Scotch novels first appeared, like a giant refreshed with sleep."[5] A dramatic—even melodramatic—moment, the passage bears witness to the rapid construction of the manly genius known as the Author of Waverley. If this author's initial appearance in 1814 was not registered in such theatrical terms, it was generally celebrated in an idiom that laid the ground for the heroic image that would soon dominate the literary reviews.

Francis Jeffrey, for example, whose *Edinburgh Review* was at the height of its power at the time of the publication of *Waverley*, opens his important review of the novel by declaring: "It is wonderful what genius and adherence to nature will do, in spite of all disadvantages."[6] The disadvantages of *Waverley*, it turns out, include hasty and often clumsy writing; extensive use of a dialect "unintelligible" to the majority of readers; historical setting in a period lacking the conventional interests of either remoteness or contemporaneity; and publication in a city remote from London and generally regarded as inhospitable to the writing and reading of fiction. Despite all these drawbacks, however, Jeffrey finds that the novel is "already casting the whole tribe of ordinary novels into the shade, and taking its place rather with the most popular of our modern poems, than with the rubbish of provincial romances" (208). In these lines Jeffrey rhetorically establishes (and approves) *Waverley* as innovative text, imaging innovation as the incursion of prestigious extratextual forces (nature and genius) into a field dominated by debased and highly conventionalized writings (the rubbish of provincial romances). "Genius" and "nature" thus challenge, in

5. Ibid.
6. *ER* 24 (1814): 208. The review of *Waverley* (208–43) appears in the issue led off by Jeffrey's review of Wordsworth's *Excursion* with its notorious opening sentence: "This will never do." On the power of the *ER* in 1814, see John Clive, *Scotch Reviewers: The Edinburgh Review, 1802–1815* (London: Faber, 1957), 43.

their unpredictability and authenticity, the predictable and artificial collectivity of "the whole tribe of ordinary novels."

When it was first published, *Waverley* looked very much like an ordinary novel. The introductions and notes with which the modern reader is familiar were added by Scott much later for the "Magnum Opus" edition of his collected works. Nevertheless, to Scott's contemporaries, this apparently routine publication was of unusual interest. Rumors of Scott's authorship surface in almost every review (including the *Edinburgh*), and their significance is apparent in the statement by the *Critical Review*: "we neither like the work nor the subject; but the name of Walter Scott claims attention" (288). The name of Walter Scott— name of a famous poet, respected scholar, and undisputed gentleman—immediately distinguished *Waverley* from "the rubbish of provincial romances" and positioned it within reach of— if not inside—the republic of letters. Hence the conventional critical move of identifying a novel as worthy by setting it apart from its genre ("this is not an ordinary novel") takes on a special cultural valence in the case of *Waverley*, as does the code of female reading and feminine writing that is inevitably the standard from which *Waverley*—and its readers—must be distinguished.

So John Scott, despite his muted initial enthusiasm for the novel, feels bound to assure his readers of both its and their distinction: "The first chapters of this work, though not likely to be the most popular, shew that the Author has both read and thought:—this is saying enough to avert the reader's indignation against us, under the idea that we were about to claim his attention to a common novel" (*Champ*, 238). For its part, the *British Critic*, whose review bears the running title "Waverley: supposed by W. Scott," implicitly invokes the trope of female reading when it declares itself "unwilling to consider this publication in the light of a common novel, whose fate it is to be devoured rapidly for the day, and to be afterwards forgotten for ever."[7] Writing in the *Monthly Review*, John Merivale is even more explicit, describing *Waverley* as "a tale which has little of the ordinary attractions of a novel to recommend it, and which

7. *BC*, n.s., 2 (1814): 204.

will therefore probably disappoint all those readers who take it up at a circulating library, selecting it at random from amid sundry tomes of *Emmeline, Castel Gandolpho, Elegant Enthusiasts,* and *Victims of Sensibility.*"[8] To establish the value of *Waverley,* then, the reviewers appeal to their own readers as precisely *not* female readers (whatever their biological gender may be), characterizing the implied reader of critical reviews as a discriminating member of an intellectual elite. If *Waverley* disappoints the frequenter of the circulating library, it is all the more likely to satisfy the serious and superior reader of literary periodicals, who chooses texts rather than selecting them at random and who reads instead of devouring them.

In general, the reviews reiterate two points about *Waverley*: its "variety" of mode, scene, and characterization; and the "fact" and "accuracy" of its historical and cultural representations. The "variety" to which most reviewers draw attention signals the novel's referential breadth and its narrative energy. Jeffrey laments at the end of his long review that even though he has "trespassed indeed considerably on space which we had reserved for more weighty matters, we have, after all, afforded but an imperfect specimen of the variety which this work contains" (*ER,* 242). And he squeezes in a list of distinctive scenes and characters that have not yet been mentioned. John Merivale also turns to a list to give his reader a sense of how the novel touches on "almost every variety of station and interest . . . at the period under review," and he too finds himself running out of room as he attempts to convey something of the range of this "bustling drama" (*MR,* 288).

It is the second point—the fact and accuracy of the novel— that most clearly establishes its positive critical value. Croker stresses in the *Quarterly* that "the interest and merit of the work is derived, not from any of the ordinary qualities of a novel, but from the truth of its facts, and the accuracy of its delineations" (377); and the *British Critic* characterizes the novel as a whole as "a vehicle of curious accurate information upon a subject which must at all times demand our attention—the history and manners of a very large and renowned portion of the inhabitants of

8. *MR,* n.s., 75 (1814): 279–80.

these islands" (204). Concentrating on the narrative skill that makes possible this informative power, Francis Jeffrey sounds a note that will be heard repeatedly in relation to the Waverley Novels when he testifies to "the extraordinary facility and flexibility of hand which has touched, for instance, with such discriminating shades, the various gradations of the Celtic character" (*ER*, 210). The painterly metaphor enters into Merivale's celebration of Scott's technique as well, as he marvels that "almost every variety of station and interest, such as it existed at the period under review, is successively brought before the mind of the reader in colours vivid as the original" (*MR*, 288). Neither the "high" color of romance nor the "chaste" color of the proper novel, here is color "vivid as the original"—perfect reproduction.

Moreover, the language of assessment for *Waverley* merges easily (if not fully) with that used for nonfictional works under review—histories, travel books, political analyses, and so forth. Several reviews draw on the stages-of-society argument popularized by the sociological historiography of the Scottish Enlightenment. The *Scots Magazine*, for example, sees the Highlands of sixty years ago as analogous to "what all of Europe was, at the distance of three centuries."[9] John Scott also assumes the stages-of-society paradigm in his primitivist argument that the clans possessed a concentrated energy "which the more diffused, and therefore weaker motives, arising from ethical theories and the rules of jurisprudence, are unequal to awaken" (*Champ*, 238). The *British Critic* stops to explain the difference between a clan and a feudal system, and it uses the occasion of the novel's setting in 1745 ("the last fatal year when the blood of our countrymen was spilt on its own shores") to express its concern lest the army which recently defeated Napoleon now turn its "gigantic force . . . inwardly upon itself" (190). Somewhat less dramatically, Jeffrey spends a long paragraph in the *Edinburgh* analyzing the cultural and historical significance of the Forty-Five. *Waverley*, then, is seen as speaking to serious political concerns of the age, a point underscored both explicitly through direct commentary and implicitly

9. *SM* 76 (1814): 524.

through the way in which it merges with respected genres of nonfiction. Indeed, as the Waverley series continued, it promoted the production of the nonfictional texts on which it partially depended. John Lockhart stresses this point in his review of Scott's *Lives of the Novelists* in 1826 when he notes that the Waverley Novels "have, with hardly one exception, been immediately followed by republications of the comparatively forgotten authors from whom he had drawn the historical part of his materials"[10]

To its invocation of nonfictional genres, Scott's fictional narrative added the authority of a very specific kind of male writing as it wove in a constant strain of allusion to the entire European literary canon, notably to the classics, so locating itself in a literary mainstream that was neither precisely modern nor exclusively novelistic. The *British Critic* noted with approval its deployment of both legal and high literary discourse: "The humorous and happy adaptation of legal terms shew no moderate acquaintance with the arcana of the law, and a perpetual allusion to the English and the Latin classics no common share of scholarship and of taste" (209). The allusion, we note, is "perpetual," implying an easy and thorough absorption of modern and ancient classics, and the reviews in general confirm Robert Colby's argument that what Scott introduced into the novel was scholarship. The details and documentation that "cram" the pages of *Waverley*, Colby notes, establish the author "as a man of learning as well as a man of letters."[11] The classics are featured prominently (if not unambiguously) in *Waverley*, notably through the figure of Baron Bradwardine; and a classical (specifically Latin) education, as Walter Ong has emphasized, long functioned in the West as a central mechanism of gender and class definition.[12]

Women who ventured into the domain of the classics were typically mocked and ruled out of order, as in the 1803 review of Susanne Necker's *Réflections sur le divorce* in the *Edinburgh.*

---

10. *QR* 34 (1826): 371.

11. *Fiction with a Purpose* (Bloomington: Indiana University Press, 1967), 34.

12. See, for example, Walter Ong, *Rhetoric, Romance, and Technology: Studies in the Evolution of Consciousness and Culture* (Ithaca: Cornell University Press, 1977).

Necker's argument against divorce and her admiration for Rousseau would have guaranteed a less than sympathetic reception in the Protestant and anti-Rousseauist *Edinburgh*, especially if the reviewer (as the Wellesley Index speculates) was the Reverend Sydney Smith. But it is significant that the reviewer chooses to make his point by deploying codes of gender rather than religion or politics, denigrating the work by comparing it to an ignorant schoolboy theme: "A woman may have read some translations of the classics, with the profound notes of Madame Dacier, or even construed part of Virgil in the original, without being able to afford much instruction to the world. She may be a sort of prodigy in her own circle, without having acquisitions beyond those of a boy of sixteen."[13]

Scott, on the other hand, already authorized in the reviews as a scholar by (to note only a few of his activities) his *Minstrelsy of the Scottish Border*, his own review essays for the two major quarterlies, and his editions of Dryden and of Swift, was definitely not a schoolboy. This did not place him beyond criticism. On the contrary, it placed him firmly inside the critical sphere by placing him beyond the condescension that—more or less tactfully—tended to exclude women writers from its contentions. When the language and style of *Waverley* are attacked, it is not immaturity or ignorance that are cited but a gentlemanly carelessness or a misplaced patriotism that indulges in "Scotticisms" unintelligible to the English reader.

But the validation of *Waverley* as a novel that satisfied the official critical idiom of value ("fact," "truth," "intellect," "nature") exists in tension with another, less authoritative valuation signaled by words like "extraordinary" and "wild." If the analytic portions of the reviews keep stressing the realist value of the novel, the plot summaries and the passages chosen for quotation keep highlighting its romantic appeal, pointing to the way in which Scott's narrative mode provided the imaginative and emotional expansiveness that a fictional mode like that of Maria Edgeworth was regarded as so conspicuously lacking.[14]

13. *ER* 1 (1803): 495. The tone of such a passage certainly recalls the writing of Sydney Smith.

14. David H. Richter hypotheses that the turn of the nineteenth century witnessed "a major shift" in reading practices from reading as a form of cognition to reading as a form of emotional and psychological release ("The Recep-

Over and over again the same passages describing the "extraordinary" life at Tully-Veolan and in the Highlands are presented
to the reader. Extracts from certain scenes are quoted repeatedly
and extensively: Waverley's entrance into the village of Tully-
Veolan and meeting with Davie Gellatly (Davie seems a particular favorite of the reviewers); the introduction of Baron
Bradwardine; Waverley's arrival at Glennaquoich and the introduction of Fergus MacIvor.

The choice of such passages is usually explained as occasioned by a rational interest in a particular "state of society" or
as somehow compelled by the exigencies of reviewing. So
Croker of the *Quarterly* introduces a lengthy passage from chapter 15, "A Creagh, and its Consequences," as part of "some
further specimens of the state of society into which Waverley
was thrown" (361); and the *British Critic* introduces the description of Bradwardine in Chapter 10 as "a curious specimen of the
manners of the days of yore" (191). The second tactic—the appeal to professional duty—is particularly telling, for it is generally invoked to excuse inattention to more domestic or proper
parts of the novel. Merivale, for example, makes this appeal in
order to account for the way in which he rapidly passes over the
proper heroine, Rose Bradwardine, and her excellent qualifications for domestic life: "while we give to those qualifications in
real life the full tribute of our sincere preference, we feel it to be
our duty on the present occasion to pass from them to the
delineation of more striking characteristics" (*MR*, 284). In a parallel passage in the *Quarterly*, Croker similarly commends
Rose's domestic virtues, then announces that he must "hasten
from the character which, in real life, would most attach us, to a
description of the uncouth personages who partook with
Waverley the wild hospitalities of Tully-Veolan" (357). As rational men and responsible critics, Merivale and Croker cannot surrender too easily to the satisfactions of fiction, which here appear clearly divorced from those of life. The tension in the
critical response to *Waverley* surfaces most obviously at the end
of John Scott's review in *The Champion*. "On looking back to our
observations," he notes with some alarm, "we see there is a risk

---

tion of the Gothic Novel in the 1790s," in *The Idea of the Novel in the Eighteenth
Century*, ed. Robert Uphaus [East Lansing: Colleagues Press, 1988], 121).

of its being thought from them, that this work is chiefly a *roman-tic Novel* . . . but this idea must not be entertained. Its chief merit is its accurate and lively delineation of character and manners" (239).

John Scott's comment underlines the struggle in the reviews to contain *Waverley* within categories that would establish its distinction from the dubious romantic fictions of the ordinary novel. This struggle was all the more intense because the "healthy" romance satisfactions of *Waverley* and its successors could not be easily distinguished from those of diseased female reading (see my argument in Chapter 8). For the moment, however, the point is that the reviews of *Waverley* record not only the contemporary male suspicion of fiction but also the male release into the satisfactions of fiction that Scott's historically grounded novels made possible. The "extraordinary" and the "wild" in *Waverley* are at once the stuff of romance and the stuff of history.[15] They offer a generic doubleness that allows male subjectivity to enter into a female genre without losing its masculine purchase on truth and fact. Scott is careful to point out in the Postscript to the novel that "the most romantic parts of this narrative are precisely those which have a foundation in fact" (340). Paradoxically, Scott's commitment to external reference— to that "fact" valorized by the reviews—permitted him to be more, not less, fictional. Francis Jeffrey, for instance, argues that an artist guided by "nature and truth," rather than by "the phantasms of his own imagination," has rooted himself in a principle whose internal consistency gives him the confidence "occasionally to risk a strength of colouring, and a boldness of drawing, upon which he would scarcely have ventured in a sketch that was purely ideal" (*ER*, 208). He can afford, in other words, the high coloring that was so questionable in the narratives of a Sydney Morgan. Defined by "risk," "strength," and "boldness," *Waverley* is marked as a liberation of the imagination from a confined and enervated space.

This space, as William Hazlitt was to suggest shrewdly, was

15. Cf. George Levine's point that history in Scott often manifests itself in the conventions of romance: "History releases Scott into romance because it anchors him firmly in fact" (*The Realistic Imagination: English Fiction from Frankenstein to Lady Chatterley* [Chicago: University of Chicago Press, 1981], 93).

in some sense the space of modern civilization itself, whose effeminacy (usually coded as "refinement") was widely assumed and often lamented in the period.[16] Scott's own passive hero, of course, is himself a mark of that anxiety about modernity, an anxiety which derived in large part from the necessity to recode masculinity under the pressure of the development of civil and commercial society.[17] The model of social evolution inherited from the Scottish Enlightenment (and underlying the stages-of-society model in the reviews of *Waverley*) posited that certain forms of energy such as imaginative energy, martial energy, and religious energy dissipated as society developed, ruling out certain kinds of (often valuable) social action and virtue.

Adam Ferguson's paradigmatic text, *An Essay on the History of Civil Society* (1767), for example, presents the "advance" of society from "rudeness" to "civilization" as a story of loss as much as of gain. So the development of property appears in Ferguson, as in most eighteenth-century models of social change, as a crucial advance. Property frees the mind from bondage to mere appetite and violent passions by bringing about a fundamental change in the orientation of oneself in time: one now acts with a view to futurity and motivated by a distant object, no longer propelled only by the immediate gratification of instinct or passion. At the same time, property introduces divisiveness, avarice, and a breakdown of community. Similarly, specialization (the "subdivision of the mechanical arts") is necessary to commercial progress, but mechanical skill for Ferguson is at odds with intelligence, so that the less skilled "savage" has more of the intelligence that grasps how things work as wholes than does his modern counterpart. "Thinking itself, in this age of separations," Ferguson remarks, "may become a peculiar craft."[18] Very much shaped by this tradition of sociohistorical thought, the Waverley Novels encode the doubleness of histor-

16. On the link between civilization and the feminization of men in the Waverley Novels in particular, see Daniel Cottom, *The Civilized Imagination: A Study of Ann Radcliffe, Jane Austen, and Sir Walter Scott* (Cambridge: Cambridge University Press, 1985), chap. 8.

17. On the passive hero, see Alexander Welsh's landmark *The Hero of the Waverley Novels* (1963; New York: Atheneum, 1968).

18. *An Essay on the History of Civil Society* (1767; New York: Garland, 1971), 281.

ical change, charting the way in which the present bears loss, as well as gain, within it.[19]

Herein lies the clue to their power for Hazlitt, whose reading of the romantic appeal of Scott's fiction is equally informed by the stages-of-society argument. In a playful but not unserious piece titled "On the Pleasure of Hating," Hazlitt muses about how the progress of civilization does not so much weaken primitive energy (as was commonly feared) as block the direct expression of certain forms, leaving intact the energy itself. His particular concern, as the title suggests, is the energy of hatred: "We give up the external demonstration, the *brute* violence, but we cannot part with the essence or principle of hostility."[20] Civilized persons therefore, restrained by "the progress of intellectual refinement," resort to the imaginative displacement of violence in rituals, texts, and fictions: "We burn Guy Faux in effigy, and the hooting and buffeting and maltreating that poor tattered figure of rags and straw makes a festival in every village in England once a year. Protestants and Papists do not now burn one another at the stake: but we subscribe to new editions of *Fox's Book of Martyrs*" (129).

The "secret" of the success of the Waverley Novels, he continues, is similar, for these novels transport readers to a less restrained time of feuds, wrongs, and revenge: "As we read, we throw aside the trammels of civilisation. . . . The wild beast resumes its sway within us, we feel like hunting-animals . . .

---

19. The doubleness of the Waverley Novels has been extensively commented on since they were first published and has by now become a standard trope in Scott criticism. The definitive modern statement remains David Daiches, "Scott's Achievement as a Novelist," *Nineteenth-Century Fiction* 6 (1951): 81–95, 153–73, reprinted in his *Literary Essays* (Edinburgh: Oliver and Boyd, 1956), 88–121. The question of Scott and the Scottish Enlightenment is rather more recent but has been much discussed since Duncan Forbes's pioneering work in "The Rationalism of Sir Walter Scott," *Cambridge Journal* 7 (1953): 20–35. See, for example, Avrom Fleishman, *The English Historical Novel: Walter Scott to Virginia Woolf* (Baltimore: Johns Hopkins University Press, 1971); Peter D. Garside, "Scott and the 'Philosophical' Historians," *Journal of the History of Ideas* 36 (1975): 497–512; and Graham McMaster, *Scott and Society* (Cambridge: Cambridge University Press, 1981), part 2.

20. *The Complete Works of William Hazlitt*, ed. P. P. Howe, 21 vols. (London: Dent, 1930–34), 12:127. Further references to this essay will be included in the text.

the heart rouses itself in its native lair, and utters a wild cry of joy, at being restored once more to freedom and lawless, unrestrained impulses" (129). The sense of freedom and unrestrained impulse to which Hazlitt refers is, of course, firmly contained by the rational and conservative structure of historical interpretation in the Waverley Novels, but it is integral to that structure. "Here are no Jeremy Bentham Panopticons," Hazlitt concludes, "none of Mr. Owen's impassable Parallelograms . . . no long calculations of self-interest" (129). Here, in other words, is release from the disciplinary virtues of an Edgeworth or a Brunton, and this release is at the core of the male romance that structures the Waverley plot. Even as the Waverley hero learns to accept his troubled modernity—his "civil" status—he must make an uncivil journey in order to do so. Rob Roy, comments Hazlitt, would have "spurned and poured a thousand curses" on Bentham's Panopticon and Owen's Parallelogram, and so, for a short while, may his modern reader.

For these first male readers, Waverley reading offered a compelling alternative both to female reading and to feminine writing. In particular, in this period of conservative reaction, evangelical revival, and the domestic-didactic novel, *Waverley* and its successors licensed a nostalgic male-inflected romance of history that offered the satisfaction of emancipation from the necessary restraints of civil society even as it effectually absorbed male subjectivity into those restraints. And central to that sense of liberation, the reviews suggest, was release from a feminized space. Suggestively, Francis Jeffrey, writing in 1817, found that the main fault of the Author of Waverley lay in his "descriptions of virtuous young ladies—and his representations of the ordinary business of courtship and conversation in polished life." He attributes this failure with "polished life" to the fact that the author's "powers" require "some stronger stimulus to bring them into action, than can be supplied by the flat realities of a peaceful and ordinary existence."[21] With their outdoor adventures, their battles, and their political intrigues, the Waverley Novels swerve outside the "flat realities" of genteel daily life. At the same time, they work within those realities, and the mas-

21. Review of *Tales of My Landlord, ER* 28 (1817): 197.

culinity that these narratives helped to construct absorbs the purity that marked femininity. Lockhart praises Scott's novels for achieving their triumphs "without for a moment departing from that firm healthiness of feeling, that sustained and masculine purity of mental vigour, of which there are unfortunately but few examples in the works of this class that intervened between Don Quixote and Waverley."[22]

Even as it was marked by unfeminine "vigour," masculinity shared with femininity the "purity" that guaranteed its "healthiness," so that both genders were constructed under the sign of restraint and both in a sense lived on deferment. As Welsh reminds us, masculinity in this period was redefined to mean "self-control under the most trying circumstances."[23] Certainly, masculinity or "manliness" stood in a different cultural place from femininity and was authorized by different discourses (politics and law, for example); it typically battled different internal and external forces (such as anger and public corruption); and it expressed its social sympathy through forms of action closed to women (as in fighting in Greece rather than visiting the local poor). But it also emerges as a more unstable sign than femininity in that it is now "bold and free" and now "pure" and restrained.

If the femininity of this period has its contradictions, as critics like Mary Poovey have argued,[24] femininity is not itself an internally contested concept in the same way. There is no contention within the concept, in other words, about what should mark femininity as there is with manliness, which not only negotiates with great unease the differing claims of traditional virility and modern masculinity but also stands in a vexed relationship to the femininity that is constituted as its "other" but with which in important ways it coincides.

Gender in the early nineteenth century is constructed within the two prominent signs of civil society—property and restraint. Both of these indicate an orientation to the future, and both encourage the evolution of a prudential morality that

22. Review of *Lives of the Novelists* QR 34 (1826): 377.
23. Welsh, *Hero of the Waverley Novels*, 25.
24. See, for example, *The Proper Lady and the Woman Writer* (Chicago: University of Chicago Press, 1984), 15–30.

makes time the medium of advantage as well as of truth. But the prudential morality of private life with which femininity was identified tended to be read, as we saw with Edgeworth, as constriction and confinement—even as a kind of meanness. Countering it stood the new public virtue of human sympathy, which denied calculation and temporal and spatial differentiations, positing an underlying core of humanity in each human being. To this core, the imagination provided privileged access, and fiction itself (whose existence in all times and in all places was routinely stressed in the period)[25] stood as a central vehicle.

In this sense, the Waverley Novels, activating in their fable of history the old alliance of fiction with romance and desire, were supremely fictional and hence morally valuable at a "deeper" level than didactic fictions like those of Edgeworth. Balancing their indulgence of the aggressive desires and emotions repressed, sublimated, or otherwise governed by civil society was their activation of the benevolence of sympathy. The radical Hazlitt himself despised the Tory Sir Walter Scott, but he celebrated the Author of Waverley, who "conversed with the living and the dead, and let them tell their story their own way."[26] Over and over again, as the Waverley series unfolds, the reviews draw attention to their powers of sympathy, highlighting the "sociality," "cordial spirit," and "social sympathy" that the novels signify and encourage. In reading a Waverley Novel, one reviewer notes in 1820, "the heart swells and yearns towards humanity; forgets the restraints imposed upon it by polished society, and communes in intense feeling with the whole human race."[27] This language recalls that of the erotic daydreams that distinguished female readers, who equally swelled and yearned and forgot the restraints of polished society. But whereas the female reader, yielding (as the *Scots Magazine* put it) to the "delusive sensations of bliss," typically returned "with

25. John Dunlop, for example, insists on this point throughout his *History of Fiction*, 3 vols. (London, 1814), as does Anna Laetitia Barbauld in the long prefatory essay to her important collection of novels, "On the Origin and Progress of Novel-Writing," *The British Novelists*, 50 vols. (London, 1810), 1:1–62.

26. Hazlitt, "Sir Walter Scott," *Complete Works*, 11:63.

27. Review of *Ivanhoe*, Gold's *LM* 1 (1820): 80.

palled senses" and a lack of interest in her domestic duties,[28] the Waverley reader is represented as returning in an expansive mood, his social sympathies invigorated and heightened.

The virtue of sympathy thus operated in conjunction with the outdoor male romance in the Waverley novels to establish the health-and-manliness matrix that increasingly came to define the Waverley Novels as the century continued (see Chapter 8). Looking back at the Waverley phenomenon in 1858, Walter Bagehot was following a standard line when he claimed for Scott a "peculiar healthiness" and linked it to his endowing his representations with "the glow of sentiment natural to a manly mind, and an atmosphere of generosity congenial to a cheerful one." "There are no such books as his for the sick-room, or for freshening the painful intervals of a morbid mind," he memorably concludes.[29] And for Bagehot, as for Scott's first reviewers, the "sick-room" from which the Waverley Novels offered relief was as much metaphorical as literal, standing for the feminized space of modernity itself.

Waverley and Female Reading

Waverley's own story of gender begins, as do the reviews of the novel, by establishing its distinction from the kinds of fictions gathered under the trope of female reading. When it clears a space for itself in the celebrated first chapter, it does so by repudiating contemporary forms of fiction and implicitly aligning itself with earlier, canonical (and more masculine) forms of the novel. In establishing its own difference from the "pages of inanity" that have marked "half a century past," Waverley takes as its particular target fictional forms like the Gothic novel and the sentimental novel that postdate the foundational period of Fielding and Richardson.

Scott's opening tactic is conventional, deploying the authenticating device that realist writers learned from Cervantes and that allowed a novelist to make room for his/her authentic rep-

---

28. "On Novels and Romances," Scots Magazine 64 (1802): 471.
29. "The Waverley Novels," Literary Studies 2: 171–72.

resentation of the real by discounting rival representations as somehow fraudulent.[30] Peculiarly characteristic, however, is the oblique way in which Scott manages the confrontation with "my predecessors" and "my readers." In discussing the title of the novel and the name of the hero, the narrator states his unwillingness to engage in "unnecessary opposition to preconceived associations" by choosing a title that would create definite expectations in readers. Instead, he announces that he has avoided the whole problem by choosing "an uncontaminated name" whose associations will be fixed by the reader. The reluctance to engage in "unnecessary opposition" leaves open, of course, the question of necessary opposition even as it suggests that in this case opposition may be unnecessary simply because the genres in question are played out. Most of all, however, the sly formulation allows Scott to mute his innovative intent in a way that Jane Millgate finds characteristic of him throughout his entire career.[31] The paradoxical tactic of nonoppositional opposition introduced in this first chapter of this first Waverley Novel will mark the series as a whole. Scott rarely directly contests the norms in place; instead, he simply shifts to another place. Here he circumvents the problem of fictional conventions and readerly expectations—the problem of pre-occupied ground, as it were—by moving to new ground, taking an "uncontaminated" name, and letting the reader "affix" its interpretation and associations.

Equally typically, the declaration of novelty and openness to interpretation is couched in a traditional image from romance: the narrator as a maiden knight with a blank shield. The mock-heroic accentuation of the image recalls Cervantes and hence the canonical line of the novel, which then echoes against the list of debased contemporary novelistic forms contained in the

30. On Cervantine realism, see Harry Levin, *Gates of Horn: A Study of Five French Realists* (New York: Oxford University Press, 1963). For more recent studies, see Levine, *Realistic Imagination*, and Walter L. Reed, *An Exemplary History of the Novel: The Quixotic versus the Picaresque* (Chicago: University of Chicago Press, 1981).

31. Jane Millgate argues that Scott, the "great originator," had a "profound distrust of innovation," preferring always to cast his innovations in a tale of continuity where they could figure as variations or extensions (*Walter Scott: The Making of the Novelist* [Toronto: University of Toronto Press, 1984], x).

series of counterfactuals that soon follows: "Had I, for example, announced in my frontispiece, 'Waverley, a Tale of other Days,' must not every novel-reader have anticipated a castle scarce less than that of Udolpho. . . . Again, had my title borne, 'Waverley, a Romance from the German,' . . . " And so on. Removing himself from the contemporary fray, the narrator frees himself to claim kinship (again obliquely) with the figure generally credited with founding the British novel—Henry Fielding. Drawing on *Joseph Andrews*, Scott's narrator authorizes his text by declaring in a well-known passage that "the object of my tale is more a description of men than manners."[32]

But the buried citation is ambiguous, for the realist text must separate itself from all rivals—even canonical ones. Scott may establish his allegiance to the canonical line of novel writing, but he distinguishes himself from it all the same. His point in the opening chapter is indeed the Fieldingesque point that the novelist concentrates on what is common (the human nature of "men") rather than on what is particular (the cultural variable of "manners"). His wording, however, inverts that of Fielding, who had written that "I describe not men, but manners; not an individual, but a species."[33] The generic point is ostensibly the same, but the formulation turns Fielding on his head, prefiguring the way in which Scott's nineteenth-century historical mode of fiction will overturn the hierarchy of men and manners affirmed by Fielding's eighteenth-century satiric fictions. Similarly, the disclaimer in chapter 5 of any attempt to imitate the "inimitable" Cervantes stresses less the modesty and prudence of the author (as he claims) than the greater realism of *Waverley*, for the new text takes as its subject a "more common aberration from sound judgment" than the "total perversion of intellect as misconstrues the objects actually presented to the senses" (18; chap. 5). No more than the Gothic novels and sentimental tales mocked in the opening chapter, then, are the canonical fictions of Fielding and Cervantes left unchallenged, but they are challenged respectfully and granted positive value in a way that the popular fictions of his own day are not.

32. Sir Walter Scott, *Waverley*, Claire Lamont ed. (Oxford: Clarendon, 1981), 4. Future references to this book will appear in the text.

33. *Joseph Andrews and Shamela*, ed. Martin C. Battestin (Boston: Houghton Mifflin, 1961), 159; bk. 3, chap. 1.

The reader of such fictions becomes the direct subject of narrative commentary at the end of the same chapter 5 that opened with the Cervantine reference. The narrator now makes the claim that his novel requires a different mode of reading than that to which most novel readers are accustomed: "I beg pardon, once and for all, of those readers who take up novels merely for amusement, for plaguing them so long with old-fashioned politics, and Whig and Tory, and Hanoverians and Jacobites. The truth is, I cannot promise them that this story shall be intelligible, not to say probable, without it" (24; chap. 5). In contrast to the opening chapter, the narrator now insists that historical particularity is the source of his story's intelligibility and probability, of its meaningfulness as both intellectual and aesthetic construct. He goes on to identify explicitly the kind of readers that he feels his historicity has discouraged: "I do not invite my fair readers, whose sex and impatience give them the greatest right to complain of these circumstances, into a flying chariot drawn by hyppogriffs, or moved by enchantment." Impatient of political and historical analysis, fair readers seek the Oriental escapism of a flying chariot ("Prince Hussein's tapestry") and chafe at a narrative that offers only "a humble English post-chaise, drawn upon four wheels, and keeping his majesty's highway." Elaborating the contrasting (realist) mode of travel offered by his narrative, the narrator announces that readers who remain with him will have to endure "the dulness [sic] inseparable from heavy roads, steep hills, sloughs, and other terrestrial retardations." There is a kind of sober heroism to realist reading, it seems, that contrasts positively with the flighty self-indulgence of female reading.

But, in a characteristic self-mocking turn, Scott undercuts the pretensions of his realist pose by promising "to get as soon as possible into a more picturesque and romantic country, if my passengers incline to have some patience with me during my first stages." Not much more patience is required: the very next page begins the description of Waverley's departure from England for the picturesque and romantic Scotland whose image had been constructed in large part for the reading public by one Walter Scott, poet.

And on the question of the romantic love privileged by female romance, Scott's narrator once again divorces the reading of his text from female reading. Chapter 54 ("'To one thing constant never'") centers on a scene of reading: Waverley's reading of *Romeo and Juliet* at a social tea where Rose and Flora are in attendance. Their contrasting responses to the story of Romeo—Rose's emotional, Flora's rational—help discourage his courtship of the latter and awaken his interest in the former, and the chapter ends with Waverley's decision to renounce Flora-Rosalind. But he is less sure whether he should court Rose-Juliet to whose hand Fergus aspires; in characteristic fashion, Waverley resolves to be "guided by circumstances" (257; chap. 54). The next chapter opens with a narrative comment: "If my fair readers should be of opinion that my hero's levity in love is altogether unpardonable, I must remind them, that all his griefs and difficulties did not arise from that sentimental source. Even the lyric poet, who complains so feelingly of the pains of love, could not forget, that, at the same time, he was 'in debt and in drink,' which, doubtless, were great aggravations of his distress" (257; chap. 55). A moment of realist puncturing, it mocks the delusion and irresponsibility of sentimental reading, and the narrator continues his lesson in right reading when he adds: "There were, indeed, whole days in which Waverley thought neither of Flora nor of Rose Bradwardine, but which were spent in melancholy conjectures upon the probable state of matters at Waverley-Honour, and the dubious issue of the civil contest in which he was engaged" (257; chap. 55).

If Edgeworth assigned to romantic love "its just limits," Scott displaced the whole plot of courtship which had remained central to the proper novel, shifting it to the periphery of narrative interest and so altering novelistic attention. That shift, registered for the most part by the nineteenth century as a shift from private to public, was decisive for the kind of authority granted to Scott. The "most striking feature" of the Waverley Novels, writes Richard H. Hutton near the end of the century, is that "they are pivoted on public rather than mere private interests and passions." This public turn allows the participation of various kinds of readers: "And this it is which gives his books so large an interest for old and young, soldiers and statesmen, the world of society and the recluse, alike. You can hardly read any novel of Scott's and not become better aware what public life and political issues mean." Indeed, Hutton adds, "no man can read Scott without being more of a public man, whereas the ordinary novel tends to make its readers rather less of one than before."[34]

Waverley itself, mixing modes and moods, appeals to a variety of implied readers.[35] More particularly, the narrator posits a whole range of narrator-narratee relationships in the various moments of address scattered throughout the narrative. So he turns now to the generic "gentle reader" featured in eighteenth-century fiction, now to the less formal "my dear reader," now to the even more intimate but still distanced "my worthy friend." Different readerships are called up at different moments of the narrative: scholars, soldiers, romance readers, Scottish patriots, enlightened moderns, and others. But all are kept at a distance, and the continual reminder of reading combines with the narrator's self-consciousness to break any tendency to engage in the absorbed flow of female reading.[36] This is not to say that the errors of reading that *Waverley* strives to correct are all female errors. Far from it, as the example of the soldier-pedant Baron Bradwardine illustrates. But female reading is paradigmatic of all such disorders, and it is the fair reader who stands *for* reading errors.

As an undisciplined and inexperienced young reader, Edward Waverley himself is a type of female reader. The description of his reading early in the novel associates him from the outset with the standard trope. Waverley's "powers of apprehension," the narrator notes, are "so uncommonly quick, as almost to resemble intuition"; he has "brilliancy of fancy and vivacity of talent" but also the "indolence" that often accompanies these and that is overcome only by immediate "plea-

---

34. *Sir Walter Scott* (New York, 1878), 101–2. For an elaboration of Scott's transformation of the privacy of novel reading, see I. Ferris, "The Reader in the Rhetoric of Realism: Scott, Thackeray and Eliot," in *Scott and His Influence*, ed. J. H. Alexander and David Hewitt. (Aberdeen: Association for Scottish Literary Studies, 1983), 382–92.

35. On this point, see Colby, *Fiction with a Purpose*, 37–38.

36. Robyn Warhol has argued that narrative distance and self-consciousness tend to mark male as opposed to female narration in the nineteenth century; see her *Gendered Interventions: Narrative Discourse in the Victorian Novel* (New Brunswick, N.J.: Rutgers University Press, 1989).

sure" and "novelty" (12; chap. 3). His self-indulgence is "in-flamed" by his "power of imagination and love of literature," but his sole motivation in reading is instant "gratification"; and he soon finds this increasingly difficult to achieve, so that "the passion for reading, like other strong appetites, produced by indulgence a sort of satiety" (13; chap. 3). The list of Waverley's preferences in reading stresses his romantic taste: in English literature, he favors Spenser, Drayton, and "other poets who have exercised themselves on romantic fiction"; in Italian literature, he peruses "numerous romantic poems"; in French literature he finds "an almost exhaustless collection of memoirs, scarcely more faithful than romances, and of romances so well written as hardly to be distinguished from memoirs" (14; chap. 3). And so it continues, with the Spanish and others adding to "his stock of chivalrous and romantic lore." Interestingly, the classical writers are mentioned only perfunctorily: "In classical literature, Waverley had made the usual progress, and read the usual authors."

In her recent study of the Waverley Novels, Judith Wilt draws attention to the way in which Scott plays with the boundaries of male identity through his passive hero, and she notes of Waverley in particular that he rides out from home "to be kidnapped, 'educated,' seduced, and otherwise feminized."[37] Certainly, Waverley tends to be carried about a great deal, as in this moment during his journey to see David Bean Lean: "Four or five active arms lifted Waverley out of the boat, placed him on his feet, and almost carried him into the recesses of the cave" (79; chap. 17). In many ways, he is best understood as a Gothic heroine in male form, and the whole Waverley series is marked by an interest in male-female interchange, as if, Wilt remarks, each gender "must journey through the experience of the other, the outlawed, gender, before either one can choose and re-fix the male or female identity appropriate to the new age."[38] So Darsie Latimer puts on female dress in *Redgauntlet*, as does George Staunton-Robertson in *Heart of Midlothian*. The young hero of *The Abbot* is bewildered by the appearance of the heroine

37. *Secret Leaves: The Novels of Walter Scott* (Chicago: University of Chicago Press, 1985), 117.
38. Ibid.

in male dress on various occasions (it turns out she has a twin brother), and Scott's outlaw women like Meg Merrilies and Madge Wildfire tend to be masculine in form and dress. The constructs of gender that have become so firm in the mid-Victorian novel of Dickens and Thackeray demonstrate a certain mobility and fluidity in the Waverley Novels.

Rose Bradwardine, for example, Scott's first domestic heroine, talks familiarly of armed conflict and regrets the disarming of the Scots even as she tends her flower garden and obeys her father. She falls in love with Waverley before he falls in love with her; moreover, she confides that love to Flora MacIvor, whom Waverley desires and who herself lives entirely outside the domestic sphere. Flora's own incompatibility with Waverley largely stems from their different relationship to the domestic world. To Flora, his "real disposition" is "exclusively domestic," despite his "dreams of tented fields and military honour" (248; chap. 52). He fails when measured by traditional standards of virility, and Flora develops a contempt for him as a result. This contempt emerges clearly in her argument with Rose over Waverley's lack of interest in the disputes of the Jacobite army in Edinburgh. When Rose defends Waverley as "so gentle, so well informed," Flora cuts in: "Yes he can admire the moon, and quote a stanza from Tasso" (249; chap. 52). It is not his ability to fight that is the issue, for to Flora all men are much the same when it comes to "mere fighting." The problem is with the set of his character as a whole: "But high and perilous enterprize is not Waverley's forte. . . . I will tell you where he will be at home, my dear, and in his place,—in the quiet circle of domestic happiness, lettered indolence, and elegant enjoyments of Waverley-Honour" (250; chap. 52). Like the proper heroine or the fair romance reader in the didactic fictions of the day, Waverley must come to recognize and accept "the quiet circle of domestic happiness." His flirtation with "high and perilous enterprize," like his flirtation with Flora, is the mark of the romance reader gendered male.

Whereas female reading was critiqued for encouraging young women to neglect their domestic duties and to long for impossible romantic relationships, *Waverley* suggests that its male enactment potentially entails even more significant social effects.

When Waverley moves into the Highlands, he "give[s] himself up to the full romance of his situation" (78; chap. 16), and from that surrender stem serious consequences. As a gentleman, Waverley risks more than the well-being of the domestic circle that is jeopardized by female romance readers: he risks the life of the men on his estate, as well as his own life, and he threatens the order of the state. Swayed by the "romantic fiction" of his youth, fired by family legends of heroic action, bored with the restrictions of his secluded English place, and unsettled by the onset of sexual desire, the hero of *Waverley* seeks to act out his dreams.[39] What he learns (as do all romance readers) is the unfitness of those dreams to him and to modern life. And he articulates the insight to which he comes in a fitting metaphor of genre change: "he felt himself entitled to say firmly, though perhaps with a sigh, that the romance of his life was ended, and that its real history had now commenced. He was soon called upon to justify his pretensions to reason and philosophy" (283; chap. 60). What is odd about this passage is that it seems to signal a choice (the choice of "reason and philosophy"), but its passive verbs undermine the notion of choice by placing in the foreground a change already in place rather than a choice: something outside Waverley has determined that romance "was ended" and that history "had now commenced."

The obvious answer to what has determined these matters is "circumstances," and that, in turn, is another name for history. But how is withdrawal from the public stage of history an entry into history? What sort of "history" does Waverley have in mind? The statement is intriguing and puzzling, but in one sense at least it does achieve a certain clarity, for Waverley articulates his sense of transition by calling on two highly connotative genres: the youthful and female genre of romance and the adult and male genre of history to whose traits of "reason and philosophy" the narrator carefully draws attention. For Waverley, the hero who rescues Ariosto from the ruins of Tully-Veolan, the literary turn here is entirely characteristic, as is his choice of the literary hierarchy as a metaphor for the achieve-

39. On the dream logic of the plot, see Robert Kiely, *The Romantic Novel in England* (Cambridge, Mass.: Harvard University Press, 1972), chap. 7.

ment of adulthood. In rejecting romance (if with a sigh), Waverley comes to a position similar to that of the generic fair romance reader, who (like *Northanger Abbey*'s Catherine Morland) also exchanges romance for another mode. But whereas a heroine like Morland comes to ethical knowledge and moves into ethical space, Edward Waverley's passage to maturity involves as well an entry into the more strictly historicist knowledge of cultural difference; hence he enters not simply ethical but historical and cultural space.

More precisely, Waverley comes to discern not simply the duplicity of words, the slipperiness of the signifier, but also the distinctiveness and relativity of signifying systems. One of his first lessons, for example, is that "in Scotland a single house was called a *town*, and a natural fool an *innocent*" (40; chap. 9). Thus begins his education in the historical variability of language, and it is followed by a whole series of lessons on words, clothes, foods, and other symbolic cultural practices, as he moves from Tully-Veolan through the Highlands to Edinburgh and back to England. He is amused by the baron's obsession with a symbolic feudal obligation that seems ridiculous in modern Scotland; he is discomfited by his own Highland dress when he faces the standard of his former English troop in battle; and he is flattered by Charles Edward's gift of a broadsword that is itself a Stuart heirloom. In these and a whole host of similar moments, Waverley discovers the cultural, psychological, and political power of signs.

Fittingly, his education in the semiology of culture ends where it began, at Tully-Veolan.[40] Waverley's story concludes with a highly charged scene of emblem-making, as the survivors of the civil discord gather at Tully-Veolan to celebrate its recent restoration and the recent wedding of Edward and Rose. In a veritable excess of signification, sign crowds upon sign in the scene, from the arrangement of the landscape to the actions (such as the drinking of toasts) in which the characters engage. Two signs dominate: the familial emblem of the restored bears of Bradwardine (including the recovered cup known as the

40. For the structural significance of Tully-Veolan, see Millgate, *Walter Scott*, chap. 3.

Blessed Bear of Bradwardine), and the painting of Fergus and Waverley in Highland dress that hangs in the dining room. What all this signals—and celebrates—is the kindly power of signs. Here Waverley exploits their restorative and consoling force, counteracting their destructive and divisive potential to which his whole Scottish experience had alerted him. In so doing, he may, as often charged, aestheticize the past into comforting pattern, but this in itself signals the important point that he now knows something about how culture—and history—are made.

4

From "National Tale" to "Historical Novel": Edgeworth, Morgan, and Scott

> To Sir Walter Scott belongs the honour of having first shown how history ought to be made available for the purposes of fiction.
>
> —T. H. Lister, *Edinburgh Review* (1832)

Edward Waverley's emergent sense of cultural process points to one way in which Scott showed how history "ought to be made available for the purposes of fiction."[1] But Scott's innovation here depended on a form of fiction already in place, on what came to be called the "national tale." And in transforming national tale into historical novel, Scott was working within a contemporary female genre. An Anglo-Irish creation, the national tale was founded by Maria Edgeworth in *Castle Rackrent* (1800), and it was transformed into national romance by Morgan's *Wild Irish Girl* (1806). Morgan, in fact, came to be more firmly linked to the category than Edgeworth herself. As a narrative form, the national tale was symptomatic of what John Wilson Croker saw as the definitive characteristic of the contemporary novel. According to Croker, contemporary fiction was distinguished from that of the previous century in taking as its object of representation "men of a peculiar nation, profession, or temper, or, to go a step further—of *individuals*." So, he claims, Tom Jones "might have been a Frenchman, and Gil Blas an Englishman, because the essence of their characters is human nature . . . while, on the other hand, the characters of the most popular novels of later times are Irish, or Scotch, or French, and not in the abstract, *men*."[2] As a sign of the new

---

1. "The Waverley Novels," *ER* 55 (1832): 65.
2. Review of *Waverley*, *QR* 11 (1814): 355.

importance beginning to be granted to national distinctiveness in the late eighteenth and early nineteenth centuries, the national tale takes its place in the matrix of (mostly) counter-Enlightenment forces that converged to form the nationalism that was to mark nineteenth-century Europe.

The Waverley Novels themselves, of course, were to play a significant role in that formation not only in Scotland but in countries as diverse as Italy and Poland where historical fictions modeled on Scott quickly assumed the status of national epics in the nationalist struggles of the nineteenth century.[3] And the national tale provides the immediate novelistic context for the reception of *Waverley*, which is consistently placed in relation to Edgeworth's work. Croker himself goes on to announce that it is "of a higher strain" than *Castle Rackrent* with its "amusing vulgarity," and he prefers to align it with what he sees as Edgeworth's best works, *Ennui* and *The Absentee*. Other reviews make other distinctions—the *Monthly Review*, for example, argues that *Waverley*'s historical setting makes it quite different from *Ennui*[4]—but most reviews locate *Waverley* in some relation to Edgeworth's Irish fictions.

In so doing, they follow Scott's own example in the postscript to *Waverley*, which defines the novel's attempt to represent the Scots as an emulation of "the admirable Irish portraits drawn by Miss Edgeworth, so different from the 'dear joys' who so long, with the most perfect family resemblance to each other, occupied the drama and the novel" (341; chap. 72). Reiterating the point in private but under cover of his anonymity, Scott wrote to Matthew Weld Hartstonge that the author of *Waverley* "must have had your inimitable Miss Edgeworth strongly in his view, for the manner is palpably imitated while the pictures are original."[5] These early tributes received powerful confirmation in the 1829 general preface when the now canonical Sir Walter Scott credited Edgeworth with having revived his interest in the

---

3. I have in mind texts like Alessandro Manzoni's *I Promessi sposi* and Adam Mickiewicz's *Pan Tadeusz*, both of which became (and to some extent still are) nationalist icons in Italy and Poland respectively.

4. *MR*, n.s., 75 (1814): 280.

5. *The Letters of Sir Walter Scott*, ed. H. J. C. Grierson et al., 12 vols. (London: Constable, 1932), 4:465.

unfinished manuscript of *Waverley* and so of having played a catalytic role in the formation of the Author of Waverley. Where the novel itself had stressed her innovative role in undermining standard modes of cultural representation, the late preface sets her up as the model of the politics of conciliation that always attracted Scott: "she may be truly said to have done more towards completing the Union than perhaps all the legislative enactments by which it has been followed up" (*Wav. Nov.*, 1:9). In his own writing, he adds, he sought to achieve a similar reconciliation between the Scots and the English by introducing the "natives" of Scotland "to those of the sister kingdom in a more favourable light than they had been placed hitherto." His goal was to "procure sympathy for their virtues and indulgence for their foibles" (*Wav. Nov.*, 1:9–10).

Such reconciliation was soon to become suspect, and both Edgeworth and Scott have come under serious criticism, especially by twentieth-century Irish and Scots nationalists.[6] But the practice of fiction by this Anglo-Irish woman and this Scotsman was instrumental in initiating the historically significant process of authorizing cultural margins in nineteenth-century Europe, a process that depended on but was not always congruent with the nationalist drive. Admittedly, the early national novel typically sought recognition for colonized groups within the current imperial arrangement of things. Even the liberal Morgan, agitating for Catholic emancipation and other national causes, was, as Barry Sloan has stressed, firmly conservative in her acceptance of Irish dependence on England.[7] For her part,

---

6. As the more successful creator of national myths, Scott has been attacked more vehemently and consistently than Edgeworth. In the course of setting up his own argument that Scott deserves to be celebrated as a pioneer of modern Scottish nationalism, P. H. Scott gives a good sense of the nationalist attack in "The Malachi Episode," prefaced to his edition of Walter Scott's *The Letters of Malachi Malagrowther* (Edinburgh: Blackwood, 1981), ix–xxxiv. The *Malachi Malagrowther* papers themselves, written in 1826, show Scott at his most nationalist, and they were instrumental in forcing the English government to change its policy on abolishing the issue of Scottish bank notes.

7. *The Pioneers of Anglo-Irish Fiction, 1800–1850* (Totowa, N.J.: Barnes and Noble, 1986), chap. 1. This chapter is a useful introduction to the cultural significance of Morgan and Edgeworth. Sloan builds on the important earlier study by Thomas Flanagan, *The Irish Novelists, 1800–1850* (New York: Columbia University Press, 1958).

Edgeworth sought principally to create a more responsible attitude on the part of the landlords, and Scott himself (however ambiguously) affirmed the Union. But in introducing cultural difference—in language, habits, attitudes—the national novels of the early nineteenth century challenged assumptions of cultural homogeneity and superiority, opening up important new spaces within—and through—their own conservative fictions for "other" questions. And here it was the Waverley Novels, rather than the Irish fictions on which they built, that became the effective medium of literary and cultural innovation. What follows sets the first novels of Edgeworth and Morgan in relation to Scott's own first novel, asking questions about discursive authority and romance structure, in an attempt to explain why this should have been so.

Discursive Authority in *Castle Rackrent* and *Waverley*

Both *Castle Rackrent* and *Waverley* make the realist claim to nonfiction, more precisely to historical value, and each couches the claim in a narrative frame. Edgeworth encloses Thady Quirk's first-person memoir of the Rackrents within a preface, coda, and glossary;[8] and Scott makes his historical claim after the conclusion of Waverley's story in the final chapter, "A Postscript, which Should Have Been a Preface."[9] In making their realist claim, both writers exchange fictional for historical discourse in a very specific way by diminishing the distance between actual author, implied author, and narrator.

Paul Hernadi's argument about the distinction between historical and fictional narrative is pertinent here. Hernadi posits that it is possible to derive a "workable theoretical distinction" between the two discourses on the basis of the different relationships they prompt the reader to postulate between the im-

8. I leave aside the notes as a secondary device, and I am also leaving aside the problem of Richard Lovell Edgeworth's contributions to the narrative frame and the documentation. Not only does his specific role seem impossible to determine, but my interest is in authorship as a discursive sign in the text.

9. Here too I leave aside the notes since these, along with Scott's introductions, were added later.

plied author and the narrative *persona* of a text. Fiction demands a distinction between the two, whereas history precludes it. Of special interest is Hernadi's point that the narrator of a work of fiction is fictional because the particular narrator "has been created for the purpose of narrating a given work of fiction."[10] One could, of course, say something similar about the narrator of a work of history, who is equally constructed in terms of a specific discourse and hence in a sense equally fictional. Nevertheless, there is an important difference in the "pledge" (to use Scott's metaphor in *Waverley*) between writer and reader that is involved in fiction and in history. And that difference has less to do with the status of the referent (X really happened) than with the status of the speaker mediating between reader and referent. This does not mean that the referent is either unimportant or fictional but simply that it is the speaker who establishes for the reader which referential and hermeneutical rules are in place. The speaker of history implicitly claims identity with the author of the text, as a fictional narrator does not, and in so doing the speaker of history grants to what is spoken a status distinct from that of fiction.

Two key self-reflexive moments in *Waverley* help clarify the point: the opening and the closing of the text. In chapter 1 the narrator establishes his credentials as a *novelist*, demonstrating in a playful and self-deprecating manner his familiarity with novelistic genres and conventions. Following his list of the types of novels he has chosen not to follow, for example, he remarks: "I could proceed in proving the importance of a title-page, and displaying at the same time my own intimate knowledge of the particular ingredients necessary to the composition of romances and novels of various descriptions. But it is enough, and I scorn to tyrannize longer over the impatience of my reader, who is doubtless already anxious to know the choice made by an author so profoundly versed in the different branches of his art" (4; chap. 1). What follows this passage is rather more serious as the narrator sets out the "object" of his tale, but the discourse remains firmly within literary, and more

10. "Clio's Cousins: Historiography as Translation, Fiction, and Criticism," *New Literary History* 7 (1976): 252.

specifically, novelistic tradition. Hence when the hidden term of the preface—"history"—finally surfaces in the last few lines of the chapter ("at the period of my history"), it is read in the novelistic context evoked by the narrative voice. "My history" is received as a standard fictional device familiar to novel readers since the early eighteenth century. While the gap between narrator and implied author opened up by irony in the first pages is not sustained over the entire narrative, this initial evocation of the rules of fiction governs the overall reading of the narrator as a fictional device. His primary function is to serve the fiction—to tell the story—and questions about his relationship to the author do not, in the normal course of reading, arise.

But in the postscript of chapter 72 the rules change, and *Waverley* moves decisively out of the fictional contract. That contract is recalled at the very beginning of chapter 72 by the Fieldingesque image with which it opens: "Our journey is now finished, gentle reader, and if your patience has accompanied me through these sheets, the contract is, on your part, strictly fulfilled. Yet, like the driver who has received his full hire, I still linger near you, and make, with becoming diffidence, a trifling additional claim upon your bounty and good nature" (339; chap. 72). But the Fieldingesque tone is reintroduced only to be abruptly abandoned when the narrative voice announces: "There is no European nation which, within the course of half a century, or little more, has undergone so complete a change as this kingdom of Scotland" (340; chap. 72). This statement signals the end of fiction and the beginning of another kind of discourse. In contrast to chapter 1, the narrative voice is now located in a specific place and in a specific historical period, and its particularization continues as it speaks of "my younger time" and "my accidental lot . . . to reside during my childhood and youth" among Highlanders. This is the voice less of a novelist than of a Scotsman, a shift to autobiography whose rules invoke a different understanding of who is speaking and of how (or what) he speaks. No longer the playful, stylized novelist of the introductory chapter, this voice draws on the conventions of personal, serious discourse as it reflects on cultural change and on the sources and production of the fiction that has just been concluded.

Here, in other words, is an authorial voice, and it is read as such whether or not one knows that the author is Walter Scott, and whether or not Walter Scott is lying or otherwise acting in bad faith. In fact, it is the possibility of making such charges that distinguishes the kinds of generic contracts evoked in the opening and concluding chapters (and accounts, perhaps, for the vehemence with which a critic like David Craig could indict Scott's novels).[11] To accuse the narrator of chapter 1 with something like betrayal, for example, would be to read inappropriately, whereas it would not be inappropriate to aim such a charge at the authorial voice of the final chapter. The difference lies in the kind of responsibility that the author-narrator takes for what he says, the kind of referential authority that he wants his words to have for the reader. Because of this voice the "Scotland" of the final pages falls under the category of history in a way that the "northern part of the island" referred to in chapter 1 does not.

The history-effect of both *Waverley* and *Castle Rackrent* depends in large part on such shifts in narrative voice. Interpretive authority in both texts is finally granted through a nonfictional voice that identifies the aim and referent of the fiction as historical. Edgeworth first indicates her historical project through the subtitle, a technique that Scott was to imitate effectively in the teasing subtitle to *Waverley*, "'Tis Sixty Years Since." *Castle Rackrent* is subtitled "An Hibernian Tale Taken from Facts, and from the Manners of the Irish Squires, before the Year 1782." The terms "Facts," "Manners," and "Irish Squires" suggest a social, nonfictional intent, but novels of the period routinely claimed such an intent, and it is only with the very specific date that Edgeworth's text begins to distinguish itself (though still not decisively) from standard procedures. The year 1782 figures prominently in both the personal history of the Edgeworths (the year of their move from England to Ireland) and in the public history of the nation (the year of the establishment of the Irish Independency). For Maria Edgeworth herself, then, the year stood as a watershed in several ways, not

11. *Scottish Literature and the Scottish People, 1680–1830* (London: Chatto & Windus, 1961).

least in the sense that "before 1782" marks a time in Ireland that she could know only as history. In public terms, the adoption of the constitution in that year meant that it served to divide former days from these days, a point stressed in the preface: "The Editor hopes his readers will observe, that these are 'tales of other times;' that the manners depicted in the following pages are not those of the present age."[12]

Despite the short chronological gap between the date noted in the subtitle and the date of actual publication (a mere eighteen years compared with the almost seventy years of *Waverley*), Edgeworth identifies her tale as an account of the vanished past; hence it falls into the category of historical narrative. But *Castle Rackrent* is rarely classified as a historical novel. More commonly, as with George Watson's edition for Oxford's World's Classics, it is recognized as "the first regional novel in English" (vii). Marilyn Butler allows that because of its material, it is "one kind of historical novel," but she argues that "at a more serious level it is the least historical of Maria's tales. There is no sense of impending future in it—no clash between the Rackrents' values and those of the people replacing them."[13] Butler's contrast is with *Waverley*, whose sense of historical process as the painful replacement of one cultural order by another has been much commented on, and it is certainly true that the history-likeness of Scott's novel depends crucially on his peculiar sense of cultural collision and transition. It depends, that is, on a certain narrative thematization or configuration, but it also depends—and this is where Edgeworth is especially useful as a contrast—on the way it merges its discourse with that of history. Where Scott absorbs the authority of official discourses like that of history, even as he modifies and on occasion subverts them, Edgeworth challenges such discourses but betrays an uneasiness in so doing that in effect leaves their authority in place.

Edgeworth's preface takes official history as its target, criticizing "the professed historian" and the critics who support his

12. *Castle Rackrent*, ed. George Watson (New York: Oxford University Press, 1964), 4. All references are to this edition, which is based on the first edition of the novel.

13. *Maria Edgeworth: A Literary Biography* (London: Oxford University Press, 1972), 357.

claims to authority by scorning the public taste for "anecdote." Edgeworth makes two related main points: official history is full of "fine fancy," and even "the best authenticated antient or modern histories" contain "much uncertainty." Those who love truth, therefore—and this is the interesting and important conclusion of the preface—look to "secret memoirs and private anecdotes": "We cannot judge either of the feelings or of the characters of men with perfect accuracy from their actions or their appearance in public; it is from their careless conversations, their half finished sentences, that we may hope with the greatest probability of success to discover their real characters" (1). Edgeworth's notion of the "real" is classically logocentric: its discovery depends on a set of binaries that privilege speech over writing, private over public, the careless over the careful, and so on. For one so committed to rationality—and her rationality, as we have seen, was much recognized and often lamented by her contemporaries—Edgeworth grants an odd primacy to the secret, the hidden, and the half finished. It is even odder if we allow that the arch-rationalist Richard Lovell Edgeworth had a hand (as he probably did) in writing this preface.

But it all proves to be somewhat less strange than it seems at first, for the downgrading of the conscious, public, and writerly sphere turns out to be a way of privileging the domestic, which for the Edgeworths stood as the measure of virtue and the source of rational social value. Noting the public interest in autobiographies, familiar letters, and diaries, the preface maintains that "we are surely justified in this eager desire to collect the most minute facts relative to the domestic lives, not only of the great and good, but even of the worthless and insignificant, since it is only by a comparison of their actual happiness or misery in the privacy of domestic life, that we can form a just estimate of the real reward of virtue, or the real punishment of vice" (2). Because the historian can seldom "consistently with his dignity, pause to illustrate this truth," we have to turn to the (presumably less dignified) biographer. The link between intimacy, lack of dignity, and the presence of truth is then imaged in a theatrical metaphor that Thackeray's *Vanity Fair* was to make famous: "After we have beheld splendid characters playing their parts on the great theatre of the world, with all the advantages of stage effect and decoration, we anxiously beg to be admitted behind the scenes, that we may take a nearer view of the actors and actresses" (2).

In all this, Edgeworth is following novelistic tradition, which had long claimed not only that the novel was a form of history but that it was a more authentic form of history than official history. Authenticity for the novel, Mikhail Bakhtin has argued, always resides in the unofficial genres,[14] and one does not have to turn Edgeworth into a carnivalesque figure in order to align her with his insight. In this preface in particular there emerges a strong sense of the value of a writing outside the official and dignified genres. What is stressed about the historian is "his dignity"; to be outside the sphere of dignity, the preface repeatedly urges, is to be authentic. Valorization of the unofficial genres reaches its height not, as might be expected, with the defense of the use of dialect but with the notion that gossip represents the model for biography. Speaking through the male voice of the editor and taking as a specific target Dr. Johnson's biography of Richard Savage, Edgeworth argues that an uneducated and untalented writer makes a better biographer because such a writer will be less capable of deceiving the reader. He will not sacrifice truth to style, nor will he be able to disguise as easily his prejudices and biases. For Edgeworth, the public is right to countenance those who "simply pour forth anecdotes and retail conversations, with all the minute prolixity of a gossip in a country town" (3). This argument is mounted to prepare the reader not only for the voice of Thady Quirk (identified here as "an illiterate old steward") but also for distance from that voice. Thady's prejudices on behalf of the Rackrents, Edgeworth declares, "must be obvious to the reader" (3–4). But the "must," hovering between indicative and imperative senses, betrays a certain anxiety about exactly how obvious it all is, and *Castle Rackrent*, notoriously, has yielded to contradictory readings: as a nostalgic lament for and as a devastating critique of the world it represents.[15]

14. The most convenient collection of Bakhtin's essays on the novel is *The Dialogic Imagination*, trans. Caryl Emerson and Michael Holquist, ed. Michael Holquist (Austin: University of Texas Press, 1981).

15. Thomas Flanagan, for example, inclines to the nostalgic and Marilyn Butler to the critical reading.

To Edgeworth, the limitations of Thady should be "obvious" because truth is obvious to all right-minded persons. It is Edgeworth's Enlightenment belief in the clarity, rationality, and uniformity of truth that allows her to fictionalize and to argue for unofficial genres like gossip. At the same time, her faith in the homogenous world of reason, as that uneasy "must" suggests, is somewhat porous. Two points in the preface are suggestive here: the definition of the role of "vernacular idiom" in the text, and the admission that to "the *ignorant* English reader" the memoirs may be unintelligible. Both acknowledge difference and discontinuity. In admitting Thady, Edgeworth has admitted not only an obviously prejudiced person (and hence a target for irony) but also one who is culturally particular. The editor notes that he has recorded Thady's "vernacular idiom" even though he had thought of translating it into "plain English." Two perceptions prevented translation, and both effectively unsettle the rationalist assumptions that the preface has also been urging: first, Thady's idiom is "incapable of translation"; second, the "authenticity" of his story would be exposed to doubt "if it were not told in his own characteristic manner" (4). To admit that a language is incapable of translation and to tie the judgment of authenticity to a characteristic manner is in an important way to question assumptions about human uniformity. It is not necessarily to deny those assumptions, but it is to make them more problematic. Like Scott, who opens *Waverley* on a Fieldingesque note affirming uniform human nature (despite historical differences) and closes it on a historicist note foregrounding radical historical difference (despite general human nature), Edgeworth struggles with opposing models of cultural understanding, and out of their friction generates the novelistic innovation of *Castle Rackrent*.[16]

Her innovation—and this is the second point unsettling the assumption of homogeneity—was directed at the English reader. As with the admission that Thady's idiom is untranslatable and essential, so the admission that the English reader will need a few notes in order to understand the story foregrounds cultural heterogeneity rather than the ideal homogeneity of the

16. On the ambivalence of Edgeworth's narrative, see Robert Tracy, "Maria Edgeworth and Lady Morgan," *Nineteenth-Century Fiction* 40 (1985): 1–22.

literary republic. The point is made even more strongly at the end of the narrative in the editor's coda and by the glossary. At the conclusion of Thady's narrative, the voice of the editor returns, reiterating his decision not to varnish "the plain round tale of faithful Thady": "He [the editor] lays it before the English reader as a specimen of manners and characters, which are perhaps unknown in England. Indeed the domestic habits of no nation in Europe were less known to the English than those of their sister country, till within these few years" (96–97). Even more strongly than in the preface, the editorial voice here merges with the authorial voice as it goes on to single out for commendation *A Tour of Ireland* by Arthur Young as "the first faithful portrait of [Ireland's] inhabitants" and adds that its own sketches "were taken from the life" (97). Concluding with some inconclusive comments on the impending union of Ireland and Scotland, the narrative proper is followed by an "Advertisement to the English Reader." Since this consists of a simple announcement that the glossary is added in order to explain terms and idiomatic phrases that might be unintelligible to "the English reader," the advertisement is oddly redundant. The point has been made several times before, and it will continue to be made throughout the commentary of the glossary, which distances itself not just from "the lower Irish" (the main subject) but also from "the English reader" (the main object). Mediating between the subject and object is a voice apart from both, providing information and linking past and present.

Edgeworth insists that the narrative of the Rackrents is a tale of other times, that the manners are not those of the present, that the race of Rackrents has long been extinct. This insistence signals not so much a historical understanding (as it will do in *Waverley*) as an ethical and political hope. Referring to the impending union at the end of the preface, she imagines the present as analogous to "a time when individuals can bear to be rallied for their past follies and absurdities, after they have acquired new habits and a new consciousness. Nations as well as individuals gradually lose attachment to their identity, and the present generation is amused rather than offended by the ridicule that is thrown upon their ancestors" (5). The final paragraph of the preface reads: "When Ireland loses her identity by a union with Great Britain, she will look back with a smile of good-humoured complacency on the Sir Kits and Sir Condys of her former existence" (5). But the coda at the end is not quite so hopeful, for here the Editor admits that "it is a problem of difficult solution to determine, whether an Union will hasten or retard the amelioration of this country" (97). Written when Edgeworth's father was in Dublin voting on this very question of union, *Castle Rackrent* is permeated with a sense of change, of the end of an order—and with ambivalence about the future.

Strangely enough, this sense of temporality does not create a sense of historical process. Instead, Thady's recital of the fall of the Rackrents over successive generations (and the rise of his own family) takes on the static, spatial contours of the rise-and-fall pattern of older histories, fables, and didactic tales. Despite her own ambivalence to historical changes and despite her techniques of local color and historical reference, Edgeworth's narrative (and this remains true of her later Irish tales as well) lacks a sense of historical time.[17] And this has a great deal to do with the way in which narrative voice in *Castle Rackrent* is awkwardly split between the first-person, specifically located Thady Quirk and the third-person, unlocated editor. Between the two is simply a gap; they seem to exist in the same narrative space but in noncontiguous portions of it. They do not exist in different times. In order for *Castle Rackrent* to register as *historical* in its approach to cultural change, Edgeworth has not only to create a third-person perspective to give the sense of temporal distance but to make that third-person perspective an active mediation. Through the editor and his apparatus she attempts something like this, but this narrative device, prompted by the valorization of the private and domestic that underlies the use of Thady's view of things, fails to effect the connections and to generate the sense of process that historical narrative requires. Not surprisingly, her later Irish tales turn to a third-person narrator even as they abandon the attempt to record historical change.

When Scott praised Edgeworth as his model in the postscript to *Waverley*, he was probably thinking more of her *Absentee* than

---

17. Sloan disagrees, finding in *Castle Rackrent* an "astonishing sense of historical process" (*Pioneers*, 3).

of *Castle Rackrent*.[18] *Waverley* certainly has a great deal in common with the later novel (from the plot centered on a journey out of England to third-person narration), but to see *Waverley* in relation to *Rackrent* is to stress the self-consciousness with which both writers approached the cultural project of their novel writing. Only in their first novels is either so explicit and so tentative about what she/he is trying to do. Furthermore, Scott's postscript provides an important contrast to Edgeworth's preface and coda, suggesting why his, rather than her, approach to "a tale of other times" registered as historical with nineteenth-century readers.

Scott's postscript, as noted earlier, quickly drops the editorial role that Edgeworth maintains in her preface, and its primary concern is less literary than cultural. Where Edgeworth worked through literary notions of genre to develop a formal justification of her choice of narrative mode, Scott justifies his narrative by abandoning literary concerns (the concerns of *his* prefatory chapter) and directly entering historical and political discourse. History as change is the first problem and the main concern of the postscript, which asserts that no European nation has undergone "so complete a change" in the last half century as Scotland: "The effects of the insurrection of 1745,—the destruction of the patriarchal power of the Highland chiefs,—the abolition of the heritable jurisdictions of the Lowland nobility and barons,—the total eradication of the Jacobite party, which, averse to intermingle with the English, or adopt their customs, long continued to pride themselves upon maintaining ancient Scottish manners and customs, commenced this innovation" (340; chap. 72). With its list of public causes, the passage establishes the authority of the author-narrator as historian and social analyst. The postscript cites references (e.g., Lord Selkirk's *Observations on the Present State of the Highlands of Scotland*) and types of change (e.g., "extension of commerce") that count as part of historical discourse in a way that the private memoirs privileged by Edgeworth do not. Where her preface attempts to discount official history, Scott's postscript (like his preface with its reluctance to engage in "unnecessary opposition") signals

18. Butler, *Maria Edgeworth*, 394–95.

acceptance of generic codes and demonstrates its own historical competence.

But even more than Edgeworth, Scott effectively undermines official history, and he does so because of his ambivalence about the paradigm of progressive historical change standard in his day. Scott's much-noticed dualism comes into prominent play in the contrasting—even contradictory—notions of change articulated in the postscript. The change in Scotland in the last century is characterized as both a violent rupture ("so complete a change") and a "gradual" evolution. The "present people" of Scotland, for example, are said to be "a class of beings as different from their grandfathers, as the existing English are from those of Queen Elizabeth's time." But the radicalness of the change suggested here is softened by the insistence that this change has "nevertheless, been gradual." Where the first model draws attention to cultural loss, the second compensates for loss with cultural gain, but Scott's emphasis typically falls on the former, as in this description of the Jacobites: "This race has now almost entirely vanished from the land, and with it, doubtless, much absurd political prejudice; but, also, many living examples of singular and disinterested attachment to the principles of loyalty which they received from their fathers, and of old Scottish faith, hospitality, worth, and honour" (340).

The contrast with Edgeworth's sense of the vanished past in *Castle Rackrent* is striking. If for her the "former existence" of Ireland ideally evoked "a smile of good-humoured complacency," for Scott the vanished Scottish past evokes neither smiles nor complacency. Its absurdities, while admitted, are of far less interest to him than the loss of the valuable code of conduct with which he associates the displaced social order. The point is not that Edgeworth somehow feels superior to the past or that Scott engages in easy romantic nostalgia. Both writers have a complex and troubled response to historical change even as they affirm its fundamental direction. But they stand differently in relation to the country whose history is their concern, and that difference produces a markedly different narrative motivation.

When Scott introduces the idea of change as gradual, he adopts a simile to make his point clear: "like those who drift down the stream of a deep and smooth river, we are not aware of the progress we have made until we fix our eye on the now-distant point from which we set out" (340). The simile suggests a position similar to that of Edgeworth's editor when he argues that the present generation is secure enough and distinct enough from the past to be able to look complacently at the past. But this image of the smooth river of history which allows one to look back at ease and measure one's progress is soon disrupted not only by the insistence on what has been lost but by the shift to a highly personal definition of preservation as the aim of the preceding narrative. Informing the reader that it was "my accidental lot" to spend much of childhood and youth among Highlanders, Scott explains: "and now, for the purpose of preserving some idea of the ancient manners of which I have witnessed the almost total extinction, I have embodied in imaginary scenes, and ascribed to fictitious characters, a part of the incidents which I then received from those who were actors in them." The historian and scholar of the previous paragraph now speaks the language of autobiography and personal witness, a shift into unofficial genres that is all the more effective for its placement after two different "official" roles: the novelistic role of good-humored guide, and the historical role of cultural analyst.

The incorporation of unofficial genres, prompted by the unprogressive notion of preservation, continues as the authorial voice turns to its sources. The accounts of the military battles in the novel, he tells us, are "taken" from the stories of "intelligent eye-witnesses" and "corrected" from John Home's *History of the Rebellion in the Year 1745*, so that the narrative base lies in unofficial genres but gives final authority to an official one. As for the representation of the Lowlands, it comes both from personal witness ("I have witnessed some remnants in my younger days") and from tradition ("partly gathered from tradition"). This account of sources is then followed by the tribute to Edgeworth, who enters as a literary model once the sources for the historical material have been acknowledged. The acknowledgment of Edgeworth raises the issue of cultural purpose and intended audience. Scott seeks to "emulate" Edgeworth in

breaking the stereotypes of the Scots that have been internalized by the English (and in part by the Scots themselves)
through literary representations in the drama and the novel.
Two "female authors," he notes, anticipated him while the unfinished manuscript of *Waverley* lay where it had been mislaid
among "other waste papers." During this time, Elizabeth
Hamilton published her novel of rural Scotland, *The Cottagers of
Glenburnie* (1808), and Anne Grant published her collection of
Highland material, *Account of Highland Superstitions: Essays on
the Superstitions of the Highlanders of Scotland* (1811). Neither,
however, offers quite the "fictitious narrative" that he contemp-
lated. Female rivals thus out of the way, Scott turns directly to
the question of audience. The audience he has in mind seems to
be primarily Scottish, for he affirms his hope that *Waverley* will
"recall" for "elder persons . . . scenes and characters familiar to
their youth," and "present" to the younger generation "some
idea of the manners of their forefathers" (341). In contrast to
Edgeworth, then, he aims his narrative at cultural insiders as
well as at the outsiders on whom she concentrates her atten-
tions. The whole notion of "preserving some idea of the ancient
manners" of Scotland makes sense primarily for a Scottish audience, so that Scott's motivation dictates a different attitude
not just to the subject of representation (Scottish manners) but
to its intended recipient as well.

Preservation, moreover, implies an acute sense of time as an
agent, and such a sense is the basis for (if not a guarantee of)
historical awareness. Certainly, the postscript to *Waverley* is permeated with images of the working of time, whereas the preface
to *Rackrent* is not. Infused with a sense of the precariousness of
cultures, Scott's final image of his narrative attempt is "the task
of tracing the evanescent manners" of his "own country." His
novel, then, comes into existence under the sign of transience:
it traces what is itself evanescent. Historically, of course, the
novel (as its very name suggests) has been linked to the temporary and the fleeting; at the same time, its link to print culture
has enabled it to fix and to preserve. Building on both associations, Scott founds his historical mode of fiction. If novels, as
critics like John Dunlop were arguing at this time, were valuable

cultural indexes and hence gained through time a nonfictional, documentary value,[19] *Waverley* anticipated the generic shift granted by time and marked itself from the beginning as a document.

The Wild Irish Girl, *Waverley*, and National Romance

In the same 1814 letter to Matthew Weld Hartstonge in which Scott declared that the anonymous author of *Waverley* must have had the "inimitable" Maria Edgeworth in mind, he commented on other recently published novels, including Sydney Morgan's *O'Donnel*: "I agree with you that Lady Morgan has fairly hit upon her forte—for O'Donnell [sic] is incomparably superior to the Wild Irish Girl—having nature and reality for it's [sic] foundation."[20] Morgan's *O'Donnel* may have been superior, but it was *The Wild Irish Girl* that made Morgan's reputation and that was crucial to the formation of the rhetoric of nineteenth-century Irish nationalism. So much so, argues Thomas Flanagan, that for several generations "the issues of Irish politics would be argued out in the terms of Sydney Owenson's rhetoric."[21] What Morgan harnessed for her nation, in contrast to Edgeworth, was the affective realm of emotion and feeling. The reviews of Edgeworth, Marilyn Butler points out, make no mention of "the emotional sense of national identity which is so strong an element in Lady Morgan and, later, in many of the imitators of Scott."[22] *The Wild Irish Girl* at once exploits and shapes the Celtic myth that was to underlie the "emotional

19. Dunlop's whole study is motivated by the notion of fiction as cultural index. He notes in his preface: "By contemplating the fables of a people, we have a successive delineation of their prevalent modes of thinking, a picture of their feelings and tastes and habits. In this respect prose fiction appears to possess advantages considerably superior either to history or poetry" (*History of Fiction*, 3 vols. [London, 1814], 1:ix).

20. *Letters*, 4:465. Cf. Maria Edgeworth's response to the same novel, which she finds a "shameful mixture" of the "highest talent" and "the most despicable disgusting affectation and *impropriety*" (Butler, *Maria Edgeworth*, 448).

21. Flanagan, *Irish Novelists*, 124. Barry Sloan, admitting the influence of Morgan's rhetoric of Ireland, finds it highly suspect, and he prefers to see *Castle Rackrent* as the "seminal" Irish novel, *Pioneers*, 3–7.

22. Butler, *Maria Edgeworth*, 345–46.

sense of national identity" in Ireland for the rest of the century. Daughter of an Irish-speaking father, Morgan knew some Irish and had learned from him various old songs. Her collection of *Twelve Original Hibernian Melodies* (1805), in fact, was the acknowledged model for Tom Moore's highly popular *Irish Melodies* (1807). Like Scott, whose *Minstrelsy of the Scottish Border* came out in 1802 and whose *The Lay of the Last Minstrel* (1805) drew on his experience with ballads, Morgan participated in the antiquarian revival of the late eighteenth century that helped shape images of national identity in the nineteenth.[23] Collecting old songs, oral tales, and bits of almost forgotten lore, both Morgan and Scott incorporated the relics of earlier Irish and Scots cultures in their fiction; the imagination of both was powerfully drawn to the past of clans and Gaels, and both were haunted by landscapes of loss.

Where Edgeworth functioned as (acknowledged) exemplary cultural realist for Scott, Morgan stands as the (unacknowledged) muse of the cultural romance which he also practiced. He may playfully recall Morgan's Glorvina in the introductory chapter of *Waverley* when he mocks literary heroines "with a profusion of auburn hair" who manage to transport harps around inhospitable landscapes, but his own harp-playing Flora and the journey structure of his novel have strong affinities with Morgan's popular tale.[24] Both narratives are built around the journey of an English hero to a Gaelic culture, an experience that serves as an initiation into adulthood and involves the crossing of various cultural and psychological borders.[25]

Since Morgan's novel is little-read, a brief outline may be useful.[26] Her epistolary story features Horatio Mortimer, impru-

23. Peter Garside draws attention to the importance of antiquarianism in the development of Scott's sense of the Scottish past in "Scott, the Romantic Past and the Nineteenth Century," *Review of English Studies* 23 (1972): 147–61.

24. For the affinities between *Waverley* and *Wild Irish Girl*, see Robert Colby, *Fiction with a Purpose* (Bloomington: Indiana University Press, 1967), chap. 2.

25. On the centrality and ambiguity of borders in Scott, see Daniel Cottom's evocatively entitled chapter "Blind Roads" in *The Civilized Imagination: A Study of Ann Radcliffe, Jane Austen, and Sir Walter Scott* (Cambridge: Cambridge University Press, 1985).

26. I refer throughout to *The Wild Irish Girl* (London: Pandora, 1986). Although not the most satisfactory edition of the novel, it is the one most easily available to the modern reader.

dent second son of the earl of Mortimer, who has been banished to Ireland so that he will concentrate on his law studies rather than on dissipation. The resentful Mortimer, full of prejudices against the Irish as a "barbarous" people, travels from Dublin to the family estate in Connaught ("which I am told is the classic ground of Ireland"). The Mortimers received the estate in Cromwell's time in reward for services that included the murder of the prince of Inismore who originally held the estate. Arriving in Connaught, the young Mortimer feels "like the being of some other sphere, newly alighted on a distant orb" (42). Here he encounters the much reduced present prince with whom he is greatly impressed, but he is even more impressed by the prince's daughter, the beautiful, highly cultivated, and refined Glorvina. An enlightened priest, Father John, rounds out the attractive trio that educates Mortimer, who has changed his name and poses as a wandering artist in order to escape identification as one of the hated Mortimers. Under the tutelage of the three, Mortimer overcomes his English prejudices; he comes to recognize both the exploitation of the Irish peasantry and the rich cultural heritage of the old Irish. After various complications (which involve a strange sexual rivalry with his father, who is about to marry Glorvina), the hero and heroine marry.

Dubbing this marriage "the Glorvina solution," Robert Tracy points out that it reconciles legal right (Anglo-Irish) and traditional right (old Irish). Such a reconciliation, he further notes, became "almost a cliche in the novels of Walter Scott."[27] But although Scott adopts the Glorvina solution, he does so with a certain hesitation and irony not found in Morgan herself, whose earnestness about the marriage trope is captured in Lord Mortimer's words to his son in the final pages of the novel: "let the names of Inismore and M—— be inseparably blended, and the distinctions of English and Irish, of Protestant and Catholic, for ever buried. And, while you look forward with hope to this family alliance being prophetically typical of a national unity of interests and affections between those who may be factitiously severed, but who are naturally allied, lend your *own individual*

27. Tracy, "Maria Edgeworth and Lady Morgan," 9.

efforts towards the consummation of an event so devoutly to be wished by every liberal mind, by every benevolent heart" (253). At this point Lord Mortimer launches into a lengthy vision of a future of national virtue and felicity which will confirm the "whole order of universal nature" (255). With these words the novel ends.

The marriage at the end of *Waverley* carries a similar political weight; the restoration of Tully-Veolan offers a Morganesque blending of legal and traditional right; and the final pages gesture hopefully toward the future. But Scott's ending is neither as ambitious nor as serious. His concluding scene moves the marriage into the background, placing in the foreground the restoration of Baron Bradwardine to his family seat. It is this restoration that bears the symbolic weight of reconciliation and justice, and the whole carefully managed event emerges as so clearly an instance of wish fulfillment that Scott has the baron exclaim (when the Blessed Bear of Bradwardine appears at the very moment when he is regretting its loss) that "one might almost believe in brownies and fairies." The baron may toast the prosperity of "the united houses of Waverley-Honour and Bradwardine!" but the narrator's more sober voice and tangled qualifications finish the story: "It only remains for me to say, that as no wish was ever uttered with more affectionate sincerity, there are few which, allowing for the necessary mutability of human events, have been, upon the whole, more happily fulfilled" (339: chap. 71).

The contrast between the two endings points to the degree to which Morgan works inside late eighteenth-century conventions of sensibility and sentiment as Scott does not. And herein lies the problem for Morgan's national tale, for the allegiance to sentiment and sensibility is at odds with the cultural and political ambitions of her narrative. The split is neatly figured by the degree to which *Wild Irish Girl* is literally two texts: the epistolary narrative (a series of apparently unanswered letters by Mortimer to his friend J. D., Esq., M.P.) that forms the bulk of the novel; and the extensive set of editorial footnotes that accompanies the main narrative. As parallel text or supplement, these notes attempt to bring to the private world of sensibility rendered in the epistolary narrative a public dimension. But the authorial and narrative worlds in the end confound each other. In the notes Morgan attempts (rather like Edgeworth in *Castle Rackrent*) to overcome the enclosure of the first person in the central narrative, for Mortimer's is in effect a first-person narration that could as easily have been divided into pieces called journal entries or chapters as letters. Through the notes the editor writes a personal story of Ireland, explaining and defending aspects of Irish culture so as to establish both her cultural competence and her patriotism. (In contrast to Edgeworth's editor, Morgan's is clearly a woman.)

These notes are authorized in various ways. A whole series depends literally on the author: some are rooted in family memory (several anecdotes are attributed to "the author's father"); others claim personal experience ("When I lived among the scenes and people here described"); still others demonstrate her own research (as in a long quotation about the modern Irish harp from a letter by "a very eminent modern Irish bard, Mr. O'Neil"). Textual authority forms another set, and the notes abound in references to a host of texts of assorted kinds: histories, antiquarian studies, poems, political writings, letters, travel writings, transactions of the Royal Irish Academy. Here learned doctors are featured prominently, as the editor invokes "Dr. Young," "Dr. Burney," "Dr. Patterson," and "Dr. Beauford," among others. But the notes are more than scholarly references; they are also political acts, at once vindicating and constructing Irish culture. The editor is clearly a partisan, seeking to build Irish pride and to counter English hegemony. An insistent motif in the notes, for example, is that Irish culture is not only "ancient" but also remarkably similar to ancient Greek culture. And the editor loses no opportunity to draw attention to the injustices and ignorance of the "English invader" with his "prejudiced aversion" to the Irish. Predictably strong is the resentment of the Scots planted in Ireland, so that when they are at issue Morgan cannot resist turning even minor matters to Irish advantage. A note on the bagpipes, for example, highlights their Roman origins and modern Irish improvement rather than their Scottish connection (141).

In the notes, then, discourses of politics and history, autobiography and fiction intersect, but their intersection does not, as in *Waverley*, succeed in attaching the fiction to the nonfictional, for underlying the whole narrative effort of *The Wild Irish Girl* is a distrust of language that signals a distrust of the mediation that enables historical discourse. To be sure, such distrust makes both the standard sentimental point of the inadequacy of words to feeling and the conventional realist point of the inadequacy of signs to their referent. So in a note attached to a letter in which Mortimer describes an Irish mass, the editor states: "I have seen many such scenes as the above, the dramatic effect of which exceeds all description" (130). A similar note later in the narrative takes as its subject the warmth of Irish hospitality rather than the "drama" of the mass: "To those who have witnessed (as I have so often) the celebration of these endearing rites, this picture will appear but a very cold and languid sketch" (193). By admitting its inadequacy, language at such moments testifies to the reality of that which it seeks to represent and embody.

But to this well-worn technique Morgan adds a special nationalist inflection—it is *English* that is inadequate—and this inflection, paradoxically, depends on premises that will threaten her cultural project. When Mortimer gives Glorvina books to read, so that "she may know herself, and the latent sensibility of her soul" (140), he does not (as Waverley does in a similar episode with Rose) include English books. Mortimer provides Glorvina with classics of European sensibility like Rousseau's *La Nouvelle Heloise*, St. Pierre's *Paul et Virginie*, Goethe's *Werter*, and Chateaubriand's *Atila*. The omission of the English tradition is deliberate and explicit: "Let our English novels carry away the prize of morality from the romantic fictions of every other country; but you will find they rarely seize on the imagination through the medium of the heart; and, as for their heroines, I confess, that, though they are the most perfect of beings, they are also the most stupid" (140).

A rejection of the English proper novel, the passage embraces not simply intelligent heroines but the antirational code of the "romantic fictions" of France and Germany in which identity is rooted in individual feelings and sensations that elude the social and rational structures of language. Signaling her sensibility, Glorvina constantly blushes; for his part, Mortimer constantly invokes "indescribable feeling" and "exquisite yet unspeakable sensation." Indeed, at one point he posits that "a similarity of refined organization" may exist between souls, producing "mutual intelligence which sets the necessity of cold verbal expression at defiance." And he continues: "May not the sympathy of a kindred sensibility in the bosom of another meet and enjoy those delicious feelings by which yours is warmed, and, sinking beneath the inadequacy of language to give them birth, feel like you in silent and sacred emotion?" (147). Bad as it is, the writing here usefully marks Morgan's attempt to write outside the English mainstream.

Morgan's remarks on the English novel in her essay "On the Origin and Progress of Fictitious History" provide a useful gloss. She argues that the "genius" of the English language and the national taste for humor work against sentiment, which for her is the generic ground of the novel. English as a language, she argues, is not well adapted "for the development of refined sentiment, for the minute analysis of tender emotion, for those varieties of manner, those shades of character, which are exhibited in the intimate intercourse of social life, and to which the delicate *nuance* of the French, the most artificial of European languages is so exquisitely adapted."[28] If Morgan's writing tends to the embarrassing rather than the exquisite, it may well be that the rhythms of English and its literary history make difficult the exquisite adaptation that she sought. Certainly, she seems constrained by English, and it is striking how often the notes to *The Wild Irish Girl* draw on other languages. Morgan's comments on English suggest that her move to multilingual quotation is not entirely a matter of authorial self-authorization. Equally at work is a desire to speak differently.

The problem for the national tale is that this desire in Morgan depends less on the potentially historical notion of cultural difference than on the antihistorical notion of essential individuality and transcendent emotion underpinning the tradition of sensibility and sentiment. This is a tradition that seeks unmediated access to the real and that holds in particular suspicion the very forms of fiction that yield the most concrete representa-

28. *NMM* 14 (1820): 27.

tions of social and cultural life. More particularly, its privileging of individual sensibility tends to turn social and cultural facts into objects of—and for—this sensibility. Coming upon the decayed chapel of the princes of Inismore, for instance, Mortimer finds the whole scene "strikingly picturesque"; witnessing the celebration of the mass there, he exclaims: "What a captivating, what a *picturesque*, faith!" Certainly, this comes early in his Irish adventure, and Edward Waverley evidences a similar aesthetic response to Lowland and Highland life. But—even leaving aside the question of irony—there is a key difference: Waverley does not have the same centrality in his narrative that Mortimer has in his. There is a real sense in which what matters in Morgan's main narrative is how and what the hero feels, which is not the case in Scott's novel. Furthermore, language in *Waverley* is more a matter of culture than of sensibility. Waverley learns of cultural difference through a series of lessons on the use of words. On his way to Glennaquoich, for example, he is escorted by Evan Dhu, and the two discuss Donald Bean Lean's daughter. Waverley regrets that she is doomed to a dismal life as "the daughter of a cattle-stealer,—a common thief!" Evan Dhu denies that Donald Bean Lean, who "never *lifted* less than a drove in his life," qualifies as a thief: "No—he that steals a cow from a poor widow, or a stirk from a cottar, is a thief; he that lifts a drove from a Sasenach laird is a gentleman-drover" (85; chap. 18). Similar scenes occur repeatedly, drawing attention to the way in which language marks cultural distinction rather than individual uniqueness. And Waverley himself does not talk much, the decentering of his voice (as much as of his actions) playing an important role in defusing the individual life as the center of narrative interest. In *Waverley* language is eventful: it is a source of energy, a form of action, and—always—an object of enormous interest. From the cacophony of Bradwardine's banquet early in the story to the skillful deployment of languages by Charles Edward to quell division in his troops much later, the text makes us aware not simply of the centrality of language in cultural life but of its animating power in the processes of history.

There is little sense of this eventfulness of language in *Wild Irish Girl*, as there is little sense of the eventfulness of time.

Morgan's novel is marked by a fundamentally ahistorical temporality. In one sense, both *Wild Irish Girl* and *Waverley* depend on an ahistorical chronotope, for both fall in important ways under the Bakhtinian chronotope of adventure-time: Mortimer in Connaught and Waverley in Scotland are suspended from the rules of everyday life, even as their holiday from ordinary time eventually spills over (as it does not in pure romance) into ordinary biographical time.[29] Neither novel, of course, exists in the category of pure adventure-time, but each draws much of its special power from the way in which it bypasses ordinary time in order to operate in the "extratemporal hiatus that appears between two moments of a real time sequence" ("Forms of Time," 91). This extratemporal hiatus is filled with the unpredictability of chance, which controls adventure-time (more so in *Waverley* in fact than in *Wild Irish Girl*). In the end, chance mediates even the return to real time, as both heroes are suspended from consequence: Waverley from the consequences of treason, and Mortimer from the consequences of lying and of family guilt. Indeed, the story-likeness (as opposed to history-likeness) of their narratives derives from this.

In the same way, space (which is marked by interchangeability in the adventure chronotope) tends to a certain abstraction and stylization. Landscape in both Scott and Morgan is highly (and self-consciously) stylized, constructed through painterly motifs and eighteenth-century aesthetic categories. Both novels invoke Salvator Rosa (whose biography, we recall, Morgan was to write), and both draw heavily on the conventions of the sublime. Morgan may cite the actual Castle of Dunluce as the model for her fictional Castle of Inismore, but Inismore (with its "mouldering turrets," "rocky basis," "and "awful ruins") is more a product of Gothic romances and sublime painting than it is of the Irish countryside (35). Similarly, Waverley's Highland journey depends as much on literary conventions as on actual topography. But Scott saturates conventional space with cultural and personal time. Whereas Morgan's descriptions are made up almost entirely of stock phrases

29. For the adventure chronotope, see Bakhtin, "Forms of Time and Chronotope in the Novel," in *Dialogic Imagination*, 84–258. Page references to this essay will be included in the text.

(hence remain abstract and monologic), those of Scott are typically shot through with particular detail, individual inflection, or parodic accentuation (hence become concrete and dialogic).

Witness, for example, the sequence describing Waverley's entry into the Highlands, which repeatedly invokes Gothic expectations only to dispel them—but without destroying the strong sense of otherness and apprehension that the Gothic is able to generate. On his way to meet Donald Bean Lean, Waverley indulges himself in "the full romance" of a situation and setting that include darkness, unknown country, and strange guides speaking in a strange tongue. He keeps in the background, the narrator wryly notes, the degrading motivation for the romantic journey: "the Baron's milk cows!" (78; chap. 16). But realist undercutting does not finally dispel the romance; Donald Bean Lean may not be the "stern, gigantic, ferocious figure" that Salvator's paintings have led Waverley to expect, but he is sinister all the same (80; chap. 17). What makes the journey resonant and particular, however, is a homely matter: the insistence that Waverley and his companions are actually *walking* in rough country late in the day. Waverley strains and stumbles as he strives to keep up with Evan Dhu, and the two engage in a contest of national and personal masculinity on the way. Thus Evan Dhu keeps offering to have Waverley carried across the brook that keeps crossing their path, and Waverley as often declines, anxious "to remove the opinion which Evan seemed to entertain of the effeminacy of the Lowlanders, and particularly of the English" (77; chap. 16). Evan Dhu shoots at an eagle to demonstrate his dexterity and the superiority of Scotland ("you have no such birds as that in England"). After missing the bird, we are told, he "covered his confusion by whistling part of a pibroch as he reloaded his piece, and proceeded in silence up the pass" (76: chap. 16). Narrative moments like this infuse the standard trope of the journey of initiation with cultural content and individual accent. Through such moments Scott moves his romance into the sphere of history, so that the chancelike ending of *Waverley*, unlike that of *Wild Irish Girl*, registers as a move out of historical time into story-time.

The ending of Morgan's novel does not register as a similar change in mode because she has already moved her whole narrative into idyllic time. With the entry into Inismore, the narrative moves into the world of the idyll—and stays there. Idyllic life, writes Bakhtin, is inseparable from a "little spatial world" that is "limited and sufficient unto itself, not linked in any intrinsic way with other places, with the rest of the world" ("Forms of Time," 225). Idyllic time is thus rooted not simply in place but in enclosed and unified place, and it is marked by three characteristics: a cyclic rhythm that blurs temporal boundaries between individual lives and between the various phases of one individual life; the limitation of life to a few basic—and softened—realities; the conjoining of human life with the life of nature ("Forms of Time," 225–26). The Inismores, driven to a remote corner of Ireland where they are known by their old name and live in the old way, live in a world outside the linear flow of modern history. In the circle around Glorvina poverty, death, and sexuality are all softened, and the link with nature is underlined both by the eternally present sea and by the communal rituals of the seasons to which large portions of the narrative are devoted. In this sense place absorbs time in the idyll. But this is not concrete or social place, for Morgan's code of sentiment gives to the idyll what Bakhtin identifies as a Rousseauistic inflection: in Rousseau the basic idyllic elements (nature, love, family) are abstracted into eternal forms of wisdom and truth whose primary function is the constitution of the isolated individual consciousness. At the world of Inismore, Mortimer is purified and healed by Glorvina; but she can teach him only in an idyllic time that by definition cannot move into the historical world. The idyllic chronotope is based on a yearning for a unity of time that denies history. Scott himself, in the little worlds of the clans, indulges the sense of idyll, but his idylls are always enclosed in and threatened by metropolitan and other worlds that have a different sense of time and value. As I will consider more fully in Part Two, the Waverley chronotope is marked by stratified space and nonhomogeneous time. Asymmetries abound even as they are finally coerced into the homogeneity of story-time (and of Hanoverian history) in the novel endings.

Behind the national romances of both Morgan and Scott lies the discovery of folklore that marked the period of their formation and in which both were actively engaged. But where Morgan intensified the link between folklore and idyllic time, thereby undermining much of the cultural project of her national romance, Scott succeeded in *Waverley* in transforming folklore into the national-historical time that was central to the development of the historical sense in the nineteenth century. In the Waverley Novels, writes Bakhtin, Walter Scott overcame the "closed past" of his poetry and achieved "the fullness of time necessary for the historical novel."[30]

30. "The *Bildungsroman* and Its Significance in the History of Realism (Toward a Historical Typology of the Novel)," in *Speech Genres and Other Late Essays*, trans. Vern W. McGee, ed. Caryl Emerson and Michael Holquist (Austin: University of Texas Press, 1986), 53.

Part Two

Defining the Historical Novel

Each new epoch gives to history new points of view and
a special form.

—A. Thierry, *History of the Conquest
of England by the Normans* (1825)

5

The Problem of Generic Propriety: Contesting Scott's Historical Novel

> So history is a vestige of vestiges; few facts leave any trace
> of themselves, any witness of their occurrence; of fewer still
> is that witness preserved; a slight track is all anything
> leaves, and the confusion of life, the tumult of change,
> sweeps even that away in a moment. It is not possible that
> these data can be very fertile in certainties.
> —Walter Bagehot, "Thomas Babington Macaulay"

The authority of the Waverley Novels and their innovative power in the early nineteenth-century literary field depended on binaries of genre as well as of gender. If, as argued in Part One, gender and genre crossed each other in the literary discourse of the period, they did not at the same time collapse into each other. The two categories have related but distinct histories, and the next three chapters will complicate the story of gender and the novel by moving into the foreground the kinds of pressure exerted by Scott's historical novel on another culturally central binary: that of history and fiction. Gender remains crucial, but the struggle is less between genders than within one gender, for the debate now is over forms of masculine discourse: what will count as history? what are the limits and rules of historical discourse? And when the debate shifts to the relationship of history and fiction, the issue of rational reading that dominated the debate about gender and the novel tends to give way to the issue of faithful writing: what is it to which history must be true? Such questions held a new urgency in postrevolutionary Europe even as they drew on one of the oldest of generic debates in Western cultures.

While Scott's historical novel was generally welcomed by its first critics as a positive expansion of the contemporary forms of fiction, its hybrid nature occasioned from the outset a certain uneasiness. John Wilson Croker, for example, concluded his review of *Waverley* in the *Quarterly* by wishing that the author had written a history instead, for historical romance, he claimed, led to "the unsettling of all accurate recollections of past transactions."[1] For Croker, history clearly stands as authoritative discourse of the past, the generator and guardian of "accurate recollections"; by "unsettling" such recollections, fiction undermines the status and authority of history. His assumptions point to the characteristic terms and structure of modern debates about historical fiction. Such debates, usually motivated (as in Croker's case) by defense of history, typically posit history and fiction as binary opposites, with history signifying rational qualities like accuracy, law, argument, and so on. Equally typically, however, the superior category of history emerges as the more vulnerable of the two, always under threat from the nonrational, oddly aggressive power of fiction.

In the wake of poststructuralism, neither the softness nor the craftiness of binaries comes as a surprise. The history/fiction binary in particular has received a great deal of attention, notably from historians following Hayden White's landmark study of the rhetoricity of history in *Metahistory*.[2] Unstable and blurred, the boundary between history and fiction has been aptly termed an "open boundary" by Suzanne Gearhart in that the domains separated by the boundary continually cross over it.[3] Both genres, she argues, depend on the open boundary even as both generally attempt to close it, to secure the borders.

1. *QR* 11 (1814): 377.

2. *Metahistory: The Historical Imagination in Nineteenth-Century Europe* (Baltimore: Johns Hopkins University Press, 1973). The literature stimulated by White is too extensive to cite, but the most useful introduction to the issues at stake remains the collection of articles edited by Robert H. Canary and Henry Kozicki, *The Writing of History: Literary Form and Historical Understanding* (Madison: University of Wisconsin Press, 1978). For a recent study that builds on White's *Metahistory*, see Hans Kellner, *Language and Historical Representation: Getting the Story Crooked* (Madison: University of Wisconsin Press, 1989).

3. *The Open Boundary of History and Fiction: A Critical Approach to the French Enlightenment* (Princeton: Princeton University Press, 1984). For an excellent meditation on the ways in which nineteenth-century history attempted to deny (and otherwise negotiate) its relationship with fiction, see Linda Orr, "The Revenge of Literature: A History of History," *New Literary History* 18 (1986): 1–

History and fiction require each other because the identity of each depends on its difference from the other; but each seeks either independence (a mutually agreed upon boundary) or dominance (an extension of the boundary). Hence the vexed and contentious historical relationship of the two genres, and hence the special—and persistent—uneasiness about historical fiction as a form that, operating right on the periphery, draws attention to its problematic status. While all generic hybrids constitute what Bakhtin calls "border violations,"[4] historical fiction violates an especially sensitive border, for the distinction between history and fiction, always uneasy and constantly re-negotiated, is one of the most deeply entrenched in modern Western cultures.[5]

Formally, this distinction is a matter of genre, and genre constitutes the battleground on which the debate about historical fiction was—and continues to be—fought. Questions of generic propriety and hierarchy are rarely matters of simply literary interest, and Scott and his contemporaries were well aware of the cultural implications of genre. Although genre for them was a literary and formal category, it was never entirely literary and formal. John Dunlop's study, for example, sets out an elaborate taxonomy of prose genres, but it always assumes that these genres are implicated in social structures and contexts. He remarks, for instance, on the connection between literary forms and the status of women in ancient Greece, and on the effect of trade patterns on the development of the Italian novella. The "fables of a people," Dunlop argues, have "an important place in the history of the progress of society." His sense of the reciprocal relationship between the two terms ("fables," "a peo-

---

22. Barbara Foley, on the other hand, concentrates on the separation rather than entanglement of the terms in her defense of the binary, in *Telling the Truth: The Theory and Practice of Documentary Fiction* (Ithaca: Cornell University Press, 1986). Foley builds in part on Barbara Herrnstein Smith's speech-act distinction between natural and fictive discourse in *On the Margins of Discourse: The Relation of Literature to Language* (Chicago: University of Chicago Press, 1978).

4. "Epic and Novel," *The Dialogic Imagination*, trans. Caryl Emerson & Michael Holquist, ed. Michael Holquist (Austin: University of Texas Press, 1981), 33.

5. For the cultural centrality of this distinction, see Louis O. Mink, "Narrative Form as a Cognitive Instrument" in Canary and Kozicki, eds., *The Writing of History*, 129–49.

ple") is summed up in his comment that chivalric romances "arose from a system of manners, and in their turn exercised on manners a reciprocal influence."[6] If Dunlop tends to be rather vague about precisely how this reciprocity works, his interest in the cultural valence of form and his sense of form as at once ambiguously formal, social, and historical typify the critical approach to genre at the time of the early Waverley Novels. Even as form and genre were treated as literary and formal categories independent of the social and political sphere, they became the object of contention because of the simultaneous perception (if not always the admission) that they were neither neutral nor independent.

In the early nineteenth-century hierarchy of genres, history held a special cognitive and political place. The often noted "historical turn" of the century meant that to know anything one had to know its history, and the success of the Waverley Novels is both a sign and consequence of this shift to historical reasoning. It also points to the political power of history in the period when the postrevolutionary wars and their aftermath were shaping the modern nation-state. Supporting that state was a story of the national past that was no "legend" or "fairytale" but reliable "history." Croker, we recall, speaks in the review of *Waverley* of the "accurate recollections" of the past provided by history. Such recollections, of course, exist as a discursive event and signal present interest rather than past reference, but the point is the way in which a national past had to present itself as "history" in order to gain sanction. Only history could authorize a past to justify or motivate the present, and so access to the prestige of history was crucial (as it still is) in the pursuit of legitimacy, particularly on the part of marginalized groups. Hence it is not surprising that *Old Mortality*, dealing as it does with a period (the late seventeenth century) central to powerful and often competing notions of national identity and legitimacy in early nineteenth-century Scotland (and England, for that matter), should have generated the sharpest critical debate of Scott's career. Published in December 1816 as part of the first series of *Tales of My Landlord*, this novel

6. *History of Prose Fiction*, 3 vols. (London, 1814), 1:ix, 2:115.

prompted an extended discussion of the role and propriety of the historical novel, raising questions about the relationship of history and fiction that have persisted into our own time.[7]

The controversy over the novel was sparked by the Reverend Thomas McCrie, dissenting Presbyterian clergyman and author of a respected biography of John Knox.[8] Deeply offended by Scott's approach to the "sacred" subject of the Covenanters, McCrie wrote an elaborate critique of more than one hundred pages in the *Edinburgh Christian Instructor*.[9] His attack was reinforced in the English press by Josiah Conder, editor of the dissenting journal, *The Eclectic Review*,[10] and it received authoritative attention when it was contested by the two powerful quarterlies. Francis Jeffrey defended Scott's novel in the pages of the *Edinburgh Review*,[11] while Scott himself, aided by William Erskine and William Gifford, responded at length to McCrie in

---

7. Witness the debate over William Styron's *Confessions of Nat Turner* in the late 1960s. Avrom Fleishman opens *The English Historical Novel* (Baltimore: Johns Hopkins University Press, 1971) with a discussion of this debate, and George Goodin draws on the same controversy, seeing it as analogous to the controversy over *Old Mortality*, in "Walter Scott and the Tradition of the Political Novel," *The English Novel in the Nineteenth Century*, ed. George Goodin (Urbana: University of Illinois Press, 1972), 14–24. For an example of the history/fiction argument applied to film, see John P. Sisk on Richard Attenborough's *Ghandi*, "Poetry and Forgetting," *Salmagundi* no. 68–69 (1985–86): 66–77. Even more closely recalling the issues raised by Scott's "sacrilegious" *Old Mortality* are the recent controversies over Martin Scorsese's film *The Last Temptation of Christ* and the notorious charges of blasphemy against Salman Rushdie's *Satanic Verses*.

8. McCrie's biography of Knox was prominently and favorably reviewed by Jeffrey in the *ER* 20 (1812): 1–23. Jeffrey declared that "we do not hesitate to pronounce [it] by far the best piece of history which has appeared since the commencement of our critical career" (4).

9. *EdCIn* 14 (1817): 41–73, 100–140, 170–201. McCrie's article appears in the January, February, and March issues, and all references are to its original publication. The article was later reprinted as a pamphlet. For a modern evaluation of McCrie's charges by a student of Scottish history, see Robert S. Rait, "Walter Scott and Thomas McCrie," in *Sir Walter Scott To-Day*, ed. H. J. C. Grierson (London: Constable, 1932), 3–37.

The reviews of *Old Mortality* in this chapter will be fully cited once; thereafter references will be included in the text.

10. *EcR*, n.s., 7 (1817): 309–36. Conder's review appears in the April issue. Conder, bookseller and evangelical, bought the review in 1814 and edited it until 1836.

11. *ER* 28 (1817): 193–259. Jeffrey's review appeared in the March issue.

the *Quarterly Review*.[12] Other journals, like the *British Review* and the *North American Review*, responded to the charges as well,[13] so that the context of the reception of *Old Mortality*, in contrast to that of *Waverley* in 1814, was one of controversy over the matter and manner of Scott's narrative.

Unlike the eighteenth-century Jacobite conflict recalled in *Waverley*, the seventeenth-century civil and religious conflict depicted in *Old Mortality* aroused passion, and it did so for several reasons. The Lowland Covenanters had a special status in Scotland, widely venerated as defenders of its civil and religious liberties. As the *Edinburgh Magazine* was to put it the following year, the Covenanters were "one of those consecrated subjects which, in this country at least, could not be approached but with the most reverential emotion."[14] This special status took on a fresh potency in the years between Waterloo and Peterloo under the double influence of religious revival and political unrest.

Politically, the period was marked (as Scott's letters of the time reflect) by the threat of revolt by those displaced by the shift to an industrial economy. These are the years of the machine-smashing Luddites and of the "Radical War" in Glasgow. More to the point, in June 1815 textile workers and artisans assembled on the spot where the Covenanters had fought the battle of Drumclog to commemorate their victory and to show their support of Napoleon on his escape from Elba.[15] Encoded as they were within the rhetoric of revolt in this

12. *QR* 16 (1817): 430–80. The review appears in the January issue of the journal, but the date is misleading, for the issue did not appear until April. On the question of the authorship of this review, see Martin Lightfoot, "Scott's Self-Reviewal: Manuscript and Other Evidence," *Nineteenth-Century Fiction* 23 (1968): 150–60.

13. *BR* 9 (1817): 184–204; [Reverend J. G. Palfrey], *NAR* 5 (1817): 257–86. These reviews appeared in the February and the July issues respectively.

14. "On the History of Fictitious Writing in Scotland," *EdM*, n.s., 3 (1818): 109.

15. Angus Calder draws attention to this gathering in his introduction to *Old Mortality* (Harmondsworth: Penguin, 1974) 10. He quotes from a contemporary account by the sheriff-substitute of Hamilton, William Aiton, who wrote *A History of the Rencounter of Drumclog . . .* (1821) to correct Scott's account of the battle in the novel. The politics of *Old Mortality* itself has been much discussed. See, in particular, Goodin, "Walter Scott and the Tradition of the Political

way, it is not surprisingly that for Scott and most of his readers, the Covenanters represented, as Harry Shaw notes, the frightening "specter" of revolution.[16] Hence the *British Critic* reads *Old Mortality* as a "warning" to Church and State and draws explicit attention to its implicit political analogy: "In times like these, when the spirit of fanaticism is abroad, and gathering the most fearful strength, the tale before us will be read with a deep and a foreboding interest."[17] The "fanaticism" to which the *British Critic* refers is not simply political but religious as well, for these years also witnessed a religious revival outside the established churches of England and Scotland. The two forms of dissent, often if not always related, worked as complementary forms of attention that renewed interest in the conflicts of the seventeenth century as the age of heroes and martyrs.[18] The Covenanters, in other words, continued to function centrally in various ideologies in the present. For someone like the Reverend McCrie, a heroic reading of the Covenanters was fundamental to his sense of the authentic inheritance and identity (what he calls the "ancient spirit") of Scotland, whereas for Scott and his allies, as the *Quarterly* review suggests, a contending version of "legitimate" inheritance and identity cast the Covenanters in a rather different mode.

The whole debate over *Old Mortality* enacts a political and ideological struggle over control of the past and therefore over the shape of the present and future. Both sides claim entry into the authentic past that gave rise to the present, and both claim equally that they are doing history in order to authenticate the past they are constructing. The rhetorical forms of this claim, notably the insistence on the separation of fiction and history, are the subject of the first section of this chapter. Ultimately, however, as I will argue in the second section, the debate

---

Novel"; John P. Farrell, *Revolution as Tragedy: The Dilemma of the Moderate from Scott to Arnold* (Ithaca: Cornell University Press, 1980); and Peter Garside, "*Old Mortality*'s Silent Minority," *Scottish Literary Journal* 7 (1980): 127–44.

16. *The Forms of Historical Fiction: Sir Walter Scott and His Successors* (Ithaca: Cornell University Press, 1983), 190.

17. *BC*, n.s., 7 (1817): 94.

18. See Rosalind Mitchison, *A History of Scotland* (London: Methuen, 1970) and Francis Hart, *The Scottish Novel* (London: John Murray, 1978), 10.

proves to be less about the distinction between history and fiction than about the social implications of fictional genres.

Transgressing the Boundaries of History

In its review of *Old Mortality*, the *Scots Magazine* noted with approval that this novel, aside from providing entertainment, "will also have the effect of introducing many readers to a better acquaintance with an interesting period of Scottish history."[19] For McCrie and Conder, that was precisely the problem: many readers were learning their history from novels. Novels, in fact, were becoming ambitious, exceeding their proper generic bounds, and their critique of Scott's novel was sparked not just by resentment at what they saw as a wrongheaded history of the period but also by the way in which the success of the Author of Waverley signaled the rapidly expanding cultural power of a dubious genre. Rehearsing familiar complaints and motifs, McCrie opens his article with a characterization of novel readers as "vacant" of mind and "morbid" in feeling, their "giddy breasts, or perhaps brains," easily gratified and manipulated (41–42). Novel writers, with a few individual exceptions, are little better, producing "insipid, stupid, and pernicious productions" for the circulating libraries. These productions are "stuffed" in the libraries and "daily tossed from hand to hand until they are literally worn to tatters." Given all this, McCrie remarks, "we cannot but think that a man of genius and taste who condescends to join such company, displays at once a great deal of courage and of self-denial, and we are not greatly surprised to find him choosing to send the offspring of his fancy into the world without his name, or under a false one" (42). The Waverley Novels (products of this anonymous "man of genius and taste") are clearly superior to the trash of the circulating library, but McCrie is nevertheless firm about their generic kinship and about the potential harm to "a numerous, and, in general, unsuspecting class of readers" of the "engaging form" used by historical fiction (47).

19. *SM* 78 (1816): 931.

Like McCrie, Conder exhibits the standard paternalism of critics of fiction, but his is a rather more dramatic imagination, and he elaborates a more sinister image of the novel as a deceptive and ambitious cultural power that will not stay in its place. Novels, Conder insists, are governed by the goal of "amusement," and they should "keep within the line of amusement" (314). Recently, however, they have begun to violate that line in various ways. First of all, they have disguised themselves as something else in order to gain a wider hearing: "Novels under the unassuming names of tales,—'Moral Tales,'and 'Simple Tales,' and strangest of all, Religious Tales,—have found their way in channels where the proscribed name of Novel would immediately have roused alarm" (310). Nor is this all. Not content with insinuating themselves into respectable domestic space, contemporary novels have threatened the discursive order more directly by invading the territory of other, more serious genres: "Imboldened by success, modern novelists have assumed a higher tone, have proceeded to give lessons in history, civil and ecclesiastical, on the principles of education and of political economy, in ethics and in divinity" (310). The problem with this incursion into the nonfictional is twofold: novels have indexical power and hence achieve a quasi-documentary status over time; second, their greater affective power weakens in their own time the cultural force of the other genres.

Conder's critique responds implicitly to the widespread critical tendency of the time to invest popular prose fictions with indexical value as signs of the culture that produced and consumed them. Such an assumption informed Dunlop's study of the "fables of a people," and Scott himself had declared in his first review article for the *Edinburgh Review* in 1803 that the "novels of Fielding and Richardson are even already become valuable, as a record of the English manners of the last generation."[20] Time, we note, has effected a generic shift, transforming novels into "records," and a similar sense of the documentary function of fiction surfaces repeatedly in the criticism of the period. So the *British Critic*, reviewing Dunlop's *History of Prose*

---

20. Review of Robert Southey's *Amadis de Gaul* and Nicolas De Herberay's *Amadis de Gaul, ER* 3 (1803): 132.

Fiction, imagines novels by Rousseau and Godwin as "documents in the hands of some future historian of our own age."[21] And the *Edinburgh Magazine,* reviewing Godwin's *Fleetwood,* claims that posterity will derive its information about the social conditions of the age "from the pencil of truth, though in the hand of fiction." Invoking the novels of Fielding, Smollett, the Author of Waverley, Hamilton, and Edgeworth, this reviewer asserts that they "leave a more vivid and lasting impression upon the mind than it is possible for the truth of history to effect."[22]

Such willingness to see fiction as a document and, more important, to accept so casually the superiority of its affective power to that of history proper was exactly what concerned Conder and McCrie. Not that they denied the affective power of the novel. On the contrary. McCrie worries that novelists "have it in their power to do much mischief" because of their "engaging form" (47). Conder is even more troubled, deploring the "facility" with which a novelist can "make any desired impression on his readers." This "facility" ensures for the novel a more far-reaching social power than that possessed by the more responsible genres, since it gives the novelist, says Conder, "a species of multiplying power in the re-production of his own sentiments, far above what is possessed by any writers who attempt to conduct their readers to a definite opinion, by means of a process of reasoning, or of the cautious details of history" (310). Fiction thus threatens to displace the rational genres of philosophy and history, and the novelist, with his sinister "multiplying power" over readers, threatens the role of the cautious reasoner and historian. With heavy irony, Conder felicitates "our modern *historico*-novelists" on their "advantages" over historians, "inasmuch as they are exempted by the license of their profession from all the anxious research, the rigorous comparison of varying testimonies, the cautious induction of obscure facts, the self-suspicious desire of correctness, that are requisite, and after all found too often insufficient, to constitute the work of an historian an unexceptionable representation of the events it records" (314). The modern historico-novelist, by implication, eschews research, rigor, and caution, producing

21. *BC,* n.s., 2 (1814): 167.
22. *EdM,* n.s., 2 (1818): 58.

cavalier pseudohistories that will mislead the vulnerable readers of fiction. Conder is writing less than three years after the
publication of *Waverley*, but already the products of the Author
of Waverley have come to represent the clearest contemporary
challenge posed by novels to the other genres in the literary
hierarchy.[23] His novels, McCrie notes, have "attracted the attention even of those who have no predilection for this species of
composition" (42). Conder adds that "nothing short of the genius which is discovered in the present work, could render the
attempt to give a false colouring to an important portion of
history by means so inadequate as a novel or a tale, a matter of
grave apprehension" (314).

Fiction, in short, emerges in the critiques of Conder and Mc-
Crie as more powerful than history despite its conventionally
secondary status. Anxious to protect what McCrie calls "the
faithful page of history," Scott's critics strive to keep history
under the sign of fidelity and to separate it firmly from the
infidelities of fiction. Both rely centrally on metaphors in order
to do so. Conder turns to eighteenth-century aesthetics as his
source, setting up an analogy that will yield the generic distinction he seeks:

> Applied to history, indeed, the art of the novelist may be considered
> as strictly analogous to landscape gardening. In his hands the most
> rugged course of events is made to sweep along in the line of
> beauty; facts the most repulsive, are, by the skilful management of
> light and shade, made to assume a picturesque aspect; graceful and
> romantic incidents planted in the foreground, serve either for relief
> or concealment to the more obstinate features of the scene; and the
> dark array of truths which frown over the page of history, are
> thrown into perspective, and mellowed down into a pleasing indis-
> tinct grandeur. (310)

Motivated by the desire for formal pleasure ("line of beauty,"
"picturesque aspect"), the historical novelist conceals and distorts at once the contours of nature and the truths of the "page
of history," both of which Conder represents through the motif

23. In some suggestive remarks on Scott, Walter Reed identifies Scott's fiction with "the romanticized novel" that sets itself against literary conventions
and official culture (*An Exemplary History of the Novel* [Chicago: University of
Chicago Press, 1981], 162–67).

of the sublime.[24] The conventional motif of the sublime stands for the real in Conder's passage, and through it he figures the notion that historical fiction coerces a difficult and dark reality ("is made to") into smooth and mellow forms of pleasure. Moreover, the metaphor of landscape (standard since the late eighteenth century) allows Conder to set up a skillful four-part homology: fiction is to nature as historical fiction is to history. The homology dissolves history (as both deeds and writing) into nature while keeping the historical novel firmly within the category of fiction. Conder posits for these two genres incompatible aims, arguing that the "genuine character" of history "must be perverted" in a novel because the latter seeks pleasure ("amusement"), not truth (313).

McCrie agrees, drawing attention to the way in which the historical novelist "does not hesitate to violate historic truth and probability" for the sake of "giving effect to a particular scene." The author of *Old Mortality*, he concludes, may have "the imagination and feeling of a poet," but he is clearly "deficient in the judgment and discriminating taste of a historian" (52). McCrie, however, makes his generic point less through an aesthetic than a juridical-political metaphor. Explicitly presenting his critique of Scott's novel as a legal charge, he structures his case on the notion of genre as territory. One of the most enduring of critical metaphors, the topos of territory figures prominently in the literary reviews of the period, which typically rely on a vocabulary of "dominion," "kingdom," and "empire" in defining the functions and relations of genres.[25] Genres are thereby not only objectified as land but transformed into quasi-juridical entities: land under rule, or, as writers in the nineteenth century liked to put it, under "jurisdiction," and their relations are then regulated according to "laws." Macaulay offers a striking example of the metaphor at work in his well-known essay on "History" for

24. Conder's point recalls Hayden White's recent argument that postromantic historiography has suppressed the sublime for the more domestic mode of the beautiful, in "The Politics of Historical Interpretation: Discipline and De-Sublimation," *Critical Inquiry* 9 (1982): 112–38.

25. The OED, incidentally, notes that the etymology of "territory" is unsettled: "usually taken as a deriv. of *terra* earth, land . . . but the original form has suggested derivation from *terrēre* to frighten, whence *territor* frightener, *territōrium* 'a place from which people are warned off.'"

the *Edinburgh Review*. He opens by defining the "province" of history as "a debateable land": "It lies on the confines of two distinct territories. It is under the jurisdiction of two hostile powers; and, like other districts similarly situated, it is ill-defined, ill cultivated, and ill regulated."[26] The two "hostile powers" are Reason and the Imagination; Macaulay, prompted by the success of the Waverley Novels, urges history to reconcile the two powers and, in particular, to give "to truth those attractions which have been usurped by fiction."[27]

Whereas Macaulay responded to the challenge of the historical novel by seeking to absorb the powers of fiction (see Chapter 7), McCrie insists on the separation of the two genres. For him, too, the genres lie side by side, but this simply means that it is the duty of criticism to secure the borders of the "province" of history from the incursions of fiction. "The guides of public opinion," McCrie writes, "cannot be too jealous in guarding against the encroachments of the writers of fiction upon the province of true history, nor too faithful in pointing out every transgression, however small it may appear, of the sacred fences by which it is protected" (47). This short passage draws on a whole set of powerful binaries to make its generic point: true/false, sacred/profane, faithful/unfaithful. Aligning the critic under the banner of fidelity (the sign of history), McCrie not only casts fiction as transgressive but invests the whole generic set with a sense of divine sanction: the boundaries of genre are marked by "sacred fences." And Conder, arguing that *Old Mortality* implicitly defines itself as a history, also draws on the sacred when he declares that Scott's obligation to historical truth is as "sacred" as if he had entitled his work a history. Set against the faithful page of history, with its generic ties to law, reason, and divine order, fiction appears as illegitimate, irrational, and irreligious.

And it is as history that Conder and McCrie wish to indict *Old Mortality*. The point of their insistence on the separation of the two genres is not simply to protect the domain of history but to allow them to contain the hybrid genre of the historical novel by

26. *ER* 47 (1828): 331.
27. Ibid., 364.

declaring it an either/or proposition: it is either fiction or history. And Scott's novel, each finds, places itself under the "laws" of history when its narrator, Peter Pattieson, announces in the opening chapter his desire "to present an unbiassed picture of the manners of that unhappy period, and, at the same time, to do justice to the merits of both parties." As a result, in the words of McCrie, the novelist "subjects himself to laws far more strict than those which bind the ordinary class of fictitious writers. It is not enough that he keep within the bounds of probability,—he must conform to historic truth" (47). After defining "historic truth" as correspondence to "the faithful page of history" and setting out the "laws" governing the writing of history, McCrie concludes: "The work before us we consider as chargeable with offences against these laws" (47).

Conder concurs, though he exchanges the language of law for the language of moral philosophy in making his case. Drawing on William Paley's speech-act approach to language, notably to his definition of lies as breach of promise in *The Principles of Moral and Political Philosophy*,[28] Conder claims that Scott's introductory chapter explicitly promises something more than fiction (whose aim is simply "diversion") and so places him under an obligation "to preserve, even in a tale, the truth of history, since his aim is not simply *to divert*" (315). That obligation he has not fulfilled; hence the text falls into a special category of lie.

Scott and his allies were more willing to admit the legitimacy of mixed genres like the historical novel, but they agreed that historical fiction does indeed invoke the historical contract and is therefore subject to the generic criterion of truth as verifiability in the archives. The value of a historical novel, all concur, depends in an important way on its historical competence, that is, on its use of sources. The historical text, Stephen Bann has observed, is characterized by its relationship to other texts (its sources), and its credence "depends radically on what we suppose to be its relationship to these absent sources."[29]

28. Conder draws on "Lies," Book. 3, Part. 1, chap. 15. See William Paley, *The Principles of Moral and Political Philosophy*, rev. ed. (London, 1821), 117–21.
29. *The Clothing of Clio: A Study of the Representation of History in Nineteenth-Century Britain and France* (Cambridge: Cambridge University Press, 1984), 34. Bann points out that specific reference to sources was a relatively new conven-

Scott himself always disclaimed any rivalry with history, saying that he was writing romances; at the same time, the only aspect of his novels that he ever defended was their historical fidelity. Responding to McCrie in the *Quarterly*, Scott cheerfully indicts his heroes, his plots, his structure—but he insists that in his representation of the Covenanters he has "acted in strict conformity with historical truth" (460). Aided by Erskine and Gifford, he lays out documentary evidence to counter the evidence presented by McCrie.

The debate, then, becomes a battle of testimonies in which each side accuses the other of being unhistorical while demonstrating its own historical competence. The point is that each wants to secure for *its* past the authority of history and to deny that authority to the other's past. So McCrie and Conder quote documents and cite facts omitted by Scott, while Scott and his allies quote documents and cite facts not mentioned by their opponents. Each defines itself as "impartial" and the other as partisan; each plays the game of citing testimony from the opposing side that supports its own case (McCrie cites Episcopalians and Scott cites Covenanters); and each creates the impression that it could go on presenting evidence indefinitely. Like most such battles, the battle of testimonies is inconclusive. The criterion of verifiability in the archives may rule out certain forms of writing as unhistorical, but, as theorists of history have emphasized, it cannot distinguish among competing stories made out of the archival materials. So Louis Mink notes that disputes about matters of historical fact may in principle be resolvable but not so their combinations: "The same event, under the same description or different descriptions, may belong to different stories, and its particular significance will vary with its place in these different—often very different—narratives."[30]

To McCrie and Conder, such a reading of the genre would

---

tion for history. Gibbon, for example, emphasizes in his *Vindication* how his history stands out from other histories because of the specificity of his references. While the debate over *Old Mortality* is in many respects less over the criterion of verifiability in the archives than over the older, more theological criterion of testimony or witness, it clearly draws on modern disciplinary notions like evidence, document, and so on.

30. Mink, "Narrative Form," 144–45.

have been unacceptable, in large part because as dissenters they lacked access to official history ("what everyone knows") and so were correspondingly more anxious to preserve their history *as* history—and not just as one possible story. From this stems the urgency with which they attempted to retain the notion of history as determinate, as a separate territory with known rules and laws. They sought, in other words, to retain their past as a *historical* subject both in the sense of significance (history as the significant past) and in the sense of determinacy (the past as determinate event with determinate meaning). On the question of determinacy, Mink points out how common sense and professional history alike assume not only that "everything that has happened belongs to a single and determinate realm of unchanging actuality" but also that "past actuality is an untold story and that there is a right way to tell it even though only in part." This presupposition very often clashes with conscious belief and always clashes with actual practice, for, as Mink also notes, historical narratives of the "same" event multiply and coexist without displacing one another as they—in theory—should.[31] If theory does not translate into practice, it does construct the characteristic rhetoric of history in that historical narratives (like realist novels or, for that matter, literary studies) typically present themselves as authentic accounts that cohere seamlessly with the real (the subject of representation), dislodging in the process other, false accounts. This is the rhetoric that McCrie and Conder take seriously, or profess to take seriously, when they attack Scott's novel. To preserve their past, they present their struggle with Scott as a struggle over *one* event, over the same space, and define his fiction as a narrative capable of displacing other, properly historical narratives in that space.

Their anxiety reflects not just their own marginal position but the more general problem of the peculiar status of the referent in historical discourse. History represents that which no longer is, making its discourse, in the often-cited words of Roland

31. Ibid., 141–43. Mink's article is highly useful for understanding what was at stake in the debate over *Old Mortality*, especially in its discussion of how historical narratives, in contrast to fictional narratives, theoretically *should* aggregate but in fact do not do so (142–43).

Barthes, "presumably the only kind which aims at a referent 'outside' itself that can in fact never be reached."[32] For Walter Bagehot, criticizing the confidence of Macaulay as historian ("It is too omniscient. Everything is too plain"), history is but "a vestige of vestiges," and time and change threaten even its status as vestige: "a slight track is all anything leaves, and the confusion of life, the tumult of change, sweeps even that away in a moment."[33] Barthes's point is the discursivity and Bagehot's the uncertainty of history, but both converge in stressing the absence that constitutes it. R. G. Collingwood put the point memorably: "Historical thought is of something which can never be a this, because it is never a here and now. Its objects are events which have finished happening, and conditions no longer in existence."[34] Whatever the problems with Collingwood's statement, it remains true that history as a genre has a special dependence on absence and on discourse that makes the referent of history highly vulnerable, threatening it with indeterminacy, fictionality, specularity. Hence the efforts by the critics of Scott to ensure that the past over which they were contending did not slip out of determinacy and into fiction.

As Conder's landscape metaphor and his derogation of the beautiful and the picturesque suggest, these critics resented in particular any transformation of the past from historical into aesthetic object. The review of Old Mortality in the British Review provides a good example of the kind of thing that Conder had in mind.[35] An Evangelical and progovernment quarterly published by Hatchard, the British Review is perhaps best remembered for Byron's scorning it as "my Grandmother's Review."

32. "Historical Discourse," in Introduction to Structuralism, ed. Michael Lane (New York: Basic, 1970), 153–54.
33. "Thomas Babington Macaulay," Literary Studies, ed Richard Holt Hutton, 2 vols. (London, 1879), 2:256.
34. The Idea of History (1946; London: Oxford University Press, 1956), 233.
35. McCrie comments on the review of Old Mortality in the British Review, but his explicit point is nationalist. In the last of his series of articles, he argues that Old Mortality has reinforced English prejudice against the Scots, citing in evidence the reviews in the British Critic and the British Review. Not surprisingly, he finds the latter "more moderate and liberal" than the former; even so, he argues, it evidences a characteristic English ignorance of Scottish history (170–71).

Despite its religious allegiance, the review was secular in its approach to most texts, and its favorable assessment of *Old Mortality* evidences little religious sectarianism or doctrinal concern. On the question of historical fiction, the reviewer agrees that historical novels must observe a "general resemblance to the truth of fact," but he regards as equally valid and valuable "the picturesque additions and embellishments requisite to produce the effect of novelty, and to communicate that intense and sustained interest which belongs to the productions of dominant genius and chartered invention" (197). The double generic allegiance that McCrie and Conder see as a contradiction leading to deception is for the *British Review* no problem at all. "Invention" has its charter, as does history, and the two can work together legitimately and effectively.

What allows the *British Review* to be so relaxed is that it situates the historical novel rather differently in the generic field, seeing it as part of an old literary tradition whose roots go back to a time before the emergence of history as a distinctive form of narrative. Rather than aligning historical fiction with history, this reviewer downplays the link with history to foreground the link with epic and ballad, hailing Scott as the "Homer of his country" and praising the literary results of Thomas Percy's *Reliques of Ancient English Poetry* (185–86). The Author of Waverley is placed not among historians but among minstrels, and the choice of context underlines the way in which the *British Review* regards the past as a poetic subject—a source of literary pleasure rather than an urgent issue for the present. In contrast to the critics of Scott, it welcomes "those authors who have thus turned back our minds upon the history and traditions of our ancestors as sources of amusement" (185). Drawing on the late eighteenth-century primitivism whose traces we saw in John Scott's response to *Waverley*, the *British Review* sees in "our ruder forefathers" a more "romantic" interest and "intense" sympathy than now exist, for they were cast "in a mould newer and less worn" (186). Such a response to the past is precisely the kind of response that McCrie and Conder despise, not least because (despite the use of terms like "ancestors" and "forefathers") it assumes difference and discontinuity. For the *British Review*, the past is a foreign country. It is delightful to take a tour there, but it has nothing to do with us. By contrast, for McCrie and Conder, who insist on continuity through their metaphors of legacy and heritage, the past has everything to do with us. And the transformation of the past from historical into aesthetic object threatens not simply *their* history but the writing of history at all, and so they insist on history as distinct and authoritative access to the past.

At the same time, history (as they well know) cannot resolve the issue between them and *Old Mortality* and its allies. The battle of testimonies in which each side has engaged in the name of "historical truth" is undecidable, infinitely expandable. Potentially, there is no end to this debate, so that the historical truth defined as normative of the genre cannot enact closure. But the writing of history is impossible without it, and closure in history, as Hayden White has argued, comes from fiction and its tropes. The most serious quarrels over historical fiction (both in Scott's time and in our own) are generally less over its history than over its fiction. And that, in turn, the debate over *Old Mortality* underlines, has a great deal to do with the way in which in any culture fictional genres themselves operate in a highly valorized social space.

The Impertinence of Fiction

The real problem with *Old Mortality* for the dissenting readers, it becomes clear, lay not in the details but in the figure that the entire narrative made. It is "upon the impression which the whole piece is calculated to make," McCrie writes, "that our judgment must be formed" (48). *Old Mortality* may, he admits, contain some accurate facts and even specific condemnation of the tyranny of the royalists, but "the general tendency" of the work is "unfavourable to the interest of religion and political freedom" (53). This he terms "our decided judgment," and when judgment (and with it justice) comes into focus, the argument about history and fiction gives way to an argument about the propriety of literary genres. Discussion shifts from problems of representation to those of signification and interpretation. Scott himself points to the two distinct grounds when he follows his comment in the *Quarterly* about having acted in strict conformity with "historical truth" with the parenthetical remark: "(whether with propriety we shall hereafter inquire)" (460).

The inquiry into propriety is conducted later in the same review by William Erskine, who articulates the specific points at issue in the case of *Old Mortality*: "two questions arise of much more importance than any thing affecting the merits of the novels [*The Black Dwarf* was also under review]—namely, whether it is safe or prudent to imitate, in a fictitious narrative, and often with a view to a ludicrous effect, the scriptural style of the zealots of the seventeenth century; and secondly, whether the recusant presbyterians, collectively considered, do not carry too reverential and sacred a character to be treated by an unknown author with such insolent familiarity" (474). The Covenanters, that is, are conventionally cast in the mode of hagiography (their "reverential and sacred" character), and to represent them in the mixed modes of realism, as does *Old Mortality*, is obviously to violate decorum in a particularly offensive way ("insolent familiarity"). If Erskine is being somewhat ironic at the expense of the critics of the "unknown author," it is nevertheless notable how carefully he and Scott's other defenders tread when it comes to the charges of undermining national heroes and profaning scripture. Erskine himself goes on to admit that there is "some risk of mischief" in the novel's use of scriptural language but claims that ridicule is the friend of "religion and virtue." On the second point, he argues that Scott's representation of the Covenanters concentrates on the extreme wing and in this respect is accurate, and he offers documentary evidence to support his claim.

Similar arguments appear in the other major quarterly where Francis Jeffrey (whose review will be discussed in chapter 7) concedes that "all jocular use of Scripture phraseology is in some measure indecent and profane" but makes the same argument as Erskine in defense of satire. More sympathetic to the insurgents than Erskine, Jeffrey makes sure that he acknowledges the Covenanters as a brave group of men "to whose efforts and sufferings, their descendants are deeply indebted for the liberty both civil and religious which they enjoy, as well as the spirit of resistance to tyranny, which, we trust, they have inherited along with them" (258). However, this group, Jeffrey notes, also included many "absurd" and "ferocious" characters, and Scott's representation, though clearly that of a Tory, is not unfair (258–59).

For McCrie and Conder, of course, the whole problem begins with the choice of fiction as a medium for writing about national heroes. Conder concludes his review by impugning the motives, honesty, and personal character of the author: "What must be the feelings of a man who could sit down coolly to turn to amusement the characters and sufferings of men whom, if he was incapable of honouring their heroic fortitude, he must regard as objects of the most poignant compassion?" (336). The result of such cynicism, Conder concludes, is a "literary outrage." It is not simply the choice of fiction over history that constitutes the "outrage"; what makes the choice outrageous is the choice of genres within the fictional field. One would have thought, Conder remarks earlier in the review, that, given the suspect decision to make the Covenanters the subject of fiction in the first place, one would choose to make them "the subject of some solemn and elevated tragedy" (316). Instead of this high and respectful mode, however, *Old Mortality* has exploited the low and degrading modes of "the ludicrous" and "the terrifico," compounding their demeaning effect by inserting "certain *fanatical* peculiarities of expression." Conder presents the novel as a mixture of fictional genres—mingling "burlesque" and "tragic horror," for example—thereby registering his discomfort at its disruption of the more decorous and homogenous possibilities of "solemn and elevated tragedy."[36]

Scott's generic choices aroused McCrie's resentment as well. Commenting on the scene of Morton's arrest early in the novel, for instance, he comments: "Thus the tragic scenes of military violence, described by the faithful page of history, sink, in the mimic representation of our author into a mere farce" (62). Because the "mimic" can be read so easily as mimetic, the forms that fiction assumes generate a special hostility. McCrie's lan-

---

36. For the subversive potential of the mixture of modes, see Alexander Welsh, "Contrast of Styles in the Waverley Novels," *Novel* 6 (1973): 218–28.

guage typically becomes emotionally charged when fictional genre is at issue in a way that it does not when historical accuracy is his subject: "we cannot consent to be tricked and laughed out of our principles; nor will we passively allow men who deserve other treatment, and to whose firmness and intrepidity we are indebted for the transmission of so many blessings, to be run down and abused with profane wit, or low buffoonery" (48).

Justice, it turns out, has something to do with literary decorum. And this is so because of the special reciprocity of literary forms to which Suzanne Gearhart draws helpful attention in her study. Literary form, she argues, is always "'beside itself,' that is, always radically and fundamentally implicated in the so-called extraformal spheres."[37] At the same time, as she also stresses, the extraformal—that which goes by the name of reality—is "contaminated" by questions of literary form and genre. It is this reciprocity that makes literary genres contentious. Not only does literary status in the generic hierarchy have a social valence ("high" tragedy versus "low" comedy), but that valence is, in turn, transferred in a recharged form back to the social sphere. Terms like "tragedy," "farce," and "caricature" signify forms of experience as much as forms of representation. The major fictional genres in a culture, trailing connotations of worth, status, and significance, are integrally tied to the self-esteem of the cultural groups that use them to define themselves and others. Encoding positive and negative values, they are central to cultural polemics, as different groups struggle for prestige and centrality. McCrie and Conder, seeking access for their past to the noble genres of tragedy and the sublime, resist its reduction to the ignoble genres.

The problem of the choice of fictional genre underlines the degree to which there is always a gap between event and meaning, experience and significance. This gap always yields various semantic possibilities, and the instability signaled by this over-determination helps explain why designations of genre so often

---

37. Gearhart, *Open Boundary of History and Fiction*, 75. Arguing for a very particular kind of reciprocity, Kenneth Burke considers literary genres as symbolic structures designed for living, in *Attitudes toward History*, 3d ed. (Berkeley: University of California Press, 1984), Part 1, chap. 2: 34–105.

arouse strong emotional responses. For instance, our indignation at how X can designate event Y as comic when it is so
clearly tragic testifies to the fact that X *can* do so. McCrie and
Conder may scorn Scott's generic choices, but they cannot rule
them out. What they are left with in the end is ad hominem
attack. So Conder concludes his review by impugning the
character of Scott, and McCrie closes his series of articles by
questioning Scott's patriotism and accusing him of feeding English prejudices "at the expence of his country's honour" (171).

The personal tone of the attack and the indignation that run
through much of the writing of McCrie and Conder point also
to another characteristic of debates of this kind: the charges
against fiction tend to be not only vehement but also intimate.
To illustrate, let me turn briefly to a rather peculiar remark by
Walter Bagehot in his essay on the Waverley Novels. Bagehot is
discussing the limitations of the historical novel as a genre, and
he comments: "We do not like to have our opinions disturbed
by reasoning; but it is impertinent to attempt to disturb them by
fancies."[38] Bagehot, we note, charges the historical novel with
violating not cognitive or ethical but social rules: it acts imperti-
nently. And impertinence is an offense against social decorum
that has a particular emotional and political charge.[39] In contrast
to the more familiar notion of impropriety, for example, it de-
notes the crossing of *vertical* boundaries. To be impertinent is
not only to be out-of-place but to move into and defy a superior
place.[40] As an intrusion from below, ranging in seriousness
from cheekiness to insolence, it signals willful aggression rather
than ignorance or error. Hence what registers its presence is
resentment, the peculiarly personal, even physical, response to
a felt invasion of the place within which one defines oneself.

38. Bagehot, *Literary Studies* 2:171.

39. The OED entry on "impertinence" identifies the following as its chief
current colloquial sense: "Interference with what lies beyond one's province;
offensive intrusion or taking of liberty; presumptuous forward rudeness, esp.
to a superior; insolence."

40. On Scott and impertinence, see Welsh, "Contrast of Styles in the Waverley Novels," 224–28. Welsh concentrates on the implications of Scott's use of
dialect, noting that "almost all of Scott's low characters are impertinent. What
they speak in dialect draws itself up against the high style and the assurance of
life that the high style connotes" (224).

Resentment of fiction, and particularly of historical and other forms of factual fiction,[41] is a recurring historical phenomenon. It emerges under different pressures at different times, but always at stake is a culturally central binary (e.g., male/female, sacred/profane, truth/lie). On such distinctions typically depends that informal, social, and bodily orientation of ourselves in the world that we call a sense of reality. The key term here is precisely "sense" (as opposed to the more formal "idea" or even "construct"), for it is precisely the perception that a concrete, immediate relationship has been violated that accounts for the peculiar intimacy of charges against fiction. One does not (usually) charge science or history with impertinence.

As McCrie's and Conder's suspicion of the popularity of the novel in general suggests, part of their resentment of historical fiction stemmed from its functioning for them as a metonymy for the new social formation that was coming to be called "public opinion" or simply "the public." Conder worries that *Old Mortality* "will doubtless fall into the hands of thousands who will not have leisure, even if disposed to take the pains, to compare them [the historical details in the novel] with authentic narrative" (336). And McCrie, we recall, feared that novelists "have it in their power to do much mischief, from the engaging form in which they convey their sentiments to a numerous, and, in general unsuspecting class of readers" (47). Re-forming hierarchies, the early nineteenth-century public threatened for McCrie and Conder the history/fiction binary on which their sense of reality depended. And in striving to keep that binary in place, they revealed its vulnerability. Even as they tied the "faithful page" of history to law, reason, and divine order, they granted to fiction (illegitimate, irrational, and irreligious) the power of initiation vis-à-vis history. Fiction is active, mobile, and aggressive; by contrast, history emerges in their account (appropriately enough for a civil discourse) as rather like a Waverley hero: passive, loyal, and oddly vulnerable. Like the Waverley hero, it may win in the end, but its victory depends on a certain kind of fiction.

41. I adopt the term "factual fiction" from Lennard J. Davis's account of the early novel, *Factual Fictions: The Origins of the English Novel* (New York: Columbia University Press, 1983).

6

Constructing the Past:
Old Mortality and the
Counterfictions of Galt and Hogg

"Is this thy adherence to the cause of thy father?"
                    —Balfour of Burley to Henry Morton

The authoritative word is located in a distanced zone,
organically connected with a past that is felt to be hier-
archically higher. It is, so to speak, the word of the fathers.
                    —Mikhail Bakhtin, "Discourse in the Novel"

The moment of *Old Mortality* witnessed a challenge to Scott's
mode of historical fiction not just in critical but also in fictional
discourse, notably in rival Covenanter novels produced by
James Hogg and John Galt. Neither Hogg's novel, *The Brownie of
Bodsbeck* (1818), nor Galt's, *Ringan Gilhaize* (1823), had much success with the public or the reviews, so that to place Scott's
successful novel in relation to these competing modes of historical fiction is to bring into sharper focus the form of historical
fiction that was received as definitive by Scott's first readers.

Hogg did not cast his Covenanter novel as a deliberate counterfiction to *Old Mortality*, claiming that *The Brownie of Bodsbeck*,
though not published till 1818, was written "lang afore" Scott's
novel. Hogg's modern editor, Douglas S. Mack, agrees that
much of the tale was in manuscript by 1813, but he concludes
that it is unlikely that Hogg had a complete version before the
publication of Scott's novel.[1] Whatever the case, the fact that it

1. Introduction, *The Brownie of Bodsbeck* (Edinburgh: Scottish Academic
Press, 1976). For ease of reference to both *Brownie* and *Ringan Gilhaize*, I cite
recent critical editions of both texts; all references to *Brownie* are thus to Doug-

was published eighteen months after *Old Mortality* meant that Hogg's narrative was inevitably read as a response. The *British Critic* (the only major journal to review *Brownie*) declared it to be "so manifest an imitation" of Scott's novel as to require some preliminary remarks on the whole question of imitation.[2]

Galt's *Ringan Gilhaize*, on the other hand, was explicitly written as a counterstatement to Scott's novel. Galt explains in his *Literary Life* that he was "hugely provoked" that a descendant of Scott of Harden (who was fined for countenancing Presbyterian practices) "should have been so forgetful of what was due to the spirit of that epoch, as to throw it into what I felt was ridicule."[3] Several of his own ancestors, Galt adds, suffered on behalf of the Covenant, and *Ringan Gilhaize* emerges as their descendant's loyal tribute, not least in its genealogical structure of grandfather—father—son.[4] Familial loyalty also played a role in shaping Hogg's narrative, as is clear from his reply to Scott's charge that *Brownie* was "exaggerated and unfair": "It is the picture I hae been bred up in the belief o' sin' ever I was born and I had it frae them whom I was most bound to honour and believe."[5]

To be "bound" to honor and believe is to adopt a relationship to the past that is traditional rather than historical, and the narratives of both Hogg and Galt are structured by the fidelity of tradition. By contrast, *Old Mortality* is shaped by an enabling assumption of distance that yields a model of history as reflection on, rather adherence to, the past. Scott's model may allow for change and difference, but for critics like McCrie and Galt there lay in it a certain kind of betrayal; hence their insistence on history as a form of faithful and loyal memory.

---

las Mack's edition and will hereafter be included in the text. For Hogg's own account of when he wrote the *Brownie*, see his *Memoirs of the Author's Life and Familiar Anecdotes of Sir Walter Scott*, ed. Douglas S. Mack (Edinburgh: Scottish Academic Press, 1972), 106.

2. *BC*, n.s., 10 (1818): 404.

3. *The Literary Life and Miscellanies of John Galt*, 3 vols. (Edinburgh, 1834), 1:254–55.

4. *Ringan Gilhaize; or, The Covenanters*, ed. Patricia J. Wilson (Edinburgh: Scottish Academic Press, 1984). Wilson points out that in the manuscript the title page reads "Ringan Gilhaize or the Scottish Martyrs" (xxi). All references are to this edition of the novel.

5. Hogg, *Memoirs and Familiar Anecdotes*, 106.

Although Hogg and Galt published their novels just a few short years after the appearance of *Waverley*, the Author of Waverley was already a normative figure in the reviews, his mode of historical fiction already paradigmatic. The reviews typically treat Hogg and Galt as inferior copyists handling a subject that, in the words of the *British Critic*, was "preoccupied ground."[6] Jeffrey's omnibus review of Galt's novels, along with several by Lockhart and John Wilson, in the *Edinburgh Review* makes Scott's priority quite clear in its title, "Secondary Scottish Novels." Jeffrey has no need to identify "their great prototype." In a similar move, the *Edinburgh Magazine* handles the same three writers under the heading "Scottish Novels of the Second Class" and refers throughout to "our Great Novelist."[7] For all the reviewers, Scott stood as the model of the historical novelist, and it is mostly in terms of their ability to handle the historical mode of fiction being established by him that Galt and Hogg were discussed.

Galt, the more extensively noticed of the two, was generally criticized for moving outside his range and into the wrong genre in attempting the historical novel. Jeffrey declares that, despite some felicities, *Ringan Gilhaize* is "heavy work—and proves conclusively, that the genius of the author lies much more to the quieter walks of humorous simplicity, intermixed with humble pathos, than to the lofty paths of enthusiasm or heroic emotion."[8] The *Edinburgh Magazine* (hostile to Galt in general) also sees him as moving into an unsuitable genre beyond his powers ("straining after effect") and producing a work which is "neither history nor novel, but combines . . . the defects of both—the flippancy of fiction without its interest, and the dulness of a chronicle, without its veracity."[9] The *Monthly Magazine* finds *Ringan* "merely a *history*. There is no domestic

---

6. Review of *Ringan Gilhaize* and *The Spaewife*, BC, n.s., 2 (1824): 240. Hogg uses the same resonant image of pre-occupied ground in describing his response to Scott's anticipation of his own Covenanting tale: "I well remember my chagrin on finding the ground, which I thought clear, preoccupied before I could appear publicly on it, and that by such a redoubted champion" (*Memoirs and Familiar Anecdotes*, 45).

7. ER 39 (1823): 158–96; EdM, n.s., 13 (1823): 1–9.

8. ER 39 (1823): 178.

9. EdM, n.s., 13 (1823): 2.

tale; and the events crowd before us without exciting the least degree of personal interest."[10]

Hogg, on the other hand, was chastised for the opposite fault of transforming history into fiction. The *British Critic* identifies his problem as reliance on local, oral history ("hearsay among the shepherds and old wives of Eskdale and Ettrick"). The consequence of relying on lowly shepherds and dubious old wives, it seems, is "that instead of reflecting upon fiction the semblance of history, he has reflected upon history the semblance of fiction." The writing of good historical fiction, the reviewer admits, is extremely difficult, for it requires a special kind of imaginative power, one that compels us to forget our own age and (in an economic metaphor) to "invest our imagination" in the "thoughts and manners, and habits and prejudices" of another age. The specificity of this genre within the general fictional field, then, lies in its ability "to carry our feelings and our fancy back into the heart and into the spirit of times that are long since past."[11]

But the success of *Old Mortality* and the failure of *Brownie* and *Ringan* suggest that to register as historical a fiction needed something more than this. After all, it is Galt and Hogg who, we will see, attempt to generate the kind of eyewitness effect to which the *British Critic* refers and which has typically functioned as an informal criterion for good historical fiction ("You felt as if you were actually there"). This is not to say that the Waverley Novels were uninterested in creating a sense of concrete immediacy in their representation of historical experience. On the contrary. Over and over again, Scott's fiction was praised in the reviews for its ability to make the past "live" for the reader. As discussed in the next chapter, one of Scott's central contributions to both nineteenth-century fiction and history was the redefinition of history as experience (versus history as event) that the Waverley Novels helped to effect. At the same time, the Covenanter controversy illustrates the degree to which that achievement depended not on reproduction of the past (assuming this as a possible discursive pole) but on its mediation. Informing the narrative act of *Old Mortality*, in con-

10. *MM* 55 (1823): 449.
11. *BC*, n.s., 10 (1818): 406–7.

trast to the narrative acts of *Ringan Gilhaize* and *The Brownie of Bodsbeck*, was a distrust of notions of reenactment and memory that was crucial to defining historical discourse for the nineteenth century.

"The Ashes of Our Fathers": *Old Mortality*, *Ringan Gilhaize*, and Patrilineal Time

In a comment on *Old Mortality*, John Buchan observed that in this novel Scott was attempting the most difficult kind of historical novel because he was dealing with a period of history "far outside living experience but furiously alive in popular memory."[12] Buchan's statement suggests an opposition between the impulse of the historical novel and that of popular memory in their relations to and of the past. At stake ultimately is a difference between history and memory as constructions of the past, and Buchan rightly senses that the classical historical novel invented by Scott negotiates that difference on the side of history. Even as the Waverley Novels incorporate various linguistic forms of popular memory—song, tale, anecdote—and the languages of cultural margins, the whole narrative effort is governed by a discursive move that defines the past as *history*: as something finished and external to the present. As Harry Shaw has argued, the "distinctively historical probability" of standard historical fiction depends not so much on a sense of history as process as on a sense of history as difference, that is, on the recognition, as Shaw puts it, of " 'the past as past.' "[13]

For Galt and Hogg, by contrast, the past is constructed under the more conservative signs of memory and legacy. Galt's novel is especially striking, for it is itself a formal embodiment of the patriarchal shape of memory and inheritance in the Scottish Calvinist tradition.[14] The narrative is a first-person "household

12. *Sir Walter Scott* (London: Cassell, 1932), 160.

13. *Forms of Historical Fiction: Sir Walter Scott and His Successors* (Ithaca: Cornell University Press, 1983), 26.

14. On the patriarchal structure of Scottish Calvinism, see Charles Camic, *Experience and Enlightenment: Socialization for Cultural Change in Eighteenth-Century Scotland* (Chicago: University of Chicago Press, 1983). Francis Hart stresses the centrality of inheritance as a theme in Scottish literature in *The Scottish Novel: A Critical Survey* (London: Murray, 1978).

memorial" written by Ringan Gilhaize in 1696. He looks back on a life spent fighting for the Covenanter cause, in the course of which he lost his entire family, notably his two sons. His narrative, cast largely in Scots,[15] records the fidelity of the Gilhaize family to the principles of true Presbyterianism over several generations, covering around one hundred and thirty years (1568–1696). It begins in the time of John Knox when Ringan's (extremely long-lived) grandfather was involved in effecting the Scottish Reformation, and the memories of this old man, of Ringan's father, and of Ringan himself structure the narrative.

Old Mortality is also shaped by notions of memory and legacy, but in a very different way.[16] With this novel Scott introduced the framed third-person narration that became a hallmark of the Waverley series,[17] and through the frame to Old Mortality he set up his novel from the outset in implicit opposition to the kind of memory inscribed by Ringan Gilhaize. It is no accident that a novel focusing on the heroes of an active and popular nationalist myth should be the first of the Waverley Novels to have an extended narrative frame and should provide its author (already under the cover of anonymity) with the added mask of not simply one but *two* fictionalized narrators: Jedediah Cleisbhotham and Peter Pattieson. One might add a third (the landlord of the title) to the series of narrators, but the point is the dense screen that Scott constructs as he moves into a subject "furiously alive" in popular memory. Anticipating its challenge and offering an advance defense, Peter Pattieson's preface carefully negotiates a space apart from that of popular memory and in so doing suggests that the history-likeness of the histor-

---

15. For a discussion of the use of Scots by Scott, Galt, and Hogg in the Covenanter novels, see Emma Letley, *From Galt to Douglas Brown: Nineteenth-Century Fiction and Scots Language* (Edinburgh: Scottish Academic Press, 1988), 28–48. Letley argues that Galt's novel has a "much deeper engagement" with Scots than either Hogg's or Scott's novels (41). The standard analysis of Scott's representation of Scots is Graham Tulloch, *The Language of Walter Scott: A Study of His Scottish and Period Language* (London: Deutsch, 1980).

16. *Old Mortality* forms vols. 2–4 of *Tales of My Landlord*, 4 vols. (Edinburgh, 1818).

17. For a recent discussion of the frames, see Marilyn Orr, "Voices and Text: Scott the Storyteller, Scott the Novelist," *Scottish Literary Journal* 16 (1989): 41–59. In an analysis pertinent to this study, Orr reads the Waverley frames as a scene of contest between different kinds of narrative authority.

ical novel is a function of the *positioning* of the narrative: as utterance, it stands at a distinct temporal distance from what is uttered. This seems obvious enough, but, as the subsequent controversy over the novel confirms, it involves a potentially contentious move because it requires the exchange of a narrative model that places temporal continuity in the foreground (the past as memory) for one that makes discontinuity the enabling narrative condition (the past as history). Whereas the past as memory turns the narrative act into commemoration or execration (its two extreme poles), the past as history defines the narrative act more self-consciously as reflection (in several senses) and interpretation. That is, history conceptualizes rather than commemorates the past. Both discourses, of course, constitute an intervention in the present and may be filled with different ideological content, and the distinction between them (much like the distinction between the larger genres of fiction and history discussed in the previous chapter) is at once blurred and necessary to both.

The figure of Old Mortality, introduced by Pattieson in the opening chapter, inhabits the mode of memory, preserving the inscriptions of the past "to warn future generations to defend their religion even unto blood." Castigating his own contemporaries as "forgetters," he strives to make time homogenous and to coerce it into an authentic line of continuity authorized by the privileged and symbolic moment of the Covenant when the nation defined itself in adherence to the sacred word of Scripture. Although Old Mortality may employ the grammatical tenses of past, present, and future when he speaks, for him these are not distinct modalities of time but manifestations of the same tense. Pattieson underlines this point when he notes of the old man's tales of the Covenanters: "One would almost have supposed he must have been their contemporary, and have actually beheld the passages which he related, so much had he identified his feelings and opinions with theirs, and so much had his narratives the circumstantiality of an eyewitness" (2:20; chap. 1). In his ability to collapse the distance between then and now and to assume the discourse of an eyewitness (a discourse marked, we note, by "circumstantiality"), Old Mortality signals his eccentricity. Abandoning the temporal

signifiers of family and community, he has left his own village
to wander alone, restoring the marks of the Covenanter past,
for him the only real time and so in a sense not memory at all.

For the villagers of Gandercleugh, by contrast, the Covenanting past does exist in the pastness of memory, but it exists as
significant emblem and motivation for the present and hence
operates in the category of living memory. Taking their sons to
the graves of the executed Covenanters (and ignoring, significantly, the tombs of the aristocrat and bishop), they typically
narrate the death of "the sufferers" and exhort the boys "to be
ready, should times call for it, to resist to the death in the cause
of civil and religious liberty, like their brave forefathers." These
"forefathers," incidentally, are not biological but cultural, for
the men buried in the graves in Pattieson's village were
strangers who had been retreating from the defeat of the Pentland Rising of 1666 when they were attacked and killed by royal
troops.

Pattieson frames his account of the villagers' veneration of
these Covenanters by two passages that underline how for him
the past stimulates neither action nor exhortation but "reflection." Reflection assumes and turns into a positive value the
whole notion of temporal distance that Old Mortality and the
villagers attempt, in their different ways, to reduce or deny.
The first passage recounts Pattieson's fondness for the small,
deserted burial ground that contains the Covenanter graves.
Himself dying, the young Pattieson draws comfort from the
graveyard, welcoming the way in which the "traces" of death
have been softened by "our distance from the period when they
have been first impressed." "Those who sleep beneath," he
continues as he elaborates an ancient literary topos, "are only
connected with us by the reflection, that they once have been
what we now are, and that, as their relics are now identified
with their mother earth, ours shall, at some future period, un-
dergo the same transformation" (2:8; chap. 1). To see the "reflection" on our common mortality as the "only" link between the
dead and the living is to move decisively out of living memory
with its insistence on the relevance of past action to present
action. But it is not to move into history, for such reflection
drains time of the social and the consequential. All time for

Pattieson here becomes the same time, even as it was—or should have been—for Old Mortality.

Nevertheless, it is the power of reflection—its ability to abstract and generalize—that is the key to the construction of the past as history, as the second passage framing the description of the Covenanter graves helps to underline. Here Pattieson reflects on the meaning of the Covenanters. Himself a Presbyterian divine, he does not, he tells us, venerate "the peculiar tenets" of the Covenanters, but his dissent from their doctrines does not mean that he depreciates "the memory of those sufferers," who well deserve praise. On the other hand, he states: "it would be unjust to forget, that many even of those who had been most active in crushing what they conceived the rebellious and seditious spirit of those unhappy wanderers, displayed themselves, when called upon to suffer for their political and religious opinions, the same daring and devoted zeal, tinctured, in their case, with chivalrous loyalty, as in the former with republican enthusiasm" (2:11; chap. 1). The heraldic image of "tincture" is a favorite one of Scott. The opening chapter of *Waverley*, we remember, had declared that human passions remain the same in all stages of society, though they are "tinctured" differently (*Waverley*, 5). Pattieson similarly stresses sameness in difference, emphasizing what is shared by cavalier and covenanter, no matter the difference in the "tincture" of their beliefs.

But Pattieson's point is less universal than national, and he goes on immediately to incorporate both groups under a single national category: "It has often been remarked of the Scottish character, that the stubbornness with which it is moulded shows most to advantage in adversity, when it seems akin to the native sycamore of their hills, which scorns to be biassed in its mode of growth even by the influence of the prevailing wind, . . . and may be broken, but can never be bended." In evoking "the Scottish character," Pattieson has performed an analytic act, moving to a higher level of generality in order to establish a commonality that (in contrast to the commonality of mortality) *is* historical. "The Scottish character" has meaning only in terms of Scottish history even as it is a category abstracted from it. This level of abstraction allows Pattieson to see

two contending historical terms ("cavalier" and "covenanter")
as different manifestations of the same principle, but only if he
assumes the pastness of the past and of its motivations—a
point to which I will return.

Pattieson's description of the sources and compilation of his
narrative also moves into the foreground the notion of history
as the narrative product of a reflection upon memory. Old Mortality is identified as his main but by no means privileged
source: "My readers will of course understand, that in embodying into one compressed narrative many of the anecdotes which
I had the advantage of deriving from Old Mortality, I have been
far from adopting either his style, his opinions, or even his
facts, so far as they appear to have been distorted by party
prejudice. I have endeavoured to correct or verify them from the
most authentic sources of tradition, afforded by the representatives of either party" (2:26; chap. 1). Like an exemplary historian, Pattieson compares and verifies, seeking to come up with
a correct account. The analytic process not only enables him to
construct "one compressed narrative" out of the disparate and
plural sources available but authorizes that construction as the
product of historical discipline and integrity. He has, after all,
consulted "the representatives of either party," and Pattieson
goes on to detail the efforts he made to locate and listen to
descendants of both sides of the civil war. He does not, oddly
enough, detail any reading or any kind of documentary research, limiting his narrative authority to his oral sources. Initiated by the encounter with Old Mortality, the narrative to follow is thus implicitly defined as a reflection on oral history, on
the living memory of the countryside.

The tendency of such reflection is to defuse living memory,
just as the tendency of living memory is to discourage reflection. Both constructions of the past have (always) a present
point. In the case of Old Mortality, Pattieson makes the point—
already implicit in the integrative move of the passage on "the
Scottish character"—quite explicit in his conclusion, which insists, almost obsessively, on the pastness of the past. "I can
hardly fear," he claims, "that, at this time, in describing the
operation which their opposite principles produced upon the
good and bad men of both parties, I can be suspected of mean-

ing insult or injustice to either" (2:29; chap. 1). Both the tangled syntax and the insistence that "I can hardly fear" testify to the very anxiety about the presence of the past that the sentence claims no one takes seriously "at this time." And the sense of unease continues as Pattieson prefaces his next statement about the distance of the past with "We may safely hope that the souls of the brave and sincere on either side . . ." This statement particularly irritated McCrie and Conder, for Pattieson now shifts to an even higher level of generality, enacting a vertical move out of temporal categories altogether as he presents "the souls of the brave and sincere on either side" as having "long looked down with surprise and pity upon the ill-appreciated motives which caused their mutual hatred and hostility, while in this valley of darkness, blood, and tears." "Peace to their memory!" he urges in closing, reinforcing this imperative by an appeal to the culturally central text of John Home's *Douglas* ("our only Scottish tragedy"): "O rake not up the ashes of our fathers! / Implacable resentment was their crime, / And grievous has the expiation been." The speaker here, Lady Randolph, is urging the special forgetting of the past on which, as the old adage has it, forgiveness depends.[18]

But for McCrie and Conder (as for Old Mortality himself), such forgetting means less forgiveness than betrayal of the past. Both of Scott's critics single out for scorn Pattieson's conclusion, rejecting the move to conciliation in order to maintain the confrontational structure on which their sense of the significance of the past (and of their present) hinges. McCrie lashes out at Pattieson in direct address, asking him what he means when, "with affected whining, and glaring self-contradiction—in the language of tragedy too," he brings in the line about the fathers: "Your fathers! If you mean the Presbyterians, they acknowledge you not; and if their persecutors, *you* only are to blame for the stirring of those ashes."[19] On his side, Conder also firmly rejects Pattieson's conciliatory gesture, castigating in particular

18. In an important article on Scott and authority, Francis Hart points out that Pattieson's desire to bring "peace" to the memory of the past is in "radical discontinuity with his traditional source" ("Scott's Endings: The Fictions of Authority," *Nineteenth-Century Fiction* 33 [1978]: 53).

19. *EdCln* 14 (1817): 60.

his placing cavalier and covenanter in the same category. Such an act, he asserts, is the product of "an equalizing principle of sceptical indifference that places the tyrant and the patriot, the ruffian and the martyr, on exactly the same level, making on either side bravery or sincerity a quality of redeeming virtue."[20]

Even more clearly than McCrie, Conder responds to the general ideological implication of the positioning of the narrative, recognizing what Hayden White has called "the morally domesticating effects of consigning an event definitively to 'history.'"[21] To move an event out of living memory is to move it out of vital, concrete connection with the present and to defuse it of a certain emotional and hortatory power. But it is also to move it out of violence, the factional violence that for Scott was the blight and sadness of Scotland's history.[22] "Peace to their memory!" says Pattieson, and *Old Mortality* makes clear that the peace whose preservation civil society makes a central concern requires a forgetting, or, to put it another way, a remembering in another mode: the mode of distance and difference rather than identity and repetition.

Living memory in Calvinist Scotland, Pattieson's preface suggests, construes the past as paternal, relying on a distinctly patrilineal concept of temporal sequence as a legacy of fathers to sons. The villagers, we recall, cited "forefathers" as exemplary for their sons, but for the female speaker of the lines from *Doug-*

20. *EcR*, n.s., 7 (1817): 315.
21. "The Politics of Historical Interpretation: Discipline and De-Sublimation," *Critical Inquiry* 9 (1982): 134.
22. John Farrell's analysis of Scott as nineteenth-century moderate draws specific attention to Scott's sense of Scotland's "tragic" (the word is Scott's own) propensity for self-destruction through factional conflict. See, for example, *Revolution as Tragedy: The Dilemma of the Moderate from Scott to Arnold* (Ithaca: Cornell University Press, 1980), 74–76. Discussion of the question of Scott and the politics of moderation, an enduring critical topic since the Scottish novels were first published, typically involves *Old Mortality* as exemplary text (for good and/or ill), as in Peter D. Garside, "*Old Mortality*'s Silent Minority," *Scottish Literary Journal* 7 (1980): 127–44 and George Goodin's "Walter Scott and the Tradition of the Political Novel," in *The English Novel in the Nineteenth Century*, ed. George Goodin (Urbana: University of Illinois Press, 1972), 14–24. More recently, Virgil Nemoianu has argued for conciliation as a mark of the Biedermeier and placed Scott's historical novel in this context, in *The Taming of Romanticism: European Literature and the Age of Biedermeier* (Cambridge, Mass.: Harvard University Press, 1984).

las the ashes of "our fathers" are best forgotten. Pattieson himself stands outside the patrilineal scheme without a father (leaving aside the pseudo-paternity of Cleishbotham) and without a son. An oddly atopic character (to adopt one of Roland Barthes's evocative terms), he is unlocated in terms of family history or family place. Being out of place and dying, he occupies the abstract space of reflection that allows him to construct his "compressed narrative." And the story that he chooses to tell is of young Henry Morton, also dislocated but very much a son. For John Balfour of Burley, in fact, who ultimately forces Morton into the action that shapes his life, the melancholy young hero exists primarily as the son of the Presbyterian soldier-hero Silas Morton.

Burley sounds the note at their first meeting when he calls on Henry to repay Silas Morton's debt to him: "Did you ever hear your father mention John Balfour of Burley?" (2:97; chap. 5). Henry, who "idolized" the memory of his father, defies the law in order to fulfill his father's obligations, thereby setting in motion the events of the story. As Judith Wilt has pointed out, Burley presents himself in this scene "virtually as the ghost of Morton's soldier-father and calls him, Hamlet-like, to join . . . in opposition to the mean-minded moderation and pusillanimous political equivocation of his uncle and the government in power."[23] The Hamlet motif informs the entire characterization of Morton, surfacing quite clearly in the strange episode of return which concludes the novel—and where Morton becomes his own ghost haunting the landscape of his youth.[24] At his uncle's house of Milnwood, Morton looks at the portraits of two brothers "as dissimilar as those described by Hamlet." The one depicts his uncle, the parsimonious laird, dressed in velvet and brocade and "looking as if he were ashamed of his own finery"; the other shows his soldier-father in armor and "with a countenance indicating his masculine and determined character" (4:249; chap. 40). Shortly after, Morton goes to meet Burley for

23. *Secret Leaves: The Novels of Walter Scott* (Chicago: University of Chicago Press, 1985), 87.

24. For a psychological reading of the strange final chapters, see Alexander Welsh, *Hero of the Waverley Novels* (1963; New York: Atheneum, 1968), 255–64; for a more political reading, see Shaw, *Forms of Historical Fiction*, 199–205.

the final time, confronting the figure who sought to turn him into the image of his father and who deftly manipulated the code of masculinity in order to effect that identification.

In insisting on the primacy of the time of the father, Burley brings to the surface the questions about the paternal past underlying Pattieson's prefatory chapter. "Is this thy adherence to the cause of thy father?" he asks Morton in chapter 22, and the appeal to the father, to the past as a male legacy of loyalty and continuity, constitutes his most powerful weapon in controlling the reluctant young insurgent. Morton's time, he implies, is owed to his father and bound to reenactment of the paternal commitment to the Presbyterian cause. That commitment is not without its ambiguities, for the Scots Presbyterians fought both against and for the Stuarts during the civil wars, and Silas Morton was representative in that respect. As early as chapter 3 we learn that he fought for the victorious Parliamentary side at the battles of Marston-Moor and Philiphaugh and then later (after the execution of Charles I) for the defeated Stuart forces at the battles of Dunbar and Inverkeithing. Henry Morton thus inherits an ambivalent legacy, but Burley (who broke with Silas Morton when he accepted the Scottish decision to support the Stuarts) ignores any complexity in order to present the son with a clear patrilineal paradigm to follow. When Morton challenges the plan to send him to lead the main body of the Presbyterian army against Glasgow while Burley remains with a small group to continue the siege of Tillietudlem (home of Morton's beloved Edith Bellenden), Burley defeats the challenge by evoking the code of manliness in which the notion of the father is central. Burley first reminds Morton that he is the son of Silas Morton, then hints at cowardice by reminding Morton that he has avoided the front lines of battle to date, and finally synthesizes the two appeals in a return to the legacy of the father: "men will say, that the son of Silas Morton hath fallen away from the paths of his father." Henry, we are informed, is "stung" by the last comment to which, "as a gentleman and soldier, he could offer no suitable reply," and he quickly accedes to the plan. And yet, the narrator adds, "he was unable to divest himself of certain feelings of distrust" (3:273–74; chap. 26). The sequence encapsulates the Hamletlike vulnerability yet resistance to the paternal plea that characterizes Morton throughout. For Morton, who will and yet will not adhere to his father, the past sanctioned by popular memory and paternal authority becomes increasingly problematic, and with it the whole question of loyalty and of the authority for action.

The novel implies that to be in history is to live *in* this problem. The strangely melancholy final movement of *Old Mortality* suggests that, whatever the resolution effected by (and for) Morton, he remains entangled in the difficulties of history in a way that distinguishes him from most Waverley heroes, including Edward Waverley. An alienated figure, Morton is strongly tempted by a Pattieson-like vertical leap out of history into high abstraction and literally by suicide, but he remains in the world and within the "civil" language that characterizes it. Earlier in the novel, Morton rebuked Burley for his "uncivil language" when Burley characterized Morton's love for Edith Bellenden as "thy lust for a Moabitish woman." Burley is "uncivil" here because he points to the sexuality that decorum prefers to ignore, but his language is also "uncivil" in a profounder sense, for it marks the Covenanter allegiance to a theological construction of the past. Like most of the Covenanter characters (Mause Headrigg is exemplary), Burley reads the world through metaphors sanctioned by the biblical text and Presbyterian scriptural tradition. What makes this language "uncivil" is not only that it assumes direct access to the authoritative word but also that it admits no distance or difference. It deploys biblical metaphor in a curiously single-minded way that recognizes no distinctions of linguistic, cultural, or temporal levels. Mause, for example, relies heavily on apposition, the grammatical form of equivalence. Apposition allows her not just to collapse distinctions but to release her enormous verbal energy and inventiveness without threatening coherence. Although her catalogs of denunciation may seem unpredictable and out of control, they are in fact predictable and controlled in the sense that her organizing categories are few and closed. For her, everything makes sense in the same way, as it does not for Morton, who has difficulty by the end of the novel making sense at all.

He has, however, succeeded in redefining the legacy whose paternal shape Burley sought so fiercely to impress on him as the ground of his own identity. Morton meets Burley for the last time in an eerie dawn setting of Gothic crags, caves, and chasms. For Burley, he remains "Silas Morton's son" and "son of mine ancient comrade" (4:302, 310; chap. 43). As in the beginning of the story, Morton accepts this identity, but this time in order to refuse Burley himself. Declining Burley's challenge to fight, he tells him that "I will not fight with the man that preserved my father's life." Nor will he yield to him. Instead, declaring that "my life I will rescue as I best can," Morton proceeds to literally jump out of the scene (4:312–13; chap. 43). He has refused to kill the sign of the father and in so doing has defined himself—but ambiguously—as his father's son. By this time, we recall, Morton has been known for a decade under his mother's name of Melville even as he has been following his father's model of the Protestant soldier on the continent. Most important, in his condition of exile, he has experienced time not simply as change but as radical break; and his return to the scenes of his youth, where signs of change and loss dominate those of continuity and gain, confirms that time is not homogenous and the past not a determinate and single line. "I am so changed," he sighs when even the dog as his uncle's house fails to recognize him, "that no breathing creature that I have known and loved will now acknowledge me!" (4:234; chap. 39). Morton turns out to be wrong, but the affirmation of continuity offered by his subsequent recognition is very fragile. If in the end Morton affirms construction of the past in the homogenous mode of legacy, the whole notion of legacy has become so tangled and obscure in the process that it is the discontinuities which linger in the mind.

Galt's Ringan Gilhaize, locating himself and his narrative in a direct patriarchal line, stands in sharp contrast to the ambivalent Henry Morton, and through his narrator-hero Galt constructs a kind of history that deliberately counters that of Scott. This is not to identify Galt with Ringan Gilhaize. Galt insisted that he was not to be confused with his narrator and declared that the "sentiments" of the novel "are not mine."[25] Modern

25. Galt, *Literary Life*, 1: 251.

readers have tended to agree, stressing Galt's technical achievement in the creation of the narrative voice. Francis Hart, for instance, finds the voice of Ringan the brilliant product of "imaginative ventriloquism."[26] Certainly, there is an ironic gap between Ringan and the reader, so that, as the editor of the new critical edition comments, "long before the end of the novel the reader knows more than Ringan."[27] But if the depiction of Ringan draws on Galt's experience in creating self-revealing narrators in earlier novels like *The Provost*, the self-exposure here is neither comic nor satiric but closer to tragic, as the bereaved Ringan moves deeper and deeper into obsession and violence.

The question remains: how to take Ringan? The hermeneutic gap opened up by the use of the first-person narrator and his historical particularity in this text remains highly problematic, and the authorial postscript with which Galt concludes his text only heightens the difficulties. Its authorial generalizations about the Scots and the English reveal an imagination and language similar to those of Ringan, though of a more secular cast, as in the declaration that the Scots are royalists but not in any "unmanly" way: "On the contrary, servile loyalty is comparatively rare among us, and it was in England that the Stuarts first DARED to broach the doctrine of the divine right of kings" (324). Author echoes hero here, for shortly before, Ringan had charged Claverhouse with "canine fidelity, a dog's love, to his papistical master" (312). Even more important, after the news about the murder of Archbishop Sharp, Ringan quotes the famous lines about liberty from the 1320 Declaration of Abroath ("but it is for liberty alone we contend, which no true man will lose but with his life," 244), and Galt reproduces the entire declaration in the postscript, noting that he is using a translation from Ringan's time and that "the sacred original is in the Register Office" (324).

Clearly, there are profound points of convergence between authorial and narrative voice, notably on political and national questions, no matter their distance on Calvinist principles and

26. Hart, *Scottish Novel*, 50–51.
27. Wilson, introduction, *Ringan Gilhaize*, vii.

other matters. And even when it comes to Calvinism, which Galt is generally supposed to have repudiated,[28] it is noteworthy that his intended audience for the novel was "the Presbyterians in particular and the devout in general." He hoped in fact that it would serve as a "Sunday evening story—like the Pilgrim's Progress." Moreover, Galt wanted the novel to be published on 2 May, the anniversary of John Knox's return to Scotland and Galt's own birthday.[29] He wanted, in other words, not only to link personal and public history but to incorporate his book into significant sequence, into history imagined as momentous repetition—the same kind of history that makes sense of time and self for Ringan Gilhaize. My point is not to transform Galt into Ringan but to suggest that what underlies the writing of *Ringan Gilhaize* is an authorial imagination and historical intuition that sharply diverge from those of Scott, construing historical time and individual significance in a very different way.[30]

The challenge to Scott begins with the epigraph from *The Sabbath*, by James Grahame:

> Their constancy in torture and in death,—
> These on Tradition's tongue still live, these shall
> On History's honest page be pictured bright
> To latest times.[31]

28. John MacQueen is something of an exception. Where most modern readers of Galt emphasize his Enlightenment background, MacQueen feels that he remained a Calvinist (though a moderate one) to the end; see MacQueen's "*Ringan Gilhaize* and Particular Providence," in *John Galt, 1779–1979*, ed. Christopher A. Whatley (Edinburgh: Ramsay Head Press, 1979), 107–19.

29. The information and quotations from Galt about his intended audience come from Wilson's introduction to *Ringan Gilhaize*, xii–xiii.

30. For recent discussions of the differences between Galt and Scott in the writing of history, see H. B. de Groot, "Scott and Galt: 'Old Mortality' and 'Ringan Gilhaize,'" in *Scott and His Influence*, ed. J. H. Alexander and David Hewitt (Aberdeen: Association for Scottish Literary Studies, 1983), 321–30; Hart, *Scottish Novel*, 50–52; P. H. Scott, *John Galt* (Edinburgh: Scottish Academic Press, 1985), 79–91.

31. Conder also quoted this passage from Grahame (rather more fully) in his review of *Old Mortality*, EcR, n.s., 7 (1817): 316. James Grahame (1765–1811), incidentally, was a lawyer and a clerk in the Church of England.

This epigraph sounds a note about the past quite distinct from that in the verse cited by Peter Pattieson. Ringan sets up his entire narrative under the sign of constancy in both an ethical and temporal sense. With "unerring constancy," he tell us, he has adhered to the Covenant since his "green years" (139). And the Covenant, in turn, is but a return to the pure principles of the Reformation for which his grandfather ("my father's father") struggled. Ringan opens his narrative with this grandfather, Michael Gilhaize, on whose stories (stories that "kindled my young mind to flame up with no less ardour than his") he bases his account of the Reformation. On him, also, he bases his own sense of identity, for Grandfather Gilhaize had prophesied that God had in store for his ardent young grandson a special task. This task Ringan comes to interpret as the killing of Claverhouse, an act he performs—or thinks he performs—at the battle of Killiecrankie when he himself, in a poignant phrase he used earlier, is a "childless father" (249). By this act, Ringan believes that he has liberated Scotland from "the papistical Stuarts" for ever. "Never again in this land," he writes in the final line of his text, "shall any king, of his own caprice and prerogative, dare to violate the conscience of the people" (322).

Central to Ringan Gilhaize's sense of himself and of his nation is the notion of reenactment. Right before he participates in the Pentland Rising of 1666, for example, he feels that "the spirit of that patriarch, my apostolic grandfather, was gathering to heart and energy within the silent recesses of my afflicted bosom" (181). Grasping his grandfather's sword, he goes out with his neighbors to rouse the surrounding farms, discovering that "master and man, and father and son, there likewise found that the hilts of their fathers' covenanted swords fitted their avenging grasps" (183). Defining and defending national identity emerges as very much the province of one gender. The narrative presents Scotland as shaped by two male figures: the compound construct of Robert-the-Bruce-and-Wallace, and the figure of John Knox. Suggestively, Mary Queen of Scots, who engages in intelligent and lively debate with Knox in the novel (as she does in historical accounts), is cast primarily as sexual sinner/victim whose erotic desires place her kingdom and peo-

ple in jeopardy. To reinforce the point, Ringan rather awkwardly includes a didactic tale of one Marion Ruet, who deserts
her husband and young children to become the mistress of a
bishop. After much degradation, Marion repents, undergoes
public humiliation (as does the royal Mary in a parallel scene),
and dies on the doorstep of the home she abandoned after her
husband shuts the door in her face. Shadowed by Marion Ruet,
Mary Stuart takes her place at the impure pole of the pure/im-
pure binary, but the point is that she and the other female
figures (including the loyal and pure Gilhaize wives) are necessarily secondary, for the Scots nation is quite literally a father-
land.

The central image of the Covenant, for instance, is articulated
through the father-son motif of legacy. Ringan records that his
father as a young boy was taken by Grandfather Gilhaize to see
the signing of the Covenant at the time of the threat of the
Spanish armada (137); and shortly after, he notes the reenactment in his own life when his father took him as a young boy to
be a party to the signing of the Solemn League and Covenant
(139). The interesting—and characteristic—thing here is that
there was no Covenant signed at the time of the armada, and
the Covenant that young Ringan witnessed was not the Solemn
League and Covenant of 1643 (which, in fact, he entirely ignores) but the National Covenant of 1638.[32] The pertinence of
this is not historical inaccuracy but the degree to which the
whole notion of the Covenant quickly assumed mythic status
among more extreme Presbyterians, who, exploiting the ancient biblical connotations of the term, read it back (anach-

32. The National Covenant of 1638, signed in churches throughout Scotland,
pledged defense of the true reformed church of Scotland against the Anglican
kinds of innovations that Charles I was attempting to introduce. The Solemn
League and Covenant of 1643 was a more clearly political document, an alliance between the Scots and the English Parliamentarians against Charles I.
This treaty pledged the preservation of the reformed church in Scotland and
(arguably) the adoption of Presbyterianism in England and Ireland. After the
beheading of Charles I, Charles II signed both Covenants in return for Scots
support but renounced them once he was restored to the throne. In Covenanting tradition, the two Covenants are often treated as one, becoming simply the
Covenant (with its deliberate connotation of an ancient and special bond between God and this people).

ronistically) into the Reformation and even earlier.[33] The resonant title "Solemn League and Covenant," in particular, tended
to be applied to earlier associations and documents, as Ringan
applies it here to give a special dignity and seriousness to the
ceremony he witnessed. A striking example of such anachronism occurs when Ringan, narrating the unpopular marriage of
Mary Queen of Scots to the earl of Bothwell in 1567, reports that
outraged nobles, led by the earls of Murray and Argyle, "entered into a Solemn League and Covenant" to avenge the murder of Darnley, her former husband, and to dissolve the new
marriage. Described first as lowercase "covenanting nobles," by
the next paragraph they and their clans have become the uppercase "army of the Covenanters," and a few lines later they are
simply "the Covenanters" (120). Given such sliding, it is not
surprising that it is difficult to pinpoint from *Ringan Gilhaize*
exactly when "the Covenant" was signed and what it was. As
its historical origin recedes, it is always in the process of being
"renewed," so that Gilhaize refers to the signing of the first
Covenant in 1638 as "the renewal, at Irvine, of the Solemn
League and Covenant" (146).

Such a pointed "retroactive realignment of the Past" (to invoke Arthur Danto's definition of history) is almost a parody of
historical reasoning, which, as analytic philosophers like Danto
remind us, interprets an event in light of its relationship to later
events.[34] For Ringan and the Covenanters, however, it is less
that the chronologically later Covenants allow one to reinterpret
the past than that the Covenants and the Reformation are really
one event manifesting an original covenant between God and
his Chosen People. The seventeenth-century Covenanters saw
themselves as restoring the pure principles of the Reformation,
which was itself a restoration. As Ringan makes clear in his
opening paragraph, the Reformation restored the sacred and
pure word of Scripture that had been corrupted by "the worshippers of the Beast and his Image." To underline the point,

---

33. In her notes to *Ringan*, Wilson points out that the anachronistic application of the Covenants became quite common (339–40).

34. *Analytical Philosophy of History* (Cambridge: Cambridge University Press,
1968), 168.

John Knox appears in Ringan's account as both Old Testament patriarch and New Testament apostle: his flowing hair and beard are "like those of the ancient patriarchs who enjoyed immediate communion with God"; he is "eager and zealous, like the apostle Peter, in his temper, and as dauntless as the mighty and courageous Paul" (64). Moreover, the Reformation is linked to national identity in a more secular and political sense as well, for it also evokes the "hero-stirring times" of the Wallace and King Robert the Bruce when Scotland achieved national independence in defiance of Edward I of England (31). Characteristically, the seventeenth-century Covenanters, swayed by their own myth, choose a Colonel Wallace to lead them at one point because "his name made him bright and resplendent to our enthusiasm" (185). This choice, Ringan admits somewhat ruefully, turns out to be "a deadly error," a warning about basing crucial decisions on something "so unsubstantial as the echo of an honoured name" (185).

Yet there is a sense in which the theology and ideology of the Covenanters rely on precisely such echoes. Authority is invested almost totally in the names and texts of the past, starting with the Bible, and analogy becomes the dominant mode of interpreting one's own time. So Ringan, as we saw, quotes the Declaration of Abroath as sanction for and key to his militant turn at the time of the Pentland Rising. Some years later when he is arrested after Bothwell-brigg and questioned about the murder of Archbishop Sharp, he replies in the words uttered by Sir David Lindsay (widely read and beloved sixteenth-century satirist) "on the similar event o' Cardinal Beaton's death" (259).[35] More poignantly, he turns to the Bible for guidance after his wife and daughters have been killed by Royalists and he has received shelter from the ultra-Presbyterian Cameronians.

35. Kurt Wittig notes that in the early nineteenth century the name David ("Davie") Lindsay was almost proverbial among the Scots peasantry, which regarded him as a champion of the common people and of the Scots tongue (*The Scottish Tradition in Literature* [Edinburgh: Oliver and Boyd, 1958], 91). David Lindsay's most famous work, *Ane Pleasant Satyre of the Thrie Estaitis*, a morality play mocking corruption of church and court, is today regularly performed at the Edinburgh Festival. Cardinal Beaton, archbishop of St. Andrews, was killed on 29 May 1546, partly in retaliation for his burning of the reforming preacher (and Knox's teacher) George Wishart.

When the biblical text opens at the passage commanding Abraham to sacrifice his only son, Isaac, Gilhaize balks at taking the analogy and sending the only child he has left, his son Joseph, to join a group that seems even to him to stand little chance against the government forces ("so poor a handful of forlorn men"). He tries twice more, but the passages that fall open reinforce the implication of the first passage and its test of faith. In great agony he sends off the adolescent Joseph who, as he fears, dies as a result, suffering execution at the hands of the government.

Here is an imagination marked by a rage for continuity, gathering detail and event under one sign, but it can do so only by maintaining a relentless dualism.[36] Governed by notions of origin, Ringan struggles to maintain the integrity of the origin (the original "father") through which he can affirm himself by construing time in terms of the binary opposition of pure/impure. This binary generates the metaphors of pollution and cleansing, restoration and falling away that structure his reading of historical events. The Reformation, for example, is generally mediated through the medically accented metaphor of pollution and cleansing: "But foul as the capital then was, and covered with the leprosy of idolatry, they [the reforming Lords of Congregation] were not long in possession till they so medicated her with the searching medicaments of the Reformation, that she was soon scrapit of all the scurf and kell of her abominations" (93). The "searching medicaments" take violent form, but the metaphor sanctions violence in the cause of restoring health and purity to the social body, imaged here as literal female body.

When violence is turned on the pure themselves, of course, it is violation rather than cure. In Ringan's account, the pure inhabit a metaphorical pastoral realm subject to sudden, arbitrary invasions of the wilderness. The biblical pastoral metaphor defines the domestic life of the Gilhaizes and the everyday life of the rural Presbyterian community to which they belong. After the success of the Reformation, Grandfather Gilhaize establishes his "domestic vineyard" (126); in Ayr's "green pastures,"

---

36. Camic stresses the centrality of binaries to Scottish Calvinism, *Experience and Enlightenment*, 22–25.

the Covenanted preachers act as "kind shepherds" tending the "confiding flocks" (145); and Ringan himself cherishes his peaceful moments in his green valley with the wife and children, who are imaged respectively as a "fruitful vine" and "olive plants round about my table" (161). With the Restoration of Charles II, however, a "backsliding generation" moves into power, and Ringan reports that "all boded danger to the fold and flock, none doubting that the wolves of episcopalian covetousness were hungering and thirsting for the blood of the covenanted lambs." Moving more deeply into the metaphoric cluster, he builds the sense of threat to an innocent, natural life: "it was manifested to every eye that the fences of the vineyard were indeed broken down, and that the boar was let in, and wrathfully trampling down and laying waste" (165).

In time, Ringan's apprehensions turn out to be justified: the metaphoric boar turns into the actual Highland Host that did lay waste to Covenanting regions. But the key point is that the controlling binary opposition, with its stock of metaphors, allows him to pull out an authentic line of continuity in his national and familial history and to make sequence signify as legacy. Thus the line depends on a hierarchy that is always in place. What generates the narrative history is a static structure that makes time monolithic, turning all times into the replay of the same event and thereby inducing the circularity of a closed system. In effect—and rather oddly—time moves forward through repetition, the oppositional structure of the binary allowing Ringan to reduce the sense of contingency and differentiation as he narrates his story covering more than one hundred and thirty years of Scottish history.

Furthermore, he frequently strikes the prophetic note, writing from that sense of outcome and end identified by Frank Kermode as crucial to transforming the simple successiveness of chronos into the charged significance of kairos.[37] Experiencing at one point a "foretaste" of the fulfillment of his grandfather's prophecy and knowing that the particular rising in which he is participating will be defeated, he records that he "yet had a blessed persuasion that the event would prove in the end a link

37. *The Sense of an Ending* (London: Oxford University Press, 1967).

in the chain, or a cog in the wheel, of the hidden enginery [sic] with which Providence works good out of evil" (191). It does not matter that Ringan may be deluded or that Galt may not hold a similar view of history. What matters is that in *Ringan Gilhaize* we have a telling of the past that illustrates the working of one kind of popular memory and uncovers the degree to which it depends on a totalizing imagination that renders time, in a sense, always present.

The Brownie of Bodsbeck and Local Memory

Whereas *Ringan Gilhaize* imagines a highly linear time charged with meaning, *The Brownie of Bodsbeck* by James Hogg— disjointed and asymmetrical—projects a fluid, inconsequential time so uniform that it can hardly be called time at all. *Gilhaize's* tight, genealogical structure gives way in Hogg to a loose, anecdotal narrative in which sequence itself carries little significance and lacks generative power. The anecdotal structure reflects in part the origin of the story. Hogg's initial plan, as Douglas Mack notes in the introduction, was to include the story in a collection of "rural and traditionary tales" exemplifying the kinds of stories told in the country on winter nights (xvi–xvii). Traces of that plan remain both specifically (as in several references to "winter evening tales") and more generally in the way in which the text as a whole foregrounds the telling rather than the representation of experience. Although formally a third-person narrative, *The Brownie of Bodsbeck* includes long first-person narrations and direct dialogues in Scots, including the rather bewildering dialogue between one Walter Laidlaw of Chapelhope and his wife, Maron Linton, into which the reader is plunged at the very opening of the tale. When a narrator takes over in the next chapter, he begins to provide a clarifying context and background, but the opening scene itself is left suspended until chapter 5 when the narrator brings Walter back to "that very night when we began with him, and where, after many round-abouts, we have now found him again" (36).

The middle-aged Walter, a comfortable Border tenant farmer, is the central figure in the novel, and the main plot stems from his discovery in the autumn of 1685 that a band of Covenanters is hiding on his farm. This is the period of the infamous "Killing Time" when Claverhouse and his troops were at their most active and brutal in pursuit of the Covenanters. Walter, neither Royalist nor Covenanter himself (we are told that he "made no great fuss about religion," 14), feeds and protects the pursued men. Claverhouse (known as "Clavers" in the area and in the text) descends on the area after the murder of some of his soldiers, killing suspected Covenanters and their sympathizers at random and arresting Walter himself, who is sent for trial to Edinburgh. In the meantime, Walter's daughter, Katharine, has been behaving strangely for some time, and there are reports that she has been seen with a malevolent local spirit known as the Brownie of Bodsbeck. As a result, her sexual purity comes under suspicion and later under threat by an unscrupulous priest, who takes advantage of the sexual rumors and attempts to rape her. She is rescued by the Brownie, a disguised Covenanter leader whose men she has been helping in secret. In the end, Walter is released in Edinburgh, the persecution wanes, and Elizabeth feels free to confess to her father that she was not consorting with a brownie but aiding a band of sick and desperate men. Walter commends her for ignoring political and religious polarities and taking "the side o' human nature; the suffering and the humble side, an' the side o' feeling" (163).

A curious amalgam of narrative traditions (oral and textual, English and Scots, folktale and novel), the *Brownie* is, as its modern editor notes, "a rather disjointed book" (xviii). The disjointedness has to do less with the variety of traditions on which it draws than with authorial control of those traditions. Francis Hart has stressed Hogg's difficulties in his longer works (with the possible exception of *Memoirs and Confessions of a Justified Sinner*) in reconciling "the traditionary storyteller and the formal novelist."[38] In *Brownie*, in particular, he finds "an interesting confusion of point of view" as the narrative seeks to integrate at least three distinct narrative positions: the distanced position of the enlightened modern narrator, who writes in standard English for an equally distanced reader; the local inti-

38. Hart, *Scottish Novel*, 27.

macy of the inhabitant of the region familiar with its language, stories, and habits; and the concrete involvement of the first-person voices, notably that of Walter Laidlaw, whose telling "in their own words" the narrator affirms.[39] These narrative stances remain unintegrated, and Hogg moves awkwardly among them, producing a general narrative uneasiness. The narrator himself constantly draws attention to his difficulties in telling his story, and this is less the playful self-reflexivity of a Sterne (or a Scott, for that matter) than the awkwardness of a writer sensing that he is somehow in the wrong genre.[40] More precisely, the "round-abouts" of the early chapters point to a continual, self-conscious problem with linear flow. "Indeed," the narrator remarks at the end of chapter 11, "all such diffuse and miscellaneous matter as is contained in this chapter, is a great incumbrance in the right onward progress of a tale; but we have done with it, and shall now haste to the end of our narrative in a direct uninterrupted line" (112). The "direct line" is immediately disrupted, however, as chapter 12 wanders off to and lingers on minor characters and scenes, including the tangential Davie Tait, whose Davie Tait's Prayer is widely regarded as one of the masterpieces of Scots prose and hence as somehow a separate piece. Finally, the narrator simply calls a halt: "And thus I must close this long and eccentric chapter" (132).[41]

If the disjointedness of Hogg's narrative derives from the tension between two kinds of authority (traditional and rational), its "eccentricity" lies in the strong pull of the traditional in the modern, textual genre within which he is working. In the introduction produced for the 1837 edition, Hogg underlines the two kinds of authority on which he draws when he states:

39. Ibid., 26.

40. In his anecdotes of Scott, Hogg declares: "As long as Sir Walter Scott wrote poetry there was neither man nor woman ever thought of either reading or writing any thing but poetry. But the instant that he gave over writing poetry there was neither man nor woman ever read it more! All turned to tales and novels which I among others was reluctantly obliged to do" (*Memoirs and Familiar Anecdotes*, 124).

41. This is the conclusion of the revised 1837 edition. In the 1818 edition the chapter ended with an English hymn prefaced by the comment that "we shall with it close this long chapter" (192). By 1837 Hogg evidently saw it as not simply long but eccentric as well.

"The general part is taken from Wodrow, and the local part from the relation of my own father, who had the best possible traditionary account of the incidents" (170).[42] The authorial statement echoes the narrator's comment in chapter 11 when he too identifies the two kinds of sources: "The narrator of this tale confesses that he has taken this account of his [Claverhouse's] raid through the vales of Esk and Annan solely from tradition . . . but these traditions are descended from such a source, and by such a line, as amounts with him to veracity, while other incidents recorded by Wodrow and Huie fully corroborate them" (105).[43] Suggestively, the clause on the textual authorities was added only to the 1837 edition. In the first edition, the narrator appealed only to tradition, thereby reflecting the way in which tradition tends in general to absorb modern, textual constructs in this narrative. Veracity, we notice, is a matter of (paternal) descent ("by such a line, as amounts with him to veracity"), and this is the veracity that matters. Truth lies in persons and not in impersonal constructs, though Hogg, as author of printed texts, is clearly somewhat uneasy about such preliterate notions and adds textual authorities to support the reports of orally based tradition.

Even the textual authorities, however, tend to function more as persons than as texts embodying rational notions like evidence and documentation, for it is to *names* that the narrative typically appeals. A notable instance occurs in the scene of Claverhouse's interrogation of one of Walter's shepherds, old John of the Muchrah in chapter 7. Old John, slyly deploying local dialect ("can ye no understand fock's mother-tongue?" 61), confounds Claverhouse, who then orders a cruel punishment. Another of Hogg's superb—and subversive—scenes in Scots, it is prefaced by the narrator's authorizing of the dialogue by an invocation of writing, witness, and expert authority. The an-

42. Hogg is referring to the Reverend Robert Wodrow, *The History of the Sufferings of the Church of Scotland*, 2 vols. (Edinburgh, 1721–22), a standard history for the pro-Covenanter reading of the period. Hogg's own father was a devout Presbyterian.

43. "Huie" refers to John Howie's *Scots Worthies*, a late eighteenth-century collection of biographies of many of the Covenanters. In his introduction to *Old Mortality* (Harmondsworth: Penguin, 1974), Angus Calder calls this work "very unpleasant" and observes that Scott was "oddly attracted" to it (17).

swers of the shepherd, he states, "as taken down in short-hand by Mr Adam Copland, are still extant, and at present in my possession. The following are some of them, as decyphered by Mr J. W. Robertson, whose acquaintance with ancient manuscripts is well known" (60). In Hogg's orally based narrative, this textual appeal (document, shorthand, scholarly expertise) becomes simply another version of the oral appeal to persons: authority lies less in the principle of evidence than in the proper names.[44] Among the specifically linguistic implications of this position is a tendency to invest authenticity in an idiolect, in the "own words" of a speaker. Thus the narrator stops early in the narrative to let Walter tell his story "in his own words" (18), and near the end he abruptly ceases his own narration to allow Walter to carry on, arguing that "such scenes, and such adventures, are not worth a farthing, unless described and related in the language of the country to which they are peculiar" (146).

In such a narrative, history becomes highly localized and personalized, its actions produced by specific agents about whom individual stories are told and retold. The narrator alerts us to the personal note early when he informs his readers in the explanatory chapter 2: "Graham of Dundee, better known by the detested name of Clavers, set loose his savage troopers upon those peaceful districts, with peremptory orders to plunder, waste, disperse, and destroy the conventiclers wherever they might be found" (10). For the borderers in the region of Loch Skene, including the narrator in his local mode, the history of 1685 is the story of arbitrary and brutal actions in their area by a demonic figure named Claverhouse. His behavior on the morning that he descended on Chapelhope, we are told, "was sufficient to stamp his character for ever in that district, where it is still held in higher detestation than that of the arch-fiend himself" (67). Narrative distance decreases sharply as the narrator recounts Claverhouse's pursuit of Covenanters in the area. The "country people," he remarks, believed Claverhouse's horse to be a devil, and in the next sentence that belief is ab-

---

44. W. F. H. Nicolaisen reminds us that tradition (as opposed to mass culture) is associated with individual bearers; see "Scott and the Folk Tradition," in *Sir Walter Scott: The Long-Forgotten Melody*, ed. Alan Bold (New York: Barnes and Noble, 1983), 127.

sorbed without irony into the narrator's own language: "The marks of that infernal courser's feet are shewn to this day on a steep, nearly perpendicular, below the Bubbly Craig, along which he is said to have ridden at full speed, in order to keep sight of a party of the flying Covenanters" (75).

Along with the sense of retelling that is integral to the structure of the *Brownie*, we have here the equally vital sense of the specificity of place. History as local memory depends very precisely on telling, locating, and naming. "Tradition," the narrator informs us, "has preserved the whole of his [Claverhouse's] route that day with the utmost minuteness" (76). The narrator himself, he notes, has often "stood over the deep green marks of that courser's hoof, plenty of which remain on that hill, in awe and astonishment, to think that he was actually standing looking at the traces made by the devil's foot, or at least by a horse that once belonged to him" (76). The reiterated demonstratives ("that day," "that courser's hoof," "that hill") signal both the narrator's familiarity—his status as insider—and narrative significance, isolating a particular day and particular place for attention. The key to the narrative stance here is that even though "that day" stands at a distance, it is a distance within familiar space. In other words, "that day" (and the events it gathers) is inside a personal compass of time, as something like "1685" or "several decades ago" is not. What makes it personal—and memorable—is its connection to place. Dates and the chronology of events in the *Brownie* are typically hazy, but place is highly specific. Like the agents of history, it always has a name. Claverhouse rode "below the Bubbly Craig" and also at a place "called the Blue Sklidder, on the Merk side" (75). Five men were killed that day, four of them being first taken prisoner "on a height called Ker-Cleuch-Ridge, who were brought to Clavers and shortly examined on a little crook in the Erne Cleuch, a little above the old steading of Hopertoudy" (76). These places, we observe, are not described or in some way located for those unfamiliar with the region; they are simply named. To locals, their names signify; to those outside, they are words to be skimmed over or to be enjoyed for their sound or linguistic interest or related concerns. The point is that local memory *is* local, basing and defining itself in the closure of locality.

Through such memory, local places become resonant, full of the stories that help constitute and perpetuate a sense of one's locality. It is entirely characteristic that part of the narrator's concern in telling the story of Claverhouse's raid on the area is to tell the story of certain places, more precisely, of certain graves. The four unnamed men who were taken prisoner in the above passage, for example, were quickly shot. Later their bodies were recovered and buried in Ettrick churchyard where they are all in a row "a few paces from the south-west corner of the present church" (79). A fifth man, also killed that day, was buried "on a place called the Watch Knowe, a little to the southeast of Loch Skene." (76). Later in the same chapter, we are directed to the grave of young Andrew Hyslop, also shot by Claverhouse's troops and buried where he was executed: "A grave stone was afterwards erected over him, which is still to be seen at Craikhaugh, near the side of the road, a little to the north of the Church of Eskdale-muir" (85). Since these graves actually exist, Hogg crosses the border of fiction. He blurs generic boundaries as he has been doing in different ways all through the work, impelled always by the memorializing and perpetuating impulse of local tradition.

The temporal structure generated by this impulse, like the model of reenactment in *Ringan Gilhaize*, renders largely formal the distinctions between past, present, and future. But where *Ringan* compresses time into a relentless line of repetition, *Brownie* diffuses it so that it becomes largely absorbed by place. It matters less *when* something happened than *where* it happened; the difference between "then" and "now" is less important than that between "here" and "there." Highly spatial and concrete, this time has affinities with (but is not identical to) the unified folkloric time celebrated by Bakhtin.[45] Bakhtin's folkloric chronotope is problematic and easily sentimentalized, but its profound concreteness usefully highlights the allegiance of Hogg's narrative to ways of shaping experience that lie outside those of textuality and history. The concreteness of folkloric time means that it does not know certain differentiations familiar to the modern world. Human time and natural time, for

45. See "Forms of Time and Chronotope in the Novel," in *The Dialogic Imagination*, trans. Caryl Emerson and Michael Holquist, ed. Michael Holquist (Austin: University of Texas Press, 1981), 206–24.

example, are perceived in the same categories. Nor, Bakhtin explains, does folkloric time recognize "a system of ideals separate from embodiment of that system in time and space."[46] To Hogg's rural laborers, Covenanter and Cavalier alike are alien in their ideological approach to experience, and they absorb them into their own concrete temporality with its profound local rootedness. From such local perspectives, Francis Hart reminds us, "time is less historic than legendary . . . while place is intensely, yet matter-of-factly, localized by name and topography."[47]

In these places, memorable events occur, yet they are oddly inconsequential. Claverhouse and the fugitive Covenanters appear and disappear, leaving stories and graves behind, but they are outsiders, and their entry into the world around Loch Skene is, like an adventure, outside the normal flow of events. Their temporal mode is the "suddenly" of the quintessential story time of adventure.[48] This disjunctive time of "suddenly" simply heightens the sense of the uniformity of time which constitutes the base mode of experience in the novel. Events occur at any time and in no particular order, and they become absorbed into the life of community as stories to be told and endlessly retold. At several points the narrator draws explicit attention to this transformation into narrative, as with Walter, who tended to tell the story of his finding the fugitive Covenanters "when any stranger came there on a winter evening, as long as he lived" (18). Walter, we later learn, was equally fond of the story of his trial, for it too "formed one of his winter evening tales as long as he lived" (112); and for the community at large the smearing of the sheep at Chapelhope by the supposed Brownie "has continued to be a standing winter evening tale to this day" (137). This community is defined and perpetuated through discourse, more precisely through its repetition "to this day." As the phrase suggests, the community gives to sheer continuity a special authority. The name Claverhouse, we recall, is "still held" in higher detestation than that of Satan in the area. And the authority of "still held" continues to compel the nineteenth-century narrator and his author.

46. Ibid., 150.
47. Hart, *Scottish Novel*, 25.
48. See Bakhtin, "Forms of Time and Chronotope," 84–110.

Hogg prefixed to the first edition of the novel some dedicatory verses to Anne Scott, daughter of his patron, the duke of Buccleuch, and in them he defines his special kind of constancy. The verses note that the Presbyterian Hogg and his Episcopalian patron differ in their creeds but urge that nevertheless "We are the same, / One faith, one Father, and one aim." This affirmation is then followed by some revealing lines that effectively summarize the narrative motivation that structures the *Brownie of Bodsbeck*:

> And had'st thou lived where I was bred,
> Amid the scenes where martyrs bled,
> Their sufferings all to thee endear'd
> By those most honour'd and revered;
> And where the wild dark streamlet raves,
> Had'st wept above their lonely graves,
> Thou would'st have felt, I know it true,
> As I have done, and aye must do. (174–75)

Thus place, family, and community—but, most strikingly, place—determine his position and authorize his story. These are the traditionary sources of Hogg's imagination, and these lines are witness to their profoundly conservative effect in the unquestioned logic whereby "As I have done" is necessarily transformed into "and aye must do." A similar logic appears in Hogg's defense of his portrayal of Claverhouse in the introduction: he argues that "it is the character I had heard drawn of him all my life, and the character of him which was impressed upon my mind since my earliest remembrance, which all his eulogists can never erase" (171).

In a different way from the theological model of *Ringan Gilhaize*, then, *Brownie of Bodsbeck*'s oral and communal model values origins, fathers, and continuity. Although Hogg is not so relentlessly binary or patriarchal in his constructions, allowing for greater heterogeneity, his telling of the past equally resists notions of change and difference. Both narratives construct the past under the signs of continuity and endurance, and both tend to close off the space for reflection that *Old Mortality* sought to open. Refusing the differentiation and discontinuities that characterize a historical reading, Galt and Hogg both grant enormous privilege to the notion of eyewitness, with Galt focusing on what passes "under the eye" of a teller and Hogg affirming the importance of narrating in the "own words" of the teller. But to know an event historically, Arthur Danto has reminded us, is precisely to know it in a way that a witness cannot.[49] It is to assume an enabling discontinuity—a different language, another knowledge. "Scott can see the past in its richness," Harry Shaw writes, "only by recognizing the great gulf fixed between himself and the object of his contemplation."[50] Recognition of that gulf, paradoxically, releases the often-noted diverse languages, differentiated time, and contesting cultural pluralities of the Waverley Novels, thereby restoring (if also containing) the perspectives of local memory and oral tradition.[51] The definition of history as distance and detachment, in other words, yields the very particularity and vividness through which the Waverley Novels, as discussed in the next chapter, helped redefine the practice of history itself.

49. Danto, *Analytical Philosophy of History*, 148–69. See also Fleishman's definition of the historical novel as the interpretation of the experience of individuals (actual or imaginary) "in such a way as to make their lives not only felt by the reader as he would feel his own existence were he to have lived in the past, but understood as only someone who had seen that life as a completed whole could understand it" (*The English Historical Novel* [Baltimore: Johns Hopkins University Press, 1971], 12–13).

50. *Forms of Historical Fiction*, 247.

51. Jane Millgate observes that as early as the *Minstrelsy of the Scottish Border*, Scott was experimenting with and integrating different kinds of access to the past, specifically those of folk tradition and written history; see her *Walter Scott: The Making of the Novelist* (Toronto: University of Toronto Press, 1984), 10.

7

"Authentic History" and the
Project of the Historical Novel

He has enriched history to us by opening such varied and
delicious vistas to our gaze, beneath the range of its loftier
events and more public characters.
—*New Monthly Magazine* on the Author of Waverley (1820)

I have always had a private dislike to a regular shape of a
house although no doubt it would be wrong headed to set
about building an irregular one from the beginning.
—Walter Scott on building Abbotsford (26 November 1816)

The Waverley Novels help mark the transformation of historical consciousness and history writing in the postrevolutionary
years in Britain and the Continent.[1] This transformation took
various and often contradictory forms, ranging from the philosophical system building of a Hegel to the concrete "resurrec-
tion" of a Michelet, but all history was marked by a special self-
consciousness. My concern is with the generic implications of
one kind of change that brought history writing and the novel
into a new relationship in the early decades of the century. Put
simply, the change was the expansion of what counted as historical. As John Farrell has argued, in the late eighteenth century there emerged a preoccupation with the difference be-

1. This is a vast and complex subject with an extensive literature. Of particu-
lar interest for this chapter are Stephen Bann, *The Clothing of Clio: A Study of the
Representation of History in Nineteenth-Century Britain and France* (Cambridge:
Cambridge University Press, 1984); Lionel Gossman, "History as Decipher-
ment: Romantic Historiography and the Discovery of the Other," *New Literary
History* 18 (1986): 32–57; Linda Orr, "The Revenge of Literature: A History of
History," *New Literary History* 18 (1986): 1–22; and Mark Phillips, "Macaulay,
Scott, and the Literary Challenge to Historiography," *Journal of the History of
Ideas* 50 (1989): 117–33.

tween idiomatic and institutional life, a preoccupation which led to a negation of the heavily political definition of historical action and replaced politics with, as Farrell puts it, "the notion of 'culture' as history's most significant content."[2] The change was neither sudden nor complete. The critical reviews of the period illustrate that official or standard history remained primarily concerned with the political sphere. But they also suggest that history was beginning to include as properly historical those signs of idiomatic life formerly regarded as beneath the dignity of a discourse that the reviewers typically characterized as "stately."[3]

Underlining the centrality of history as a genre for the reviews, the *Edinburgh Review* chose for the lead article in its very first issue a review by Francis Jeffrey of a study of the French Revolution by J. J. Mounier (president of the first National Assembly). Jeffrey's review makes the point of the new and old history. His critique of Mounier centers on what Jeffrey sees as the "simplicity" of Mounier's strictly political reading of historical causation, especially when such "complicated" events are involved. The problem with Mounier's political account for Jeffrey is that it overlooks the significant causal forces that derived "from the change that had taken place in the condition and sentiments of the people; from the progress of commercial opulence; from the diffusion of information, and the prevalence of political discussion."[4] These are the categories of the new history championed by Jeffrey, a history which supplements the political with the sociological, the economic, the technological, the cultural (as in the public sphere of "political discussion"),

2. *Revolution as Tragedy: The Dilemma of the Moderate from Scott to Arnold* (Ithaca: Cornell University Press, 1980), 82. The roots of this change lie in the French Enlightenment, in the work on culture by writers like Voltaire and Montesquieu. On French Enlightenment historiography, see Suzanne Gearhart, *The Open Boundary of History and Fiction: A Critical Approach to the French Enlightenment* (Princeton: Princeton University Press, 1984).

3. See, for example, the reference to the "stately narratives of the historian" in the review of *The Abbot*, NMM 14 (1820): 422. Suggestively, this reviewer commends the Waverley Novels for placing readers "in" and "below" the "stately narratives" of history. See also Lister on "stately political history" vis-à-vis Scott's historical fiction (ER 55 [1832]: 78).

4. Review of Mounier's *De l'influence attribuée aux philosophes, Francs-Maçons, et aux illuminés, sur la revolutions de France*, ER 1 (1802): 8.

and so on. History practiced in this mode worked to redefine notions of the past and of historical significance, for the past now appeared not only as action and crisis but also, as Mark Phillips has recently pointed out, as experience and process.[5] That which was excluded from action and that which lay outside crisis, in other words, came to achieve historical value, and the Waverley Novels (for all their fascination with crisis) were instrumental in bringing about this new valorization.

Francis Jeffrey was one of the first, and certainly the most influential, of Scott's early readers to draw attention to the way in which the Scottish novelist's representation of the past implicitly challenged what Jeffrey called "authentic history." The occasion, once again, was the debate over *Old Mortality* discussed in Chapter 5. Jeffrey's main point in this debate was that *Old Mortality* was a novel, not a history; moreover, *because* it was a novel it offered historical insight and a valid if implicit critique of history writing. Jeffrey's argument is obscured by condescension: he affects great astonishment, for instance, that a work of mere fiction would become the object of "serious" historical and theological debate. His argument is also obscured by evasion of the important points about the responsibility and distinction of genres raised by Scott's critics. At the same time, it suggests a readiness to interrogate official history and to grant to the historical novel a historical subject that derived less from historical discourse than from its own novelistic roots in what eventually would be known as realism. The Author of Waverley, Jeffrey points out in his review, "makes us present to the times in which he has placed them [i.e., his characters], less by his direct notices of the great transactions by which they were distinguished, than by his casual intimations of their effects on private persons, and by the very contrast which their temper and occupations often appear to furnish to the colour of the national story."[6] Jeffrey here draws attention to the obliqueness of Scott's approach to the standard material of history, and he attributes to this very obliqueness (the "casual intimations," the "con-

5. See Phillips, "Macaulay, Scott and the Literary Challenge to Historiography."
6. *ER* 28 (1817): 216. Further references will be cited in the text.

trast" between private and public stories) Scott's much-celebrated historical vividness.

Furthermore, in that obliqueness, Jeffrey goes on to suggest, lies a critique of "authentic history": "Nothing, indeed, in this respect is more delusive, or at least more woefully imperfect, than the suggestions of authentic history, as it is generally—or rather universally written—and nothing more exaggerated than the impressions it conveys of the actual state and condition of those who live in its most agitated periods" (216–17). As in his very first article for the *Edinburgh*, Jeffrey's interest lies in socioanalytic categories like the "state" and "conditions" of the people rather than in standard historico-narrative categories like "action" and "event." It is event that absorbs official history, which, Jeffrey charges, notices only "great public events." The problem with such a focus is that great public events actually have "little direct influence upon the body of the people"; moreover, they are generally not central even for those who are in some way involved in them. Summing up his argument—and anticipating Georg Lukács's point about the continuity of daily life in civil war[7]—Jeffrey asserts that even in those times when violent, public events are dominant, "a great part of the time of a great part of the people is spent in making love and money—in social amusement or professional industry—in schemes for worldly advancement or personal distinction, just as in periods of general peace and prosperity" (217). Most people, it turns out, live life as if it were a realistic novel ("making love and money"); history, by contrast, is governed by "the tragic muse." To the retrospective view of the tragic muse, whole tracts of time will appear "one thick and oppressive cloud of unbroken misery," but this distorts the experience of those who lived through "the whole acts of the tragedy," for they will turn out to have enjoyed "a fair average share of felicity" despite the pressures of crisis (217).

If Jeffrey tends to trivialize historical conflict and suffering

---

7. *The Historical Novel*, trans. Hannah Mitchell and Stanley Mitchell (1937; Harmondsworth: Penguin, 1962), 37–38. Lukács points to Scott's "realist" recognition that no civil war produces absolute polarization and that large groups of people experience "fluctuating sympathies" and carry on the daily life of the nation, thereby ensuring cultural continuity. Lukács stresses that continuity does not preclude change.

and to rely rather too heavily for poststructuralist taste on metaphors like the "eternal channels" of the "quiet under current of
life," he also authorizes for historical fiction a critical space vis-
à-vis standard history. Taking as his principal target the single-
mindedness and abstraction of "authentic history," he allows
the concreteness of the historical novel to counteract (to some
degree) its "delusive" representations. In so doing, he points to
the way in which Scott's historical fictions participated in the
emerging conviction that forces outside those conventionally
featured in the discourses of history (whether it be political,
legal, military, or ecclesiastical) had historical import. Not that
the orthodox forces were—or could be—dismissed. Far from it,
as the Waverley Novels themselves demonstrate. But the incorporation by these novels of a whole complex realm of non-
institutional action and effect into history was central to their
innovative power. Through this move, they transformed the
import of the old category of "historical novel" to such an extent
that in 1832 T. H. Lister could maintain that all novels called
"historical novels" before the publication of *Waverley* had been
"misnamed."[8]

Into the Periphery: The Waverley Novels
and the Problem of Beginning

In order to focus some of these generalizations more precisely
and to bring into view how Scott's texts themselves tended to
negotiate their oblique relationship to history, I want to consider a specific narrative problem: the problem of beginning.
Scott's difficulties with beginning (and the related narrative
matter of ending) are notorious and were quite apparent both to
him and to his contemporaries.[9] T. H. Lister expressed the crit-

8. "The Waverley Novels," *ER* 55 (1832): 64.
9. For modern readers, the problem is compounded by the fact that most
modern editions open with a mass of prefatory material from the later "Magnum Opus" edition published by Robert Cadell after Scott's bankruptcy. This
prefatory material is a separate issue, and my concern here is with the pre-
Magnum texts, that is, with the opening scenes and narrative frames that
launch the story. For a compelling account of the Magnum edition as itself a
significant innovation in publishing, see Jane Millgate, *Scott's Last Edition: A
Study in Publishing History* (Edinburgh: Edinburgh University Press, 1987).

ical consensus when he remarked in his survey for the *Edinburgh Review*: "They [the Waverley Novels] are usually languid in their commencement, and abrupt in the close; too slowly opened, and too hastily summed up."[10] Scott himself had drawn playful attention to his structural asymmetry as early as his first novel when he had the narrator of *Waverley* stop his rapid narration late in the novel to draw a mock-apologetic analogy between the progress of a narrative and that of a stone rolled down a hill. Such a stone, the narrator writes, "moveth at first slowly . . . but when it has attained its full impulse, and draws near the conclusion of its career, it smokes and thunders down . . . becoming most furiously rapid in its course when it is nearest to being consigned to rest for ever" (331; chap. 70). Again and again, the Waverley narrators comically bemoan their tardiness at getting going and the unseemly speed of their conclusions. Scott, of course, is always ready (as in his self-review in the *Quarterly*) to admit formal incompetence— gentlemen generally are. But the easy admission also defines a more complex narrative stance. In part it reflects Scott's sense that spontaneity was the mode of his imagination (so rendering "inimical" any kind of planning),[11] and in part it signals his distrust of the norms of formal unity and regularity. More particularly, however, Scott's persistent and self-conscious violation of structural symmetry points to the special problem and the special project of his historical mode of fiction.

The historical novelist intervenes in a field that already exists as an authoritative discourse, no matter how contested portions of that discourse might be, and the pressure of the already-written and the already-known is most acute at the moments of beginning and ending narration. Scott's endings generally co-operate with both historical and literary expectations, although they do so with some irony by typically assuming their own predictability. Witness the romance ending of *Waverley* or the notorious final chapter of *Old Mortality* where Pattieson allows Miss Buskbody the outcome she has anticipated and desired.

10. Lister, "The Waverley Novels," 71.
11. See, for example, *The Journal of Sir Walter Scott*, ed. W. E. K. Anderson (Oxford: Clarendon, 1972), 86, and the introductory epistle to *The Fortunes of Nigel*.

His beginnings, by contrast, work to disconcert expectation and prediction, functioning as agents of differentiation rather than assimilation. In his suggestive preface to *Beginnings*, Edward Said muses that beginning is *"making* or *producing difference;* but—and here is the great fascination in the subject—difference which is the result of combining the already-familiar with the fertile novelty of human work in language."[12] To begin a historical novel is to enter the historical field but to do so with a difference, and the difference initiated by the Waverley Novels vis-à-vis history is the opening up of the periphery of what Jeffrey called "authentic history." Through Scott's protracted, tangled, and often reluctant beginnings, he sets up the crucial move of his narrative out of known into relatively unknown and uninterpreted historical spaces, and it is largely through this move that he establishes the distinctiveness of his "species" of composition.[13]

The move out of the known is initiated even before actual narration commences, for it begins with the first words that a reader generally reads: the title of the novel. *Waverley* is paradigmatic, not only in its choice of title but in its self-consciousness about that choice. To prepare us for the attention to be devoted to novel titles in the first chapter, the novel opens with the mock-solemn declaration: "The title of this work has not been chosen without the grave and solid deliberation which matters of importance demand from the prudent." Prudently, the narrator has chosen for his titular hero "an uncontaminated name," forestalling (as we saw in Chapter 3) the reader's "preconceived associations." The model of genre here is a contractual one, and the authorial figure assumes the role of shrewd but responsible dealer. Hence, aware that the subtitle pledges the author to "some special mode of laying his scene, drawing his characters, and managing his adventures," the narrator invents a new type

12. *Beginnings: Intention and Method* (Baltimore: Johns Hopkins University Press, 1975), xiii.

13. Lukács sees a similar significance in Scott's novels when he draws attention to their mediocre hero and to the "minor compositional role" of great historical figures (*Historical Novel*, 39). On this latter point, however, he cites Balzac's comment that Scott's novels marched toward the great heroes in the same way as history itself has done when it required their appearance. My point is rather that they march away from them.

of subtitle in "'Tis Sixty Years Since," one that will not arouse definite expectations and so make him liable for their fulfillment. In his very first novel, then, Scott establishes the resistance to titles activating strong reader expectations that will mark his entire career.

The expectations explicitly at issue in the opening chapter of *Waverley* are literary, but as the Waverley Novels take hold, the expectations in question become less novelistic than historical. Scott's fiction, that is, comes to compete less with other fiction than with nonfictional discourse, notably the discourses of history and tradition, and the titles to be resisted are primarily those denoting strongly interpreted historical persons and events. The one exception, *Rob Roy*, was agreed to by Scott very reluctantly under pressure from the publisher Constable. On that occasion Scott reportedly told Constable that, as a general rule, he did not wish to "have to write up to a name," preferring "a title that told nothing."[14]

A double prudence motivated this authorial stand: commercial and generic. In commercial terms, Scott did not want to ruin the market for his fiction by arousing expectations likely to be disappointed, as he makes clear in his discussion in the 1831 introduction to *The Abbot* of the problem of choosing what he calls a "taking title." There he notes that he did not think it "prudent" to proclaim in the introductory epistle to this 1820 novel "the real spring" by which he hoped to attract interest and make up for the failure of *The Monastery* earlier in the same year. The "real spring" to which he refers is the prominence in *The Abbot* of Mary Queen of Scots, a figure who belongs for Scott in the category of those "peculiar historical characters, which are, like a spell or charm, sovereign to excite curiosity and attract attention, since every one in the slightest degree interested in the land which they belong to, has heard much of them, and longs to hear more" (*Wav. Nov.*, 11:5). For an author, however, such characters are risky since readers are easily alienated: "it cannot be denied that we are apt to feel least satisfied with the works of which we have been induced, by titles and

14. Edgar Johnson, *Sir Walter Scott: The Great Unknown*, 2 vols. (New York: Macmillan, 1970), 1:570.

laudatory advertisement, to entertain exaggerated expectations. The intention of the work has been anticipated, and misconceived or misrepresented" (*Wav. Nov.*, 11:6). In such a case, Scott remarks, the bookseller may sell all his stock, but the author faces ridicule and anger. After "losing ground" with *The Monastery*, however, he decided to risk such an outcome and selected a subject he thought would be "most likely to procure a rehearing" (*Wav. Nov.*, 11:6). Even so, we notice, he did not choose a "taking title."

Related to this commercial prudence was the generic prudence that made Scott reluctant to compete with the more prestigious genre of history. The focal relationship in this case is that between texts rather than that between author and public, and a telling illustration of this second form of prudence, also touching on the matter of Mary Queen of Scots, comes in the "Introductory" of the late novel *The Fair Maid of Perth* (1828).[15] Here Chrystal Croftangry, Scott's most fully characterized narrator, and Mrs. Martha Bethune Baliol, the courtly relic of an older Scotland who supplies Croftangry with many of his tales, debate the question of appropriate subjects for historical fiction. Mrs. Baliol wants Croftangry to "novelize," as she puts it, the story of Mary Stuart and David Rizzio, but Croftangry argues that the events in question are "too well known . . . to be used as vehicles of romantic fiction"; moreover, they have been fully represented in the "elegant and forcible narrative" of the celebrated Scottish historian William Robertson. Mrs. Baliol does not see what Robertson's history has to do with Croftangry's novel, asking what relation "the classic Robertson" could have to "a romantic historian" like Croftangry. Drawing on metaphors of illumination, she underlines the point of generic difference: "The light which he carried was that of a lamp to illuminate the dark events of antiquity; yours is a magic lantern to raise up wonders which never existed. No reader of sense wonders at your historical inaccuracies." But Croftangry, while agreeing that he does have "immunities" as a teller of tales, nevertheless does not enjoy being "found out": "Now, this is the reason why I avoid in prudence all well-known paths of

15. *Chronicles of the Canongate, Second Series*, 3 vols. (Edinburgh, 1828).

history, where every one can read the finger-posts carefully set up to advise them of the right turning." In her reply, Mrs. Baliol takes up his topographical metaphor: "There are plenty of wildernesses in Scottish history, through which, unless I am greatly misinformed, no certain paths have been laid down from actual survey, but which are only described by imperfect tradition." Taking her advice, Croftangry announces that he will set his story in "a remote period of history, and in a province removed from my natural sphere of the Canongate" (19–21).

The Waverley Novels in general follow Mrs. Baliol's advice and Croftangry's prudence, the two acting here as mirror images of each other: Croftangry puts in the negative terms of avoidance of confrontation what Mrs. Baliol articulates positively as a journey into uncharted territory. Both locate the historical novel in the same place: in the interstices left by official history. Hence the concessive gesture to historiography in the Waverley Novels, a gesture that rapidly became a convention of historical fiction.[16] "It is not our purpose to intrude upon the province of history," declares the narrator of *Waverley* as he declines to provide a general narration of the march of the Jacobite army into England (263; chap. 57). "It is not our object to enter into the historical part of the reign of the ill-fated Mary," echoes the narrator of *The Abbot* as he refers his readers to Chalmers's *Life of Mary Queen of Scots* for the appropriate details.[17] Conceding such matters to historians, the novelist places himself alongside, outside, or at an angle to events that historiography has appropriated. This concessive gesture suggests (not entirely disingenuously) that the enterprises of history and of historical fiction stand in tangential rather than tangled relationship. As so often in Scott, the implications of this gesture are complicated and even contested by other gestures of the narrative, but the deferential stance to history is central to the structure of his fiction.

16. Galt's *Ringan Gilhaize*, for example, repeatedly uses the gesture. Gilhaize stops at several points to refer "the courteous reader" to "the annals and chronicles of the times" or to "true British histories." See, for example, *Ringhan Gilhaize; or, The Covenanters*, ed. Patricia J. Wilson (Edinburgh: Scottish Academic Press, 1984), 146, 304.

17. *The Abbot*, 3 vols. (Edinburgh, 1820) 3:306; chap. 37.

The Waverley Novels both cooperate with and disorient the official discourse of history. At their most general level of implication (that is, at the level of historical paradigm and romance pattern), they leave in place the established reading of historical events and the model of historical evolution derived from the Scottish Enlightenment that was standard in Scott's time whatever the disagreement over specific events and contents.[18] The official, inscribed plot of history, in fact, serves as their enabling assumption: the story of the progress of civil society and of the British state (virtual synonyms) that culminates in the "Glorious Revolution" of 1688.[19] But the oblique and specific approach of his fiction to this plot—most obvious in Scott's concentration on obscure communities and minor events—inevitably novelizes, in Bakhtin's rather than Mrs. Baliol's sense of the term, the historical genre.[20] It does so by placing in question the adequacy of a paradigmatic understanding and by uncovering the "singular" stories inevitably lost in the generalizing sweep of standard narrative history.[21]

It is entirely fitting that the novel introduced by the Croftangry-Baliol debate about the spheres of history and fiction should concentrate on a clan that was literally obliterated toward the end of the fourteenth century. *The Fair Maid of Perth* is largely concerned with the end of Clan Quhele, a clan remembered for a bizarre incident in the reign of Robert III. Two rival clans (Clan Quhele and Clan Kay) agreed to depute thirty cham-

18. On Scott and the Scottish Enlightenment, see Chapter 3, Note 19.

19. The most influential study of this aspect of the Waverley Novels is Alexander Welsh's *Hero of the Waverley Novels* (1963; New York: Atheneum, 1968), though Welsh stresses the Burkean shape of this plot rather than its Scottish affiliations. See also George Levine, who argues that Scott's confidence in the intelligibility and progress of history provided the security that allowed him to present "the muddles, the contrasts, the variousness of the simple facts of everyday life" (*The Realistic Imagination: English Fiction from Frankenstein to Lady Chatterley* [Chicago: University of Chicago Press, 1981], 96).

20. On the novelization of genres, see "Epic and Novel," *The Dialogic Imagination*, trans. Caryl Emerson and Michael Holquist, ed. Michael Holquist (Austin: University of Texas Press, 1981), 5–9.

21. In her study of the Waverley frames, Marilyn Orr argues that the textual authority of Scott as both historian and novelist rested ultimately on the oral notion of storytelling; see "Voices and Text: Scott the Storyteller, Scott the Novelist," *Scottish Literary Journal* 16 (1989): 41–59.

pions each to settle their quarrel in a fight before the king in 1396 at Perth. What struck Scott about this old story was not just the way in which the clans were caught up and exploited in a power struggle between the crown and certain earls but, characteristically, two very specific and peculiar details: "Two features of the story of this barrier battle on the Inch of Perth—the flight of one of the appointed champions, and the reckless heroism of a townsman, that voluntarily offered for a small piece of coin to supply his place in the mortal encounter—suggested the imaginary persons, on whom much of the novel is expended" (1831 preface, *Wav. Nov.*, 22:2). Approaching the crucial encounter through these two details, Scott constructs two atypical Waverley heroes: the introverted, sensitive chief of the Clan Quhele, highly uneasy with the code of masculinity defining his social role, who flees the battle; and the blunt, violent artisan who takes his place and marries the proper heroine of the title. A brooding novel attentive to the personal anguish of cultural alienation in both the young chieftain and the young heroine (who is equally out of place in her culture), *The Fair Maid of Perth* stands as one of Scott's most compelling historical constructs, notably in its subtle tracking of shifts in power among at least four classes; in its unusual interest in the emergence of urban consciousness; and in its concern with history as constraint.

The novel thus addresses central historical issues, but it does so in characteristic Waverley fashion: by moving off-to-the-side and by exploiting the power of fiction. Scott underlines the latter point in his 1831 preface to the text when he explains why he chose this particular subject. At the time he wrote *The Fair Maid of Perth*, he reports, the presses "teemed" with publications about "the Scottish Gael," but there had been no attempt to sketch their "manners" during the period when the archives ("the Statute-book, as well as the page of the chronicler") begin to present evidence of the increasing difficulties of the crown in the face of the power of the house of Douglas in the south and that of clan chiefs in the north. Scott's wording when he makes the point about manners is suggestive: "no attempt had hitherto been made to sketch their manners, as these might be supposed to have existed at the period when the Statute-book . . ." Highland "manners," that is, do not enter into statute-books and chronicles; hence they can only be "supposed."

Certainly, the historical record provides a frame (in this case the political frame) in which to conduct the supposition, and this kind of framing, as earlier chapters have suggested, is essential to the history-likeness of Scott's novels. At the same time, the frame releases an activity of imagination that fills in the gaps and silences of the historical record, and this too is crucial to the history-effect. It signals, of course, a different kind of history, but it does not displace official history, for the meaning of the recovered stories and details depends on the *relationship* between them and official history. It is this sense of relationship that was missing in Galt and Hogg, and, in a rather different sense, in Edgeworth and Morgan as well. As a result, their texts did not for their contemporaries intersect with historical discourse as the Waverley Novels did. "He has enriched history to us," commented the *New Monthly Magazine* on the Author of Waverley in 1820, "by opening such varied and delicious vistas to our gaze, beneath the range of its loftier events and more public characters."[22] The comment is symptomatic, underlining the widespread sense among Scott's first readers that his fiction constituted an enrichment of the historical genre. That sense of enrichment was generally registered, as it is here, as an "opening" of territory outside the "loftier" and "more public" regions of standard history whether in its analytic or narrative form.[23]

The implications of this "enrichment" for historiography will be discussed in more detail in the next section. I return now to the narrative problem with which I began in order to clarify in terms of Scott's own texts the notion of intergeneric relationship. In his complex project of working at once within and counter to (or at least alongside) official history, beginnings play a critical role, for the beginning must at once invoke the matrix of official history and negotiate a route out of it into the unofficial areas where fiction can move more freely, where it might exercise its generic right to "suppose." *A Legend of Montrose* (1819) offers a striking example of how Scott manages such

22. "On the Living Novelists.—No. 11," *NMM* 13 (1820): 548.
23. On these two forms of historiography in the late eighteenth century, see James Anderson, *Sir Walter Scott and History with Other Papers* (Edinburgh: Edina Press, 1981). See also James C. Simmons, *The Novelist as Historian: Essays on the Victorian Historical Novel* (The Hague: Mouton, 1973).

negotiation.[24] Unusually concise for a Waverley Novel, it is also unusually explicit in its strategies. The title of the novel neatly sums up the oblique historical approach of Scott's fiction, naming a Scottish historical figure who played a minor (if brilliant) role in the English Civil War in support of Charles I and indicating, through the generic designation of "legend," the local, oral, and perhaps dubious nature of the story. Moreover, the indefinite article (*a* legend) suggests that this story is only one of several possible stories and does not have special authority as "*the* legend" would have. Thus the title page already deflects standard or definitive expectations.

The novel itself offers three distinct beginnings in three different modes. In the opening narrative frame, the nineteenth-century narrator, Peter Pattieson, writes a memoir of an old Highland mercenary, Sergeant More M'Alpin. M'Alpin stopped in Gandercleugh with his sister, Janet, on their way to Canada to which they were emigrating because their native glen had been emptied by the Clearances. Finding Gandercleugh to their liking and lacking the energy to continue with the emigration, the M'Alpins remained in the village and died there. Pattieson used to walk and talk with M'Alpin in the elm-shaded graveyard where the old soldier is now buried, and it is out of the "numerous Highland traditions" and "curious particulars" recounted by M'Alpin on these occasions that he has created the narrative we are about to read. Pattieson dryly notes that the wars of Montrose "have been less commemorated" among the Highlanders "than any one would have expected, judging from the abundance of traditions which they have preserved upon less interesting subjects" (3:146–47; intro.).

Pattieson's frame is followed by a discursive first chapter offering an impersonal general analysis of the interaction of various historical forces that led to the divided role of Scotland in the English Civil War. "It was during the period of that great and bloody Civil War which agitated Britain during the seventeenth century, that our tale has its commencement," the narrator begins, and he then proceeds to provide an account of the

24. *Legend of Montrose* forms part of *Tales of My Landlord, Third Series*, 4 vols. (Edinburgh, 1819).

various interests, alliances, and divisions that accounted for the
agitation of the period. In this chapter characters like M'Alpin
and his sister give way to the Scottish Estates of Parliament, the
Solemn League and Covenant, Cromwell, King Charles, and
other institutional forces in a complicated story of Scotland's
route to civil war.

The second chapter, drawing on motifs of romance and satire,
provides a dramatic representation of a chance meeting of
strangers in a Highland pass and sets in motion a series of
particular and unpredictable events. "It was towards the close
of a summer's evening," the chapter begins, "during the anxious period which we have commemorated, that a young gentleman of quality, well mounted and armed, and accompanied
by two servants, one of whom led a sumpter horse, rode slowly
up one of those steep passes, by which the Highlands are acces-
sible from the Lowlands of Perthshire." Despite its embedding
of the scene in "the anxious period" and its realist gestures (the
sumpter horse, the signs of local familiarity), this opening sentence signals a highly conventional literary moment (dusk, journey, gentleman), triggering expectations of adventure and romance. The "young gentleman of quality," we discover, is the
earl of Menteith, the proper hero who turns out to be even less
significant than most Waverley heroes, fading quickly into the
background of the novel. Coming toward him in this opening
scene he sees "a single horseman" in full armor who proves to
be Dugald Dalgetty, eccentric mercenary and, as he hastens to
inform Menteith, former student at Mareschal College of Aberdeen. At once comic and sinister, appealing and appalling,
Dalgetty is, as Jane Millgate observes, something of a grotesque, and this grotesque then violates expectation by coming
to dominate the narrative.[25] A Legend of Montrose, as readers
from Scott's time on have remarked, is really the story of Dalgetty,[26] and the oddness of the narrative focus is underlined by the

25. Walter Scott: The Making of the Novelist (Toronto: University of Toronto
Press, 1984), 186–88.
26. Francis Jeffrey, for example, commented: "There is too much, perhaps,
of Dalgetty—or, rather, he engrosses too great a proportion of the work,—for,
in himself, we think he is uniformly entertaining" (Review of Ivanhoe, ER 33
[1820]: 5). Most of Jeffrey's own paragraph on Montrose is devoted to Dalgetty,

fact that a minor—and totally silent—figure in the opening scene turns out to be James Graham, marquis of Montrose himself in disguise.[27]

Clearly, these three beginnings draw on different idioms, operate at different degrees of narrative distance and levels of generality, and suggest at least three kinds of, or approaches to, history (as both event and writing). The crucial point is that they set into play a multiplicity of perspectives that blocks the closure of a simple, unitary understanding. Any moment, they imply, is multiple, existing simultaneously in several contexts and available to different kinds of understanding.[28] All the beginnings cohere in indicating that the focus of the narrative will be a local event (the organizing of northern royalist support), but they embed that event differently. For the memorialist Pattieson, that event exists in the context of lost Highland traditions and of the Highland Clearances of his own time. A man of feeling, Pattieson tends to filter loss through the literary language of sentiment: "The fires had been quenched upon thirty hearths—of the cottage of his fathers he could but distinguish a few rude stones—the language was almost extinguished—the ancient race from which he boasted his descent had found a

---

and Scott was so struck by Jeffrey's remarks on the character that he reprinted them in his 1830 introduction to the novel. On Dalgetty as narrative flaw, see Francis Hart, *Scott's Novels: The Plotting of Historic Survival* (Charlottesville: University of Virginia Press, 1966), 117–27.

27. Scott uses the Montrose technique even more dramatically in the opening of *Quentin Durward* (1823) where King Louis XI appears in disguise. In the later novel, however, Scott is more clearly exploiting the old folk motif of the disguised king. For a lucid analysis of the beginning of *Quentin Durward*, see Bann, *Clothing of Clio*, 144–45. In general, Bann sees the Waverley Novels as more homogenous structures than I do, and in his discussion of *Quentin Durward*, he wishes to draw attention to the opposite narrative movement: "We are conducted from an intimate and private scene to an ever broadening canvas of historical events, a process which culminates in the (authentic) episode of the assassination of the Bishop of Liège, and the battle before the city which ensues" (145).

28. In *Forms of Historical Fiction: Sir Walter Scott and His Successors* (Ithaca: Cornell University Press, 1983), Harry Shaw emphasizes the heterogeneity of Scott's novels, and he usefully aligns Scott's narrative with Siegfried Kracauer's theory of the nonhomogenous structure of history in *History: The Last Things Before the Last* (New York: Oxford University Press, 1969).

refuge beyond the Atlantic (3:138; intro.)."[29] But loss yields a less poetic language when Pattieson follows the description of the deserted hearth with an alternative formulation: "One southland farmer, three grey-plaided shepherds, and six dogs, now tenanted the whole glen, which in his youth had maintained in content, if not in competence, upwards of two hundred inhabitants" (3:138; intro.). Time in this introductory frame is a continual reenactment of loss, the dark downward-moving shadow of the upward-moving spiral of the major Romantics celebrated by Meyer Abrams.[30]

For the historian of chapter 1, the northern event is understood through two analytic models. The primary model is a synchronic, political model of "concurrent causes," which defines the Scottish event as the subset of a set of events known as the English Civil War. A secondary, diachronic model of "stages" is also at work, reading the event in terms of the theory of the evolution of civilization developed by Scottish historiography. We are informed, for example, that the clan chiefs who joined with certain northern nobles in a plan to disrupt the Scottish Parliament's active support of the English Parliament did so for three main reasons: they "conceived their interest and authority to be connected with royalty"; they had "a decided aversion to the Presbyterian form of religion"; and they "were in that half savage stage of society, in which war is always more welcome than peace" (3:150; chap. 1). Breaking up Scotland into regions and spheres of influence (the formidable influence of Argyle in the west and that of the Gordons in the north, for instance), the narrator outlines the disposition of Scottish power as the members of the Convention of Estates perceived it when they decided to continue their support for the English Parliament. The decision to continue then raises the question of why the decision to commit Scottish military support was made in the first place. The narrator, who has already established his historical competence through his language and type of reasoning, now explicitly aligns himself with historical discourse: "The

29. Millgate draws attention to Pattieson's literary affinities with Henry Mackenzie and the Gray of "The Deserted Village," in *Walter Scott,* 186.
30. *Natural Supernaturalism* (New York: Norton, 1971).

causes which moved the Convention of Estates at this time to take such an immediate and active interest in the civil war of England, are detailed in our histories, but may be here shortly recapitulated" (3:154; chap. 1). And so the chapter continues, working confidently at a high level of abstraction as it analyzes the political institutions and conditions that informed Scotland's divided interest in and response to the struggle between Charles Stuart and the English Parliament. Time here is linear: it moves in one direction, consolidating apparent divergence into the convergence implicit in the whole notion of "concurrent causes."

Chapter 2 exchanges the language of history and politics for that of romance, replacing the rationality of "causes" with the motifs of adventure and chance. The unnamed young gentleman and his servants are making their way at sunset along a "broken path" beside a lake, surrounded by steep hills, and overshadowed by "fragments of huge rock." Drawing attention to the conventional contours of the scene, the narrator establishes it as the exotic space of romance: "In present times, a scene so romantic would have been judged to possess the highest charms for the traveller; but those who journey in days of doubt and dread, pay little attention to picturesque scenery" (3:165; chap. 2). To confirm the difference in the kind of traveling, the heavily armed Dalgetty rides into the scene. Challenged by Menteith to declare his allegiance (Menteith readily announces his own commitment to "God and King Charles"), Dalgetty replies that his standard is as yet uncommitted. The young royalist is shocked: "I should have thought . . . that, when loyalty and religion are at stake, no gentleman or man of honour could be long in chusing his party" (3:171; chap. 2). Unperturbed by the slur, Dalgetty announces that he will prove that his uncommitted position "not only becometh me as a gentleman and a man of honour, but also as a person of sense and prudence." He then launches into the episodic narrative of his military adventures on the Continent that takes up the rest of the chapter.

Romance gives way to satire as Dalgetty, deploying the vocabulary of "honour" and "valour," exposes the sordidness of his "noble profession of arms." He notes, for example, that he

disliked serving the Dutch despite their admirable (and unusual) promptness of payment because they did not allow for
"peccadilloes": "So that if a boor complains of a broken head, or
a beer-seller of a broken can, or a daft wench does but squeak
loud enough to be heard above her breath, a soldier of honour
shall be dragged, not before his own court-martial . . . but before a base mechanical burgo-master." He has returned to Scotland, he reports, because he heard "that there is something to
be doing this summer in my way in this my dear native country" (3:189; chap. 2). In contrast to chapter 1, the context here is
that of individual experience as defined by conflicting social
codes (honor versus prudence, for example), and it brings to the
questions of war and allegiance the problem of personal choice.
Both Menteith's romantic honor and Dalgetty's problematic
prudence, however, operate outside the temporality of everyday life. Theirs is the amorphousness of Bakhtinian adventure-
time: discontinuous and inconsequential, even as it serves to
thematize problems of continuity and consequence.

All three beginnings thus invoke familiar categories, but their
abrupt juxtaposition and uncertain relationship induce a sense
of disorientation that prepares for the subsequent move of the
narrative through the romance plot into the unofficial world of
the Highland clans.[31] And here we come to the center of the
novel where we find the dark hero, Allan M'Aulay, in whose
story the connection with Montrose is of peripheral interest.
M'Aulay's story is based on an actual, enigmatic event: the murder of Lord Kilpont, eldest son of the earl of Menteith, by his
close friend James Stewart of Ardvoirlich in 1644 when both
were in Montrose's army. The motive for the murder was never
known, though various speculations were circulated, and Scott
appends to his 1830 introduction a letter from a descendant of
James Stewart giving the family "tradition" of the incident,
along with the line of oral transmission by which this tradition
has been handed down. Scott himself uses the introduction to
announce that he wrote *A Legend of Montrose* "chiefly with a
view to place before the reader" the "melancholy" and "singular

31. The rarely discussed *Montrose*, incidentally, offers perhaps Scott's most
politically astute analysis of the clan code, as Lukács (*Historical Novel*, 64–65)
and Shaw (*Forms of Historical Fiction*, 131–33) have recognized.

circumstances" of the fate of Kilpont and "the birth and history" of James Stewart (*Wav. Nov.*, 6:7). Characteristically, then, Scott has backed into the real subject of his novel, moving from the recollective, meditative nineteenth-century tones of Pattieson's memoir through the analytic eighteenth-century diction recalled in the historical opening and the chivalric motifs operating in the romance opening into the older, folkloric world that contains M'Aulay.

M'Aulay's story points to what Kathryn Sutherland has called the "unreadable core" of the Waverley Novels, where the outcasts, gypsies, and madwomen exist in the discursive eccentricity of their fragments of song, dark sayings, and opaque tales.[32] A troubled and brooding figure, Allan M'Aulay appears abruptly in chapter 4, entering the room where Menteith and his party are dining, only to ignore them all and seat himself silently before the fire for the rest of the chapter. Allan's story (recounted by Menteith) begins before his birth in bloody feud and maternal madness. His mother's brother, in feud with a broken clan known as the Children of the Mist, was ambushed and killed by them. Cutting off his head and wrapping it in a plaid, they set off for the M'Aulay seat, Darnlinvarach Castle, where they decided to exhibit it in a macabre fashion. On being offered reluctant refreshment by their victim's sister, they placed her brother's head on the table while she was out of the room, put a piece of bread between the jaws, and joked about the meals the head had eaten there. When the sister (pregnant at the time) returned, the sight of her brother's head sent her into a frenzy, and she fled into the woods where she wandered undetected for several months despite all efforts to find her. Meanwhile her husband and his allies hunted down the Children of the Mist, cutting off heads in their turn. Eventually, she was discovered and gave birth to Allan, her second son, on whom she doted for the rest of her short life and to whom she transmitted the duty of vengeance against the Children of the Mist, a duty that he pursues relentlessly from early adolescence. Allan is a fierce and violent soul, gifted with second sight

32. "Fictional Economies: Adam Smith, Walter Scott and the Nineteenth-Century Novel," *ELH* 54 (1987): 121.

and prone to dark trancelike states which can be dispelled only by the presence and harp of Annot Lyle, the fair-haired and fairylike heroine of the novel. Hers is a tangled story: kidnapped by the Children of the Mist from their enemies the Campbells as an infant, she was raised by them and then attacked by the vengeful Allan in one of his raids on the broken clan, escaping death only at the entreaty of Menteith. Brought back to the castle, she is treated as an adopted daughter by the M'Aulays and becomes the object of love for both Allan and Menteith.

Gaelic is the primary language of this clan world, an "unreadable" language for English and Scots readers. Hence this world can be only mediated, not re-presented, and Scott emphasizes this point by drawing attention to the necessity for translation, notably when Annot Lyle sings her Gaelic songs to soothe Allan's troubled visions. Allan himself, incidentally, speaks the rhythmic, formal English of most of Scott's seers, and its stylized tones also underline that this is an "other" way of being.[33] Two narrative comments on scenes of singing will illustrate this point. The one is rather playful, the other somewhat more serious. Annot Lyle enters the novel in chapter 6 with her harp, ready to dispel Allan's dark mood. "The air was an ancient Gaelic melody," the narrator informs us, "and the words, which were supposed to be very old, were in the same language; but we subjoin a translation of them, by Secundus M'Pherson, Esq. of Glenforgen, which, although submitted to the fetters of English rhythm, we trust will be found nearly as genuine as the version of Ossian by his celebrated namesake" (3:274–75; chap. 6). The allusion to the famous scandal of James MacPherson's forgeries, an inside joke by the enlightened modern narrator for his contemporaries, produces an oddly disconcerting moment of self-undermining in the narrative. But it makes the point of distance and difference, and after the supposed translation, the

33. I am interested in narrative moments that induce in the reader (either explicitly or implicitly) a conscious sense of stylization and translation. As Graham Tulloch has demonstrated in *Language of Walter Scott: A Study of His Scottish and Period Language* (London: Andre Deutsch, 1980) even the apparently authentic Scots for which Scott's fiction was so celebrated is a stylized and modern construct.

scene unfolds as if Annot Lyle's song possesses all the healing power that the M'Auley clan claims for it. But we never hear, or rather read, Annot's actual words.

A few chapters later, she sings again, and again the narrator brings in Secundus M'Pherson: "she executed the following ballad, which our friend, Mr. Secundus M'Pherson, whose goodness we had before to acknowledge, has thus translated into the English tongue" (4:12; chap. 9). The ballad is titled "The Orphan Maid," and to it Scott added a note in the first edition, a rather unusual gesture for him in 1819: "The admirers of pure Celtic antiquity, notwithstanding the elegance of the above translation, may be desirous to see a literal version from the original Gaelic, which we therefore subjoin; and have only to add that the original is deposited with Mr. Jedediah Cleishbotham" (4:13–14; chap. 9). A comparison of the first verse of "The Orphan Maid" and opening paragraphs of the prose "Literal Translation" illustrates the marked difference between the two versions:

> November's hail-cloud drifts away,
>   November's sun-beam wan
> Looks coldly on the castle grey,
>   When forth comes Lady Anne.   (4:12; chap. 9)

> The hail-blast had drifted away upon the wings of the gale of autumn. The sun looked from between the clouds, pale as the wounded hero who rears his head feebly on the heath when the roar of battle hath passed over him.
> Finele, the Lady of the Castle, came forth to see her maidens pass to the herds with their leglins. (4:14; chap. 9)

The "literal version" with its dialect and unmodern rhythms teases the imagination as the "elegance" of the rhymed version does not, promising entry into a remote world. But the important point is less the specific differences between the two inscriptions than the *fact* of two different inscriptions, for this narrative choice underlines the way in which not simply Annot Lyle's song but the whole world of the clans stands at an inevitable remove from the forms of representation available to the Anglo-Scots writer.

Scott thus directs explicit attention to the "unreadability" of the core of his narrative, moving into it through multiple contexts of understanding and representation that may help to make it visible but never make it available. And it is entirely fitting that at the end of the novel Allan M'Aulay, fleeing from his stabbing of Menteith, should simply disappear. Whereas the historical James Stewart joined the Covenanters after his murder of Kilpont, the fictional M'Aulay (who does not, of course, succeed in killing the proper hero) bursts into the room of his enemy Argyle in a dramatic but pointless act, utters a few words, and leaves: "and from this moment nothing certain is known of his fate" (4:323; chap. 15). The narrator reports two speculations: he was killed by the Children of the Mist "in some obscure wilderness," or he went abroad and died a Carthusian monk. But "nothing beyond bare presumption could ever be brought in support of either opinion" (4:324; chap. 15). In an equally characteristic move, the novel omits from its ending the figure of Montrose himself, whose "exploits and fate," the narrator announces, "are the theme of history." Conveniently, the publisher prefaced this final volume with an advertisement for a new reprint of George Wishart's standard account of Montrose, *Memoirs of the Most Renowned James Graham, Marquis of Montrose* (1756). And the volume itself ends with a postscript in which the Author of Waverley bids a premature farewell to his readers, registering his satisfaction that many readers "hitherto indifferent upon the subject, have been induced to read Scottish history, from the allusions in these works of fiction" (4:330).

Through stories like that of Allan M'Aulay and the Children of the Mist, Scott opened up a whole realm of unofficial historical memory and record for both fiction and history. The local worlds at the core of the Waverley Novels are preserved through oral forms—song, legend, joke, family tradition—and in marginal kinds of writing and print like the letters, tracts, pamphlets, and private memoirs on which Scott draws so heavily in his novels. Emphasizing the degree to which Scott's imagination was marked by a fascination with "the strange varieties

and motley composition of human life," Walter Bagehot linked
his imagination with the texts to which it was drawn: "From old
family histories, odd memoirs, old law-trials, his fancy elicited
new traits to add to the motley assemblage."[34] The surplus that
Scott generates (the "new" that he "adds" to what already exists) depends on the miscellaneous traces of what once was (the
"old family histories," "odd memoirs," and so forth). Consequently, the past itself, as rendered in local event through his
historical fiction, seems to exist as surplus. The historical novel
supplements official history and in so doing generates a surplus. This sense of surplus and supplement is crucial to Scott's
achievement in reinvesting the past with something of the un-
tidy, excessive, and motley details which history has to sup-
press or absorb in its ordering of events into meaningful pattern. In what may now seem a Derridean moment, Scott
comments in the final chapter of A Fair Maid of Perth (where
another Highland figure disappears much as Allan M'Aulay
disappears from Montrose): "A varying tradition has assigned
more than one supplement to the history" (3:344; chap. 36).
Although Scott's "supplement" is a long way from that of Der-
rida, there is a sense in which the mischief that the poststructuralist French philosopher generates in relation to philosophical ideas of origin and center through his deployment of the
supplement is anticipated in the mischief for official history
(with its notions of origin and center) that the Author of Waverley generates through the very form of his historical fiction; that
is, through the supplementarity that locates it outside the authoritative closure of history.

   For Scott, historical comprehension depends very much on
paying particular, as well as general, attention. As Harry Shaw
has stressed, his historical vision encompasses both the gener-
alities of historical process and the concreteness of "historical
particularities."[35] If his originality lay in the latter, his success
with his contemporaries depended on the coexistence of both
poles: the orthodox reading of historical process allowed read-

   34. Literary Studies, ed. Richard Holt Hutton, 2 vols. (London, 1879), 2:139,
140.
   35. Shaw, Forms of Historical Fiction, 249–50.

ers to register the novels as historical, while the vivid particularities invested that process with anxieties and desires that
struck responsive chords in a period becoming acutely aware of
its own historicity. Even as they exploit the explanatory power
of large paradigms, the Waverley Novels insist on initiating a
process of particularization. Their beginnings are crucial to this
process not only because they establish the oblique angle of the
narration but also because they define the whole idea of beginning *as* a problem. Scott's reliance on words like "compound,"
"concurrent," and "mixture" illustrates his sense that any
event, moment, or sequence is multiform, the complex product
of causal forces that exist at different experiential and temporal
levels. Beginnings are elusive—perhaps delusive—since any
sequence is so entangled and embedded in various other se-
quences that it loses the distinctness that allows us to identify
its beginning.

Beginnings in the Waverley Novels, as Nassau Senior noticed,
tend to be oddly dispersive in their effect. Senior remarked of
The Monastery that "even when the narrative is at last set flowing from the capacious cistern of the first volume, it breaks,
almost immediately, like a stream in a flat country, into three or
four independent channels."[36] *The Heart of Midlothian* is even
worse, for it suffers from a confusing multiplicity within the
beginning itself: "The beginning, or rather the beginnings, for
there are half a dozen of them, are singularly careless." The
problem, Senior explains, is that the author "introduces us at
the point where the different interests converge; and then, instead of floating down a united stream of events, we are forced
separately to ascend each of its tributary branches . . . until we
forget, in exploring their sources, the manner in which they
bear on one another."[37] As not only Nassau Senior has noticed,
the opening of *Midlothian* seems deliberately to defy all notions
of followability as Scott jumps around for the first eleven chapters among various apparently unrelated events and characters,
confusing chronology and obscuring relationship. Extreme as
its discontinuities may be, they are not atypical, and its involu-

36. Review of *Ivanhoe* and others, QR 26 (1821): 137.
37. Ibid., 116–17.

ted procedures exemplify the tendency of Scott's beginnings to step *into* rather than toward the middle. Even the more linear and schematic *Legend of Montrose* exploits its analytic and romance openings to make the point that the story that will emerge (and it does not much matter which particular story that will be) exists in unstable national and local contexts of ongoing and contradictory events whose roots stretch obscurely into the past. The chance meeting of Menteith and Dalgetty, we soon realize, does not so much begin a story as precipitate entrance into a story that has already begun.

As a result, the opening scenes in the Waverley Novels incline to the functional rather than the definitive mode of beginning. They are usually highly conventional—chance meeting, leaving home, enactment of a social rite—and Scott allows them to remain conventional, so that they can signify the arbitrary point of entry into the story. The contrasting fictional mode is that of particular, conclusive beginning, as in *Jane Eyre* and *Great Expectations*, where the opening moment is highly individualized, charged with intimations of inherent significance, and definitive for both the meaning and end of the story. It is the difference in narrative mode between "Once upon a time" and "There was a moment when . . ."

Behind Scott's open and inconclusive starting points lies a profound distrust of the whole idea of the moment. This distrust is dramatized most sharply in the narrative frame of the novel included with *Legend of Montrose* in the third series of *Tales of My Landlord*, *The Bride of Lammermoor*. In this frame Peter Pattieson and his friend, the painter Dick Tinto, debate the question of the hermeneutic potential of a single scene. Tinto shows Pattieson a sketch of a scene containing three figures: an apparently frightened, beautiful young woman in Elizabethan dress watches what seems to be a confrontation between her impatient mother and a proud young man. When Pattieson fails to find the scene immediately illuminating, Tinto complains: "you have accustomed yourself so much to these creeping twilight details of yours, that you are become incapable of receiving that instant and vivid flash of conviction, which darts on the mind from seeing the happy and expressive combinations of a single scene" (1:32; chap. 1). Pattieson replies that even were he able to "peep" into the actual scene that the sketch depicts, "I should not be a jot nearer guessing the nature of their business, than I am at this moment while looking at your sketch" (1:33; chap. 1). Like that of his creator, Pattieson's imagination is profoundly a narrative imagination, depending on what Jacques Barzun (in a recent article on the "atrophy of the historical") has called a sense of "how things go." Suggestively, Barzun like Scott turns to painting to clarify his term: "An analogy with a painted scene—or indeed any human scene glimpsed in medias res—makes the point. A Descent from the Cross shows what is happening only to those who know what went before and came after; the human altercation or dalliance that is overheard cannot be interpreted aright unless one knows the participants, their habits, and the customs of the country—how things go."[38]

Similarly, moments for Scott have neither constitutive nor inherently revelatory power. They exist as traces, as highly complex traces of the working of diverse and unobservable forces that it is the business of the historical novelist to attempt to uncover. To be sure, there are crucial moments in the Waverley Novels, as in Waverley's meeting of Charles Edward Stewart or Jeanie Deans's interview with the queen. But these moments take on power and significance precisely because of the way that the narrative has embedded them in contexts. In Scott's fiction a moment is never single, never pure; it is always heterogeneous, always contaminated. It may bring forces into focus, coalesce certain powers, but it is never itself generative. Its significance lies in its symptomatic nature: it acts as clue, sign, record. The opening scene of *The Bride of Lammermoor* is one of the most striking and dramatic in the Waverley Novels. It depicts the highly charged moment during the illegal funeral of old Ravenswood when Edgar Ravenswood and his Episcopalian friends draw their swords in defiance of the officer sent to enforce the Presbyterian law forbidding such ceremonies. Having described the scene, Pattieson then deliberately "paints" it in a reminder of the debate that framed his story. "The scene was worthy of an artist's pencil," he remarks, and proceeds to pro-

38. "The Critic, the Public, and the Sense of the Past," *Salmagundi* no. 68–69 (1985–86): 221.

vide a painterly redescription (1:53; chap. 2). But the scene itself—under either description—cannot be understood without the "creeping twilight details" of family and political history that surround it, and it is in the release of this kind of specificity that the Waverley Novels, drawing on history, made in turn their contribution to it.

The Dignity of History: Thierry, Macaulay, and the Waverley Model

In 1847 the irreverent Tory *Fraser's Magazine* published the article "Walter Scott—Has History Gained by His Writings?"[39] The answer was "No," and it is worth recalling how *Fraser's* came to this conclusion, for in the process the anonymous writer tells a story about the role of critical discourse in defining the Author of Waverley. The article opens by reminding its readers of the "bad odour" of the novel prior to the publication of *Waverley*. Scott's "irresistible popularity," however, "completely changed" the status of the genre, thereby forcing Jeffrey and the other critics of the day to account for how a genre "which was of late shunned by all, had now become the resort and delight both of the undiscerning public and of their critical selves" (345). Being generally conservative in literary matters, these elite "critical selves" deployed their favorite strategy when confronted with innovation: explaining the new by reference to "recognized standards." The recognized standard in this case was history, and *Fraser's* presents a mocking account of the critical reasoning that ensued: "Now, History was a good thing: for had it not been so said by them of old? and a Waverley Novel was a good thing, in virtue of one of those facts on which it is impossible to reason. It followed, therefore, that Scott's merits were exactly measured by the degree in which the inherent value of History overbalanced the intrinsic worthlessness of the novel" (346). Thus, to signal the way in which the Waverley Novels converged with but remained subordinate to history, the

39. *FM* 36 (1847): 345–51. Further references will be included in the text. The article is reprinted in *Scott: The Critical Heritage*, ed. John O. Hayden (London: Routledge, 1970), 382–93.

critics invented for Scott's fiction (*Fraser's* mistakenly but appropriately claims) the term "Historical Novel." So successful was this critical strategy, the essayist remarks, that a "belief in Scott's services to History" has "almost passed into a literary canon." As a result, Scott has had a powerful "influence" on history, but this is an entirely separate issue from the question of his "furtherance" of it.

On the question of "furtherance," *Fraser's* is firm: the Waverley Novels have had a deleterious effect. In England they have destroyed "systematic History" and encouraged the entry into the historical field of "a swarm of essayists, article-writers, and inditers of Historic Fancies," while in France a new generation of historians (Jules Michelet, Prosper De Barante, and Augustin Thierry) has been trying to write history as if it were a Waverley romance. The main problem with all this for *Fraser's* is that under the influence of Scott, history writing has come to substitute "life-like portraiture and clear, intelligible description, for philosophical comparison and analysis" (346).

The charge is a familiar one, but it forms part of a more interesting (if rather muddled) argument that the problem with Scott is his failure to mediate the past properly: he either collapses all distance, transporting nineteenth-century types into the fifteenth century, or he sets up an absolute distance, dwelling on the peculiarities of the past. He is not able, in other words, to establish the connection of each period to that which precedes or follows it, and his failure here stems from the particular cast of his mind. To illustrate the point, *Fraser's* recalls Francis Bacon's distinction in the *Novum Organum* between two kinds of minds—*ingenia subtilia* and *ingenia discursiva*—and identifies Scott as a type of the first: "He loved to linger on the *gradus rerum*, on those small particulars, which, at some period in the mental experience of all, are full of interest and even of beauty" (350). As exemplary figure of the second type (and hence as the sign of a true historical sense), the essayist names David Hume, who possessed "a distinct historical theory, and a full comprehension of national progress and social advance." Consequently, Hume was able to demonstrate both historical process (how the "mere indications" of one age became the "sharply-defined characteristics" of the next) and the purpose and unity of history (the "fore-ordained aim and ultimate union and convergence" of all the "particulars" that for Scott and his school remained "distinct and isolated facts"). Scott's history lacks the explanatory power of Hume's, for it scatters and disperses what history, properly practiced, unifies and rationalizes. As Walter Bagehot was to note a few years later, the Waverley Novels typically focused their interest "rather in the accessories than in the essential principle—rather in that which surrounds the centre of narration than in the centre itself."[40]

From the Waverley challenge to centripetal notions like "union" and "comprehension" stemmed the novelistic influence on historiography that *Fraser's* identifies and regrets. Scott's novels, Stephen Bann points out, generated "perturbation" among a whole generation of European historians, from the German Leopold von Ranke and the English Thomas Babington Macaulay to the French Augustin Thierry.[41] Ranke, for instance, read Scott (notably *Quentin Durward*) and was compelled to do otherwise, resolving to avoid "all imagination and all invention and to restrict myself severely to the facts." As a negative model, then, the Author of Waverley lies behind Ranke's influential and much quoted goal of showing what really happened (*wie es eigentlich gewesen*).[42] By contrast, Augustin Thierry, tangled up in the writing of his history of the Norman conquest, read *Ivanhoe* and found in Scott not simply the encouragement to continue his specific project but, more generally, a model of the kind of historical understanding through which he was seeking to renew French historical discourse.[43] For the young historian, as he was later to recount in

40. Bagehot, "Thomas Babington Macaulay," in *Literary Studies*, 2:253.
41. Bann, *Clothing of Clio*, 23.
42. Ranke's notorious *wie es eigentlich gewesen* appeared in the preface to *Geschichten der romanischen und germanishcen Volker von 1494 bis 1514* (1824). The comment on resolving to avoid "all imagination" after reading *Quentin Durward* comes from Ranke's autobiography as quoted by Bann, *Clothing of Clio*, 23.
43. Preface, *Dix ans d'études historiques*, in *Oeuvres complètes*, 8 vols. (Paris, 1851), 6:1–24. Thierry here refers specifically to Scott's boldness in showing Saxon and Norman still full of mutual resentment 120 years after the conquest. He also praises the effectiveness of Scott's poetic coloring, which encouraged his own goal to combine art and science in his history writing. For Thierry, Scott was "l'homme que je regarde comme le plus grand mâitre qu'il y ait jamais eu en fait de divination historique" (9–10).

his preface to the collection *Dix ans d'études historiques*, the reading of Scott was central to his discovery of his vocation, which he here defines as a war (*guerre*) on established French historiography in the name of a thoroughgoing reform of its assumptions and practice.[44]

The early text in which Thierry outlined his program for history, the introduction to his landmark *History of the Conquest of England by the Normans* (1825), serves as the first of two key texts by historians that will be discussed in this section.[45] The second is another text from the 1820s by another young man who would make a difference to nineteenth-century history: Thomas Babington Macaulay's early article "History" for the *Edinburgh Review* in 1828.[46] Written some twenty years before the appearance of his own monumental—and enormously successful— *History of England from the Accession of James II* (1849–61), this long article explicitly takes up the challenge to history posed by the Waverley Novels.[47] Like Thierry, Macaulay responded to the example of Scott's historical novel by seeking to absorb its insights for history proper, and he too cited Scott in the name of reform of the genre. If Macaulay's proves in the end a different inflection of the Waverley model from that of Thierry, both reflections on history writing highlight the degree to which Scott's novels helped to direct the attention of nineteenth-century historical discourse to what had generally stood outside its purview.

Thierry makes the point most fully, for what he found in *Ivanhoe* was confirmation of his sense that the smooth narrative line of standard history depended on erasure, its sense of unity and continuity on the repression of multiplicity and difference. Modern historians, he states in his introduction to his story of conquest, not only typically tell history from the viewpoint of

44. Ibid., 10.

45. *History of the Conquest of England by the Normans*, trans. William Hazlitt, 2 vols. (London, 1856). This is a translation of the 1846 Paris edition (the seventh edition), and all references will be included in the text.

46. "History," ER 47 (1828): 331–67. Further references will be included in the text.

47. See Phillips, "Macaulay, Scott, and the Literary Challenge to Historiography." On Scott and Macaulay, see also A. Dwight Culler, *The Victorian Mirror of History* (New Haven: Yale University Press, 1985), 20–38.

the conqueror but present conquest as accomplished all at once. "Thus," he writes, "for all those who, until recently, have written the history of England, there are no Saxons after the battle of Hastings and the coronation of William the Bastard; a romance writer, a man of genius, was the first to teach the modern English that their ancestors of the eleventh century were not all utterly defeated and crushed in one single day" (xxiv). Scott's medieval story has a modern and political point, for immediately after invoking *Ivanhoe*, Thierry turns to contemporary events: "The resuscitation of the Greek nation proves how great a misconception it is to take the history of kings, or even that of conquering peoples, for that of the whole country over which they rule" (xxiv). Whatever the specific import of *Ivanhoe* for "the modern English," for the young Frenchman its historical lesson was that in order to understand a "whole country," the historian had to develop a model of historical process that took into account contestation, asymmetry, and diversity. Disrupting the smooth narrative line of history (and the life of conquering peoples) was the fact that pockets of resistance persisted after conquest. Thierry notes two sources of resistance: forms of action (guerrillas, martyrs) and forms of language (legends, traditions, ballads). Since all of Europe has been marked by conquest in one way or another, Thierry maintains that an adequate history of a country or period must pay attention to these sources of resistance and recognize the existence of distinct cultures gathered under one name. This is what he has attempted to do with his own history of the Norman conquest, a history which not only grants significance to "facts before unperceived or neglected" but also gives "an entirely new aspect and signification to events celebrated in themselves, but hitherto incorrectly elucidated" (xxv). Here, Thierry in effect claims, is history (almost) from the other side.

Taking a cue from the Author of Waverley (among others), Thierry constructs a model of history that highlights cultural plurality, local event, and unofficial genres. In particular, he takes as his target the notions of homogeneity and unity posited by historians. So he claims to have produced the history "not merely of one, but of several conquests, written in a method the very reverse of that hitherto employed by modern historians" (xxiv). Previewing his method, Thierry opens his introduction by invoking and then fracturing totalities. "The principal states of modern Europe have at present attained a high degree of territorial unity," he writes, "and the habit of living under one same government and in the bosom of one same civilization, seems to have introduced among the population of each state an entire community of manners, language, and patriotism" (xvii). But this apparent homogeneity contains "living traces of the diversity of the races of men which . . . have combined to form that population," including differences of idiom or accent, variegated local traditions, and the "instinctive hostility" that the population of one particular district will feel toward that of another. The farther back one goes, Thierry continues, the more clearly one perceives "the existence of several peoples in the geographical circumscription which bears the name of one alone." The one name is quite literally a cover for "several peoples," and Thierry's whole sense of historical process is largely shaped by his awareness of the kind of erasure and coercion signaled by reduction to one name.

Through a prose that relies heavily on terms like "juxtaposition," "layers," and "admixture," Thierry effectively replaces the linear model of historical time (stages, progress, and so on) with a geological (or, more precisely, paleontological) metaphor of cultural strata: "the conquered of various epochs have become, so to speak, ranged in layers of populations, in the different directions taken by the great migration of peoples" (xviii). Like Scott, he has an interest in social structures and their transformations, noting, for instance, that conqueror and conquered frequently turn into the higher and lower classes of a later social structure, thereby recapitulating in a different modality the original story of invasion, dispossession, and struggle. This structural interest produces a similar temporal form in both the historical novelist and the narrative historian: a sense of time as a differentiated series rather than a single line. This is not to deny their reliance on a linear model but to emphasize the degree to which their narratives are attracted less to the coherent evolution of historical process than to the collisions and struggles that blur the clarity of the line and undercut assumptions of cultural unity and cohesion.

Certainly, both assume commonality and a certain uniformity of human nature. Without some such assumption, history is hardly possible. When Scott makes the point of "passions common to men in all stages of society" in the first chapter of *Waverley*, he does so in the context of historical difference, using it to bridge but not to erase difference.[48] To understand the violent medieval baron and the litigious modern peer whose conduct he here cites as analogous, one has to recognize both what joins and what separates them. And when Scott moves outside the sphere of the modern (and outside his own country) in *Ivanhoe*, he invokes the notion of translation to defend his move and his method. In his defense of historical fiction in the dedicatory epistle to the novel, the narrator-figure of Laurence Templeton admits that he cannot offer "complete accuracy" in either minor matters like "outward costume" or major ones like language and manners.[49] To do so (even were it possible) would be to be unintelligible. In order to achieve intelligibility, he has "as it were, translated [the past] into the manners, as well as the language, of the age we live in" (1:xvii). Templeton places limits on this "translation" (the author may not, for example, introduce anything "inconsistent with the manners of the age"), but what allows for translation in the first place is the assumption of a "neutral ground" that is formed partly by history (the handing down of culture) and partly by "the principles of our common nature" (1:xix). Interestingly, the opening scene of the novel (which, we are told, is "translated" from the Anglo-Saxon) makes not so much the point of "common nature" as it does the point of language as a sign of class and power. As Gurth the swineherd and Wamba the jester, thralls of the Saxon lord Cedric of Rotherwood, discuss the way in which words register the divisions of power between Saxon and Norman, the assumption of "translation" that enables the narrative releases a scene of historical specificity and contention.

48. The question of Scott's position on uniformity has been much debated. For a useful recent discussion, see Shaw, *Forms of Historical Fiction*, 142–45.

49. *Ivanhoe; a Romance*, 3 vols. (Edinburgh, 1820), 1:xvi. Further references will be included in the text. For the notion of the historical novel in the dedicatory epistle, see David Brown, *Walter Scott and the Historical Imagination* (London: Routledge, 1979), 173–81 and Chris R. Vanden Bossche, "Culture and Economy in *Ivanhoe*," *Nineteenth-Century Literature* 42 (1987): 46–72.

Thierry finds in the case of the Saxons under Norman rule an analogy to that of modern Greeks under Turks, thereby effecting his own "translation." But as a historian, he insists rather more than does Scott the novelist on accuracy and preservation of forms of the past. He closes his introduction, in fact, by singling out for particular emphasis his retention of the orthography of the names of different races and nationalities in order to "keep constantly marked out the distinction of races, and to secure that local colouring, which is one of the conditions, not merely of historic interest, but of historic truth" (xxx).[50] Local coloring is not just an antiquarian "interest" but the condition of "historic truth." In concentrating on the central and the national, conventional history has overlooked the truth contained in the local, and when he makes this argument, Thierry links the "truth" of his method to justice. "Without assigning to the great facts of history less importance than they merit," he writes, "I have applied myself with peculiar interest to the local events relating to these hitherto neglected populations [i.e., the Welsh, Irish, Scots, Bretons, and others], and . . . I have done this with that sort of sympathy . . . which one experiences in repairing an injustice" (xxiii).

Most great modern states, Thierry explains, have been established by force, and in the course of the "recomposition" that their development has entailed, large masses of people have lost not only their liberty, but "even their name as a people, replaced by a foreign name." In a passage that recalls Scott's own ambivalent view of historical change, Thierry adds: "Such a movement of destruction was, I am aware, inevitable. However violent and illegitimate it may have been in its origin, its result has been the civilization of Europe. But while we render to this civilization its due homage . . . we may regard with a certain tender regret the downfal [sic] of other civilizations that might one day have also grown and fructified for the world, had fortune favoured them" (xxiii).[51]

50. On the notion of local color in the historiography of the period, see Bann, *Clothing of Clio*, 24–31, 38–40.

51. For Scott's similar sense of national and political origins as violent and contaminated, see Judith Wilt, *Secret Leaves: The Novels of Walter Scott* (Chicago: University of Chicago Press, 1985).

To reconstruct something of the "other civilizations" and to achieve the local coloring that is a condition of historic truth, Thierry, like Scott, looks largely to unofficial genres as historical sources. More specifically, he follows the Scottish poet and novelist in looking to the traces of oral culture for his constructions of the past. So Thierry claims to have traced out the history of the Anglo-Saxon race "where no one previously had sought it, in the popular legends, traditions, and ballads" (xxiv). Such sources are central to his achieving the proper goal of history: the assigning to each period of the past "its true place, its colour, and its signification." To achieve this end, Thierry has consulted two kinds of archives: "original texts and documents," and "national traditions of the less known populations and old popular ballads" (xxi). He has relied on the first archive for details of "circumstances" and for "the characters of the persons and populations that figure in them." The second archive has provided "infinite indications of the mode of existence, the feelings, and the ideas of men at the period and in the places whither I transport the reader." This second archive, then, has functioned as a way into the idiomatic life that we call "culture" by providing signs of feelings, ideas, and modes of existence. Both archives—and their differing discourses—are necessary for the work of Thierry's history, and both are the source of the "detail" on which he lays such stress throughout the introduction.

Lionel Gossman has pointed to a distinctive tension in romantic historiography between sameness and difference, continuity and discontinuity. This was an age, Gossman observes, that was peculiarly fascinated by "the historical particular, the discontinuous event or phenomenon in its irreducible uniqueness and untranslatableness." At the same time, it was equally eager to "translate it, represent it, define its meaning, and thus, in a sense, domesticate and appropriate it."[52] In their doubleness, the narratives of Thierry and Scott are symptomatic of this tension. Equally symptomatic is that both locate their innovative power on the side of particularity and difference. What compels the imagination of the French historian and the Scot-

52. Gossman, "History as Decipherment," 40.

tish novelist is that which disrupts the continuities that both at the same time affirm. In a characteristic moment, Scott muses in his 1829 introduction to *Rob Roy* (1817) on the incongruity of a figure like his titular hero in eighteenth-century Britain. Rob Roy, he notes, was "playing such pranks in the beginning of the 18th century, as are usually ascribed to Robin Hood in the middle ages," and he was doing so within forty miles of the commercial and university city of Glasgow in the Augustan Age of Queen Anne and George I. "Addison, it is probable, or Pope," Scott comments, "would have been considerably surprised if they had known that there existed in the same island with them a personage of Rob Roy's peculiar habits and profession" (*Wav. Nov.*, 4:3). Edward Waverley experienced precisely this kind of surprise after the cattle raid on Tully-Veolan: "It seemed like a dream to Waverley that these deeds of violence should be familiar to men's minds, and currently talked of, as falling within the common order of things, and happening daily in the immediate neighbourhood, without his having crossed the seas, and while he was yet in the otherwise well-ordered island of Great Britain" (72–73; chap. 15). Such cultural discontinuities and juxtapositions intrigue both Scott and Thierry, and for them history writing is very much a matter of surprising both naive readers like Waverley and sophisticated ones like Addison and Pope into an awareness of those "layers" of culture to which Thierry draws such insistent attention in his introduction. For them, historical narration works not just to remind readers of the differences *in* the past or the difference *of* the past but also to alert them to recognize *within* their own present the kinds of stratifications, sedimentations, and frictions represented in the narration of the past.[53]

When Thierry sums up the historical project of his *History of the Conquest of England by the Normans*, he stresses the concreteness and particularity of his method, a method that obstructs but does not finally deny an accompanying linear sweep that moves to fusion and incorporation: "I propose, then, to exhibit in the fullest detail, the national struggle which followed the

---

53. On the implications of this point for the notion of literary unity in particular, see Ina Ferris, "Story-Telling and the Subversion of Literary Form in Walter Scott's Fiction," *Genre* 18 (1985): 23–35.

conquest of England by the Normans established in Gaul; to reproduce every particular afforded by history of the hostile relations of two peoples violently placed together upon the same soil; to follow them throughout their long wars and their obstinate segregation, up to the period when, by the intermixture of their races, manners, wants, languages, there was formed one sole nation, one common language, one uniform legislation" (xxii). The plot that Thierry outlines here—violence and conflict leading ultimately to "intermixture" and then to unity—could well describe not just the typical Waverley Novel (*Ivanhoe* is paradigmatic) but also Macaulay's *History of England from the Accession of James II*. The plot of history in all three writers is much the same; what creates the distinctive note of each is precisely the degree of interest in this plot.

Where for Thierry and Scott the movement to uniformity was at best problematic and at worst suspect,[54] the imagination of Macaulay was enchanted by the centripetal drive whereby English history revealed its inherent Whiggish shape. His own prose, with its confident, rolling rhythm, signals a special pleasure in the act of sweeping up details into unified harmonies. In the famous opening of the *History*, for example, he outlines his vision of English history in a long sentence that unpacks a series

54. As a Scotsman, Scott was enormously suspicious of the whole notion of uniformity, and this suspicion marks his entire literary career. As early as the *Minstrelsy of the Scottish Border*, he was articulating his fear that the "peculiar features" of Scottish manners and character were "daily melting and dissolving into those of our sister and ally" (introduction to *Minstrelsy*, ed. T. F. Henderson, 4 vols. [Edinburgh: Blackwood, 1902], 1:175). The popular narrative poems that grew out of the experience of collecting, editing, arranging, and translating for the *Minstrelsy* respond to the same sense of dissolution, as do the novels that followed (as the postscript to *Waverley* makes clear). But Scott's strongest statement on behalf of Scottish peculiarity and against British uniformity comes in *The Letters of Malachi Malagrowther* (1826). The political polemic here (directed at the English plan to abolish the Scottish issue of bank notes) is rooted in scorn for the doctrine of uniformity that was used to make the case against the Scottish issue. A characteristic passage reads: "But till Ben-Nevis be level with Norfolkshire, though the natural wants of the two nations may be the same, the extent of these wants, natural or commercial, and the mode of supplying them, must be widely different, let the rule of uniformity be as absolute as it will" (*Malachi*, ed. P. H. Scott [Edinburgh: Blackwood, 1981], 33). On Scott's political writings, including the rarely discussed *Malachi*, see Graham McMaster, *Scott and Society* (Cambridge: Cambridge University Press, 1981), 78–100.

of parallel clauses: "I shall relate how the new settlement . . . how, under that settlement . . . how, from the auspicious union of order and freedom . . . how our country, from a state of ignominious vassalage, rapidly rose . . . how her opulence and her martial glory grew together."[55] And so it continues, establishing the continuity and progress of English civilization. At the same time, Macaulay's centralizing drive coexists with a fascination with specificity and an avid curiosity about the texture of life in the past: its architecture, food, ballads, plays, diaries, and other assorted matters. In drawing on such sources, Macaulay (like Thierry) sees himself as breaking historical conventions. After announcing that he will describe the "history of the people as well as well as the history of the government," Macaulay declares: "I shall cheerfully bear the reproach of having descended below the dignity of history, if I can succeed in placing before the English of the nineteenth century a true picture of the life of their ancestors."[56]

Macaulay's conviction that a "true picture" of the past required a redefinition of history that potentially threatened its conventional "dignity" in the hierarchy of genres had been articulated many years earlier in one of the articles for the *Edinburgh Review* that helped establish his name. Like Thierry in his introduction, Macaulay in his essay "History" invokes the model of Scott in the context of a critique of what standard history overlooks, and he makes his point, appropriately, by way of an anecdote from "tradition." In Lincoln Cathedral, Macaulay reports, there is a beautiful window said to have been made by an apprentice out of pieces of glass rejected by his master. When the master saw this window, a window superior to all others, he killed himself—so the story goes—in mortification. Modern historians, Macaulay notes, are in a similar predicament: "Sir Walter Scott, in the same manner, has used those fragments of truth which historians have scornfully thrown behind them, in a manner which may well excite their envy. He has constructed out of their gleanings works which, even considered as histories, are scarcely less valuable than theirs" (365). The priority of

55. *History of England from the Accession of James II*, 9th ed. 5 vols (London: Longmans, 1853–61), 1:1.
56. Ibid., 1:3.

history, we note, is carefully (if precariously) maintained even as Macaulay pushes for its reform by invoking the example of a writer of fiction.

The model of Scott allows Macaulay to emphasize two main points: the need for a historiography with affective power rather than conventional "dignity"; and the urgency of integrating into historical discourse the still largely ignored new sense of ordinary life as a historical force. A historiography reformed in this way would appeal to both imagination and reason, and it would allow for a more accurate "prognosis of political events" (367). Much more clearly and directly than Thierry, Macaulay is interested in the social and political power of history as a discourse. He sees in Scott a cultural potency that history would do well to appropriate, or, rather, to reappropriate for itself. A "truly great historian," he observes, "would reclaim those materials which the novelist has appropriated" and give to truth "those attractions which have been usurped by fiction" (365, 364).

If it is to take back what has been usurped, however, history must reinterpret that "dignity" by which it has defined its status. By standing on its dignity, Macaulay argues, the genre has lost ground. Historians, for instance, have ignored to their loss the "immense popularity" of biography and memoirs, thinking it "beneath the dignity of men who describe the revolutions of nations, to dwell on the details which constitute the charm of biography" (362). Having imposed on themselves "a code of conventional decencies," historians have omitted or softened the "most characteristic and interesting circumstances . . . because, as we are told, they are too trivial for the majesty of history" (362). Dismissing this "majesty" with an anecdote about the king of Spain who died because the proper dignitaries were not on hand to help him, Macaulay proceeds to build his case that history will maintain its power only if it admits change into its discourse.

Central to this case is his recognition that the significant processes of history are generally initiated and sustained by what he calls "noiseless revolutions." Occurring in ways and places outside the usual categories of historical change, these revolutions are "rarely indicated by what historians are pleased to call important events" (363). They are not, Macaulay remarks, enforced by armies or senates, and they are not recorded in treaties or archives. Nor, he adds, does the "upper current" of society provide a clear guide for judging the "direction" of the "under current," as historians typically assume. To assume that it does is to misunderstand "the body politic" and to see only "the surface of affairs, and never think of the mighty and various organization which lies deep below" (363). What history ignores, fiction has appropriated, and Macaulay stresses the degree to which the failure of history has led to the splitting of historical discourse into fiction and history. Readers, he argues, "have to look for the wars and votes of the Puritans in Clarendon, and for their phraseology in Old Mortality; for one half of King James in Hume, and for the other half in the Fortunes of Nigel" (365). It is in terms of this split that Macaulay positions his project for a reformed historiography that would overcome the current bifurcation, so that the "history of the government, and the history of the people, would be exhibited in that mode in which alone they can be exhibited justly, in inseparable conjunction and intermixture" (365).

Macaulay's "intermixture" recalls the language of Thierry, but Thierry's "intermixture" signals a different orientation and valence. For Thierry, the aim of history is to underline that unities (whether generic, cultural, or political) are always "intermixtures"; hence he tends to fragment unities in order to accent (if not finally to privilege) multiplicity and contestation, placing in the foreground notions like "juxtaposition" and "struggle." For Macaulay, by contrast, "intermixture" points to a still deeper coherence and level of intelligibility: the "organization which lies deep below" and structures the events that appear on the stage of history. Although the "noiseless revolutions" come about in a variety of places—Macaulay mentions schools, churches, shops, and firesides—these form a coherent set, one that is either parallel or counter to the set constituted by armies and senates. The point of attention to the unofficial is to uncover the logic and movement of the "under current" that has hitherto been neglected by standard history, and for Macaulay in 1828 the "under current" had much to do with the unenfranchised middle class whose political status the 1832 Reform Bill was shortly to alter. Even as he responded to the same focus on the particular and on idiomatic life in the Waverley Novels as did Thierry, Macaulay worked to the opposite end, seeking always to integrate and to render coherent. For him, historical time flows smoothly, absorbing irregularities and differences, and the primary function of history writing is to protect and ensure that flow.

In a suggestive moment at the end of "History," Macaulay transforms the "body politic" which is the subject of history into a literal body for the historian to diagnose: "An intimate knowledge of the domestic history of nations, is therefore absolutely necessary to the prognosis of political events. A narrative, defective in this respect, is as useless as a medical treatise, which should pass by all the symptoms attendant on the early stage of a disease, and mention only what occurs when the patient is beyond the reach of remedies" (367). The historian-physician must know the idiomatic life of a people (their "domestic history") in order to cure the disease that political life represents. Where Thierry found in the Waverley Novels a new historical truth wedded to justice, Macaulay discovered a technique for making more efficient its disciplinary power.

8

Establishing the Author of Waverley:
The Canonical Moment of *Ivanhoe*

> His facility in composition was almost as great as that of
> Mrs. Henry Wood, of modern repute. But it was the fashion
> among his critics to attribute this remarkable fact rather to
> his transcendent strength than to the vulgarity of his task.
> —Henry James on Scott, *North American Review* (1864)

If, for Augustin Thierry, the Author of Waverley was "a romance writer, a man of genius," for Henry James in 1864, he
was simply a romance writer. Intent on establishing the difference of his own generation and the authority of a new critical
voice, the young James took the occasion of a review of Nassau
Senior's essays on fiction to demystify the honorific sign of the
Author of Waverley by aligning it with the debased sign of a
female novelist who produced notorious best-sellers of little
literary repute like *East Lynne*. In a curious migration of gender,
the masculine Scott has become entangled in female signs, and
the change in gender signals a change in status. As James's
critical move suggests, the divisions of the novelistic field articulated through gender early in the century (see Chapter 1) remained firmly in place in the later decades. Indeed, the lines of
gender and genre were now more firmly drawn, the salutary
incoherence and mobility of romantic critical discourse now
much reduced and regularized. In this critical field, Scott was
being relocated, and James attaches "old-fashioned, ponderous
Sir Walter" not just to sensational female romance but to naive
children's stories. The Waverley Novels, he remarks, are "capital books to have read," and in order to enjoy them once more,
"we must again become as credulous as children at twilight."[1]

1. "Senior's Essays on Fiction," *NAR* 99 (1864): 580–87. The quoted phrases
are on 583–87.

Thus relegated to the lowly, unliterary sphere inhabited by children and women and mere storytelling, Scott is expelled from the literary space for fiction that his own novels had helped forge. This is not to say that Scott ceased to matter. He remained a highly significant figure throughout the nineteenth century, though he came to function increasingly as beloved rather than exemplary novelist.[2] Nor is it to deny that James's condescension was shaped by a particular circle and a particular moment in the cultural history of the eastern United States, not to mention by James's own peculiar psychology and ambition. But it is to suggest that his dismissal of Scott is made possible by the very terms in which the Author of Waverley was canonized by his first readers. James works within a rhetoric made available by the early reviews; it supplies the categories he deploys and enables the dismissal he effects. The reviews constructed the figure of the Author of Waverley as manly genius, but the male trope turns out to depend on its apparent opposite, the trope of female reading. This doubling helps explain how a writer, declared in 1820 to be the "alpha and omega of novelists,"[3] could be moved so easily later in the century into the category of the romantic, the superficial, and the naive.

The year 1820 is central to my analysis of the link between the rhetoric of canonization and that of expulsion in the critical construction of the Author of Waverley. In that year there was an outpouring of reviews and general articles following the publication very late in 1819 of *Ivanhoe* and of the first collection of Waverley novels, the twelve-volume *Novels and Tales by the Author of Waverley*. In January, John Scott produced for the *London Magazine* the celebratory piece that Hazlitt called "the most elaborate panegyric on the *Scotch Novels* that had as yet appeared";[4] in May, Colburn's *New Monthly Magazine* lauded the

2. On Scott's critical reputation later in the century, see John Henry Raleigh, "What Scott Meant to the Victorians," *Victorian Studies* 7 (1963): 7–34.

3. "On the Living Novelists," Gold's *LM* 2 (1820): 265.

4. [John Scott], "The Author of the Scotch Novels," *LM* 1 (1820): 11–22. Hazlitt makes his remark on John Scott in his own essay on Walter Scott, in *The Complete Works of William Hazlitt*, ed. P. P. Howe, 21 vols. (London: Dent, 1930–34) 11:59. Ironically, John Scott died less than a year after writing his article on the Waverley Novels as the result of a quarrel that indirectly touched their author. John Scott died of wounds received in a duel with a man named

Author of Waverley in a series on contemporary novelists;[5] and in August, Gold's *London Magazine* joined the chorus of praise in its own series on "Living Novelists."[6] *Ivanhoe* itself sold briskly (despite a high new price of thirty shillings), and it was extensively reviewed, with the *Edinburgh* taking the lead. The January issue opened with a fifty-four page-review by Jeffrey bringing up to date the notices of the Waverley Novels and honoring the "new school of invention" founded by their anonymous author.[7] Of the major journals, in fact, only the *Quarterly* did not distinguish the occasion of *Ivanhoe*, waiting until October 1821 to include a long, omnibus review by Nassau Senior of the novels from *Rob Roy* to *Kenilworth*.[8]

The moment of *Ivanhoe* marks the culmination of the critical process of legitimation that began with *Waverley* just over five years earlier.[9] It is not so much that *Ivanhoe* itself was greeted with special enthusiasm. Although the reviews were generally favorable, the novel was received with a degree of reservation. Two objections dominated: the well-worn subject matter and the stylized language necessitated by the remoteness of the period. In his review Jeffrey noted that the novel relied on "the vulgar staple" of armed knights, jolly friars, imprisoned damsels, lawless barons, collared serfs, and household fools; but he claimed that the author had reanimated these stock fig-

---

Christie, but the duel itself grew out of a confrontation with Scott's son-in-law, John Lockhart, in connection with his writing for *Blackwood's*, Tory rival of John Scott's own *London Magazine*. For a recent account, see Patrick O'Leary, *Regency Editor: Life of John Scott* (Aberdeen: Aberdeen University Press, 1983).

5. "On the Living Novelists.—No. II. 'The Author of Waverley,'" *NMM* 13 (1820): 543–48.

6. "On the Living Novelists," Gold's *LM* 2 (1820): 262–70.

7. *ER* 33 (1820): 1–54. Further references will be included in the text.

8. *QR* 26 (1821): 109–48.

9. James T. Hillhouse's study of the reviews, *The Waverley Novels and Their Critics* (Minneapolis: University of Minnesota Press, 1936), suggests that critical attention to the Waverley Novels peaked around 1820. In terms of the novels themselves, *Ivanhoe* is generally regarded as in some sense a benchmark. For different readings of its significance in the career of Scott, see Marilyn Butler, *Romantics, Rebels and Reactionaries* (New York: Oxford University Press, 1981), 149–51; Jane Millgate, *Walter Scott: The Making of the Novelist* (Toronto: University of Toronto Press, 1984), 189–91; Judith Wilt, *Secret Leaves* (Chicago: University of Chicago Press, 1985), 18–26.

ures (7). The *British Review* was less generous, opening its list of standard ingredients by observing that the novel "consists very much of descriptions of forests and tournaments, of men of big bones and portentous looks, of chivalric parade and equipage."[10] On the question of language, the *Eclectic* sounded a recurring note in regretting the absence of the colloquial and regional idiom that gave "spirit and effect" to the earlier novels, a point that the *Monthly Review* made in a different way when it observed that "the dialogue of 'Ivanhoe' belongs to no precise age, but bears the nearest affinity to that of Elizabeth and of Shakespeare."[11] The character of Rebecca, on the other hand, was greeted with extraordinary superlatives, and the general tone of the response is indicated by the generalization in the *Edinburgh Monthly Review*: "In the whole range of fictitious composition, we hold Rebecca unsurpassed. She is in moral as well as personal beauty a matchless creature."[12]

If *Ivanhoe* itself was not "matchless," its move outside Scottish history marked a significant departure for the Author of Waverley, and this prompted general assessment and celebration of his achievement to date. Once again, Jeffrey set the tone. In 1814 he had opened his review of Scott's first novel by declaring that it cast "the whole tribe of ordinary novels into the shade and [took] its place rather with the most popular of our modern poems, than with the rubbish of provincial romances."[13] Separating the text from its genre here, Jeffrey distinguished *Waverley* by placing it in the more prestigious category of "modern poems." By early 1820, however, apparent anomaly had turned into seminal text. "In the period of little more than five years," Jeffrey now proclaims, "he [the "Author of Waverley"] has founded a new school of invention; and established and endowed it with nearly thirty volumes of the most animated and original composition that have enriched English literature for a century" (1). The novelist is imaged as benevolent philanthropist, founding and endowing a new "school"; and the novel now participates in and contributes to "English literature." Con-

10. *BR* 15 (1820): 395.
11. *EcR*, n.s., 13 (1820): 527; *MR* n.s., 91 (1820): 79.
12. *EMR* 3 (1820): 197.
13. *ER* 24 (1814): 208.

firming the admission into the literary sphere, Jeffrey opens his review by invoking the supreme sign of canonicity in British criticism: "Since the time when Shakespeare wrote his thirty-eight plays in the brief space of his early manhood . . . there has been no such prodigy of fertility as the anonymous author before us" (1). Admitting that a comparison with Shakespeare has become a routine critical move, Jeffrey recharges the motif by announcing that the Waverley Novels "save it, for the first time for two hundred years, from being altogether ridiculous" (2).

Jeffrey's awe at Scott's rapid and prodigious output is echoed in review after review, and it constitutes a leading motif in the construction of the Author of Waverley as "genius." Such facility, however, as the example of Henry James suggests, can easily be recoded to signal the vulgarity that opposes genius. In their excess, high and low oddly double one another, and the canonical sign of the Author of Waverley is constructed in much the same terms as the trope of female reading. The *British Review*, in fact, places the "extraordinary" author inside the commercial matrix of supply and demand, arguing that "it is somewhat cheering to see that, at a time when almost the whole world can read, and novel-reading is the most general of all reading, there has arisen among us an extraordinary person, who has shown himself able to supply the universal demand from the inexhaustible magazine of his genius; to keep, in short, the immense population of this class of consumers so occupied, with a description of articles comparatively innocent in their effects, as to allow them scarcely any time for ruining the constitution of their minds with adulterated and poisonous goods."[14] As he fulfills the demand of this "class of consumers," the Author of Waverley may counteract the debilitating effects of female reading, but he does so in the same space. In 1820, most reviews (unlike the *British Review*) recoded that space as the space of genius rather than commerce.

As Waverley volume followed Waverley volume, the reviews read Scott's prolific production as index of a remarkable liberality, and in their construction of his literary sign, they absorbed

14. Review of *Ivanhoe* and *The Monastery*, BR 15 (1820): 393–94.

and revalorized two key negative motifs of female reading: prolixity and proliferation. As Jeffrey develops the Shakespearean
motif, for example, he acclaims the novels for what they share
with the Elizabethan plays, and he includes in his list "the
inimitable freedom and happy carelessness of the style in which
they are executed, and . . . the matchless rapidity with which
they have been lavished on the public" (2). Where the prolixity
of the ordinary novel signaled a lack of discipline and art, of
education and knowledge, the prolixity of a Waverley Novel
becomes an index of generosity, abundance, and gentlemanly
ease. Where the proliferation of ordinary novels—the undifferentiated "hordes" and "shoals"—figured a promiscuous
and dark energy linked to female sexuality, the proliferation of
Waverley Novels affirms a directed and positive energy linked
to male potency. The Author of Waverley, marvels Gold's *London
Magazine*, "pours forth his exhaustless energies with the impet-
uosity of a mountain torrent."[15] Indeed, his rejuvenating effect
on both the reading public and the literary field is typically
articulated in metaphors of life-giving rivers, springs, and foun-
tains, which stand in contrast to the sinister images of inundation attached to the ordinary novel.

Thus linked to motifs of refreshment and rejuvenation, the
Author of Waverley signals the health-and-manliness that
counteracts the disease not just of female reading but of rival
male romance, notably that produced by what Jeffrey calls the
"the Genius—or the Demon, of Byron" (1). Aristocratic and
transgressive, the demonic masculinity of Byron served as a
standard foil in the period for the healthy masculinity of the
Waverley mode, replaying in male terms the female rivalry between domestic and demonic womanhood.

The (anti-Tory) *New Monthly Magazine* offers a striking illustration when it commends the Waverley Novels for the
"fresh spirit of health" through which they have "counteracted
the working of that blasting spell by which the genius of Lord
Byron once threatened strangely to fascinate and debase the
vast multitude of English readers."[16] To set up its argument of

15. Review of *Ivanhoe*, Gold's *LM* 1 (1820): 81.
16. "On the Living Novelists," *NMM* 13 (1820): 543. For the Scott-Byron
contrast, also see Lister, "The Waverley Novels," *ER* 55 (1832): 73 and Hazlitt's
essay on Byron in *The Spirit of the Age*, in *Complete Works*, 11:69.

counteraction, the *New Monthly* claims that men had been "seduced" by "their noble poet"; as a result, they had begun "to pay homage to mere energy, to regard virtue as low and mean compared with lofty crime, and to think that high passion carried in itself a justification for its most fearful excesses." In this asocial thrust, Byron is positioned as negative contrast to the highly social Author of Waverley: the poet offers an anarchic valorization of "mere energy," whereas the novelist encourages "human sympathies"; the poet replicates the disease of modernity by stimulating a "diseased" curiosity and inducing a sterile introspection, whereas the novelist offers "a keen and healthful relish for all the good things of life." Defined by impurity, Byron represents the dark underside of manliness ("mere energy") and threatens national order: "The genius of our country was thus in danger of being perverted from its purest uses to become the minister of vain philosophy, and the anatomist of polluted natures." The rescue of the nation has been effected by an oddly maternal Author of Waverley, who has "gently weaned it from its idols, and restored to it its warm youthful blood and human affections." His novels stand in absolute opposition to Byron's "inward revolvings" and "morbid speculations," and they eschew—in their coolness and freshness—Byron's "burning passion" and "feverish gratifications."[17]

What they offer is the outdoor male romance of invigoration outlined by Hazlitt in the passage from "On the Pleasure of Hating" discussed in Chapter 3. Hazlitt, we recall, defined Waverley reading as release from the feminized space of modern civilization, a return to the "wild beast . . . within us" and a restoration of "freedom and lawless, unrestrained impulses."[18] "Days how different from our own!" enthuses *Blackwood's*, as it celebrates the setting of *Ivanhoe* in "times of energetic volition—uncontrolled action—disturbance—tumult—the storms and whirlwinds of restless souls and ungoverned passions."[19] The passions, of course, are not ungoverned; nor (as Hazlitt well knew) are the impulses lawless. But the peculiar "healthiness" of the Waverley romance for its early readers had a great deal to

17. *NMM* 13 (1820): 543.
18. Hazlitt, *Complete Works* 12:129.
19. *BM* 6 (1819): 263.

do with the way in which it released—and managed—passion and impulse.

John Scott makes the point in his tribute to the Author of Waverley when, like Hazlitt, he images Waverley reading through metaphors of the hunt: "We join the course of his lively and rapid narrative in the true spirit of the *chace*; we there find men and animals, all at full cry, displaying their natural instincts and dispositions in the ardour of cheerful exercise; the scenery around is fresh and invigorating; health and manliness are made to circulate through our frames."[20] Here is the complex of motifs that makes up the Waverley romance: nature, freshness, invigoration, the active body, and—not least—a group of participants ("men and animals"). To engage in a chase is to join the tribe in a way that to engage in the "lofty crime" of Byronic romance is not; Byron may offer nature, but he does so to a solitary subject who is all restless mind and soul. Furthermore, John Scott emphasizes that the Author of Waverley constructs the variegated world of his fiction "without ever shocking the principles of conscience, or violating any one rule of civil or sacred authority." When confronting evil ("creatures which in their natures are noxious and dangerous"), for instance, the Waverley reader is not encouraged to feel either hostility or "false sympathy"; nor is he "exposed to any contagious influence from their propensities."[21] The space of manliness is thus a space of order and purity, even as it is the natural and open space of energy and invigoration.

It is also the social space of the new public virtue of human sympathy (see Chapter 3), for if the Waverley reader is not encouraged into a "false sympathy," he is prompted into what John Scott calls "good humour with whatever [the author] offers to our attention." By 1820, this virtue has become the keynote of the authority of the Author of Waverley, and it is an effect not just of the actual representation (the depiction of characters, marginal cultures, and so forth) but of the author implied in the narrative act. The critics responded with special warmth to what John Farrell has called the "sense of fellowship" that

20. Scott, "Author of the Scotch Novels," 12.
21. Ibid.

marks Scott's authorial presence.[22] So Gold's *London Magazine* draws particular attention to the "trait of sociality that endears him [the Author of Waverley] to us all," casting the author as a genial host who enters "cordially" into the feelings of his characters, "shakes hands with them as his oldest and best acquaintances," and then "seats himself down with his companions in the evening." He does not "disgust with egotism, or a vain display of superiority"; in fact, he is like Shakespeare himself in his receptivity and humanity: "This was the disposition of our Shakespeare; he was flesh and blood like ourselves."[23] When the reviews invoke Shakespeare, they generally do so (as here) in order to signal the special power that derives from a generous imagination and absence of personal pretension. "Of all men who have ever written, excepting Shakspeare [sic]," comments the *New Monthly Magazine*, "he has perhaps the least of exclusiveness, the least of those feelings which keep men apart from their kind."[24] And John Scott offers a similar formulation when he remarks: "More than any other writer, except Shakspeare [sic], and not less than Shakspeare himself, he renders the reading of his works encouraging to human nature."[25] John Scott goes on to elaborate the comparison at some length, careful to maintain the priority of Shakespeare but ready to claim for the Author of Waverley a similar loss of self and "universal" sympathy.

In activating rather than denying the social virtues, Waverley reading distinguishes itself from both Byronic and female reading, producing a different trajectory of reading from either of the competing modes. Where the latter encourage isolation and so duplicate the malady of modernity by further weakening social ties, Waverley reading strengthens the bonds of human sympathy by virtue of the "cordial spirit" and "social sympathy" it encourages. Herein lies the source of Scott's manly

22. *Revolution as Tragedy: The Dilemma of the Moderate From Scott to Arnold* (Ithaca: Cornell University Press, 1980) 286. Farrell rightly argues that the empowerment of Scott as an author largely depended on this "sense of fellowship."
23. "On the Living Novelists," Gold's *LM* 2 (1820): 268.
24. "On the Living Novelists," *NMM* 13 (1820): 543.
25. Scott, "Author of the Scotch Novels," 12.

power. At the same time, however, he is linked as the Author of Waverley to magic, passion, fertility, and sensibility in ways that align him (as they do Byron in a different way) with female signs.[26] His "marvellous fertility"[27] affiliates him with maternity as well as paternity. If Jeffrey turns him into paternal founder of "a new school of invention" in the *Edinburgh Review*, the *Monthly Review* playfully protests "the prolific rapidity with which he increases his intellectual family." Hardly had he finished his review of *Ivanhoe*, the reviewer complains, when "another romance burst into life, glowing with the ruddy freshness and stamped with the vigorous features of the same parentage. It should seem, also that the press is by this time teeming with another birth."[28] Literalizing a stock metaphor, the reviewer turns the act of writing (or, more strictly, publishing) into parturition, the author into a mother who is also a father, giving birth to a male child whose "ruddy freshness" mimics his own.

Similar migrations of gender occur in most attempts to define the power of the Author of Waverley. So the reviews typically draw on the female connotations of "charm," "bewitchment," and "witchcraft" to indicate the unusual force of his fiction even as they also deploy male images of wizardry, empire, and conquest. Such overlap, of course, helped make the case for the Waverley Novels as "broad" and "universal," defining them through the code of gender (as they are more explicitly defined through the code of genre) as generous and inclusive. Both codes are at work, for example, in John Scott's statement that the novels are "valuable as history and descriptive travels for the qualities which render these valuable; while they derive a bewitching animation from the soul of poetry, and captivate the attention by the interest of romantic story."[29] His response to the "valuable" genres of history and travel, we notice, is perfunctory, but the fictional genres of poetry and romantic story

---

26. On Byron and femininity, see Sonia Hofkosh, "The Writer's Ravishment: Women and the Romantic Author—the Example of Byron," in *Romanticism and Feminism*, ed. Anne K. Mellor (Bloomington: Indiana University Press, 1988), 93–114.

27. Review of *Ivanhoe*, EMR 3 (1820): 163.

28. Review of *Monastery*, MR, n.s., 91 (1820): 404.

29. Scott, "Author of the Scotch Novels," 16.

prompt the interested and sensuous language of captivation and bewitchment. Making a similar point about the synthesis offered by the Waverley mode, Gold's *London Magazine* commends their "peculiar quality, of blending romance with reason, and the most exquisite sensibility with the most scrupulous judgment." As with John Scott, the romance side of the synthesis assumes priority, underlining the degree to which the Waverley mode recuperated for male readers the poles of feeling and emotion signaled by "exquisite sensibility." "A man does not like to be made a fool of without sufficient cause," Gold's reviewer remarks at one point; "give him reason for his sensibilities; set them to work on a prudent foundation, and the desired effect will be produced." If, for a male reader, sensibility is not possible without reason, reason and prudence still stand in the *service* of sensibility and folly: a man is simply waiting to have a reason for his sensibilities. The pull of romance is especially clear when the reviewer goes on to discuss a passage featuring the "wild visionary character" of Meg Merrilies. Summing up, he argues that the passage "shows the power of the novelist over the most delicious feelings of our nature; and proves that, even in the midst of horror and romance, his presence of mind and judicious confidence can always restore to us the pleasant feelings of our reason."[30] While the syntax may affirm the power of reason, the language ("delicious feelings" versus "pleasant feelings") places romance in the semantic foreground.

As it is constructed in the reviews, then, the trope of Waverley reading turns out to be a positive, male-inflected form of the well-established negative trope of female reading. Absorbed, repetitive, and escapist, Waverley reading validates romance by giving it a different gender and taking it to a different end. But the journey is much the same as in female romance, so that, in validating romance, the manly and healthy Author of Waverley partakes oddly of that which his fictions were credited with expelling. Even as the Waverley Novels remained distinctly masculine, they incorporated a kind of power typically encoded as female, and this means that the literary sign of the Author of

30. "On the Living Novelists," Gold's *LM* 2 (1820): 265–67.

Waverley occupied a potentially ambiguous discursive space. Standing opposed to female reading, it was largely constructed in its terms, recoding its categories and motifs. But revalorized categories and motifs are potentially reversible, and this reversal is precisely what begins to occur in Thomas Carlyle's landmark essay on Scott for the *London and Westminster Review* in 1838, an essay that set in place the terms in which Scott's critical decline later in the century (and virtual erasure in our own) would be registered.[31]

Carlyle learned a great deal from the Waverley Novels, not least from *Ivanhoe*,[32] but his troubled and apocalyptic imagination was profoundly incompatible with that of Walter Scott. In his own memorable phrase, he could find "no healing" in the fictions of the worldly historical novelist (76). It is questionable, of course, whether Carlyle could have found healing in any novelist, given his frequently expressed objections to the genre, but the fictions of Scott were particularly disquieting, for their enormous popularity and influence stood for Carlyle as a vivid sign of cultural decay. To be sure, Carlyle draws on and promulgates the standard image of the healthy and manly Author of Waverley that he inherited from the early reviewers. Carlyle's essay, in fact, was largely responsible for the regular Victorian insistence on Scott's healthiness,[33] and it deploys the motif of health with the extravagance typical of Carlyle's prose: "healthy in body, healthy in soul; we will call him one of the *healthiest* of men" (38). The products of such a man are themselves healthy, and Carlyle's description of the novels activates the entire Waverley matrix established by the reviews: "a free flow of narrative," "easy masterlike coherence," "genial sunshiny freshness," "glowing brightness." Carlyle sums up: "In joyous picturesqueness and fellow-feeling, freedom of eye and heart; or to say it in a word, in general *healthiness* of mind, these Novels prove Scott to have been amongst the foremost writers" (74). But health is not a first-order quality for Carlyle. "The healthy

31. "Sir Walter Scott," *Critical and Miscellaneous Essays*, 5 vols. (London: Chapman and Hall, 1899), 4:22–87. Further references are to this edition and will appear in the text.

32. On Carlyle and Scott, see Wilt, *Secret Leaves*, 9–10.

33. See Hillhouse, *Waverly Novels and Their Critics*, 217.

man is the most meritorious product of Nature," he declares but immediately adds, "so far as he goes." And that is not very far. Carlyle awards health to Scott as a consolation prize after having denied him the quality of greatness because of an absence of soul: "His life was worldly; his ambitions were worldly. There is nothing spiritual in him; all is economical, material, of the earth earthy" (35). Material and earthy, Scott can only intensify the disease of modernity, and in making his case Carlyle himself intensifies the male/female binaries of earlier critics as he splits apart the critical synthesis that had allowed the Author of Waverley to function across (but not outside) gender.

In Carlyle, the Waverley romance (offering "vigorous whole-life" in an age of "stinted half-life") becomes more clearly a phallic fantasy: "The reader was carried back to rough strong times, wherein those maladies of ours had not yet arisen. Brawny fighters, all cased in buff and iron, their hearts too sheathed in oak and triple brass, caprioled their huge war-horses, shook their death-doing spears; and went forth in the most determined manner nothing doubting" (56). Rather like the "high-colored" Sydney Morgan (though in a different direction), Carlyle strains the English language and pushes received images to the point of parody. Here is the gigantism of Hollywood technicolor—huge men, huge horses, huge spears.

But if the masculine content of the fiction is highlighted, the imaginative transport and absorption that marked Waverley reading from the outset begin to resume their female signification: "The reader, what the vast majority of readers so long to do, was allowed to lie down at his ease and be ministered to" (57). Comparing such reading to having a Turkish massage, Carlyle translates Waverley reading into female reading, replacing the active body of male reading with the languorous, erotic body characteristic of the female trope: "What the Turkish bathkeeper is said to aim at with his frictions, and shampooings, and fomentings, more or less effectually, that the patient in total idleness may have the delights of activity,—was here to a considerable extent realised" (57). Like female readers, the reader of the Waverley Novels is represented as possessing a "languid imagination" and as peculiarly attached to sofas. But the gender, if not the posture, of this reader has changed.

Carlyle invokes "indolent languid men" (73) as the practitioners of this debilitating reading, and his rhetoric (in contrast to that of the first reviewers) has no room for a female subject. The scene of reading is now exclusively male, pointing to the hardening of gender boundaries even as its homoerotic undertones testify to the anxiety over gender generated by that very hardening. In Carlyle the battle is over male reading and writing. And here the Waverley Novels—as both writing and reading—stand for the shallowness, effeminacy, and mechanization that have overtaken men in these sorry times.

In constructing his case, Carlyle manipulates the standard critical binaries (surface/depth, high/low, inside/outside) to re-inflect the Waverley motifs established by his predecessors. He invokes the routine comparison with Shakespeare, for instance, only to emphasize a crucial difference: "Equally unconscious these two utterances: equally the sincere complete products of the minds they came from: and now if they were equally *deep*? Or, if the one was living fire, and the other was futile phosphorescence and mere resinous firework?" (55). The "deep" utterance of Shakespeare contrasts with the superficial saying of Scott, his "living fire" with the fiery illusions of the Waverley Novels. To reinforce the point, Carlyle deploys another version of the same binary: "your Shakspeare [sic] fashions his characters from the heart outwards; your Scott fashions them from the skin inwards, never getting near the heart of them!" (75).[34] The problem with the Waverley Novels, he concludes, is that "they do not found themselves on deep interests, but on comparatively trivial ones; not on the perennial, perhaps not even on the lasting" (76). So he mocks Lockhart's biography of Scott for dwelling on "his *Abbots*, *Pirates*, and hasty theatrical scene-paintings; affectionately analysing them, as if they were Raphael-pictures, time-defying *Hamlets*, *Othellos*" (32–33).

Thus placed under the signs of temporality and triviality that governed the trope of female reading, the motifs constructing the Author of Waverley (such as proliferation and prolixity) return to their original coding of transience and commercialism. Scott's productivity becomes a special concern of Carlyle's es-

34. Hazlitt's reservations about the Scott-Shakespeare comparison are also typically articulated in terms of depth/surface. See his "Sir Walter Scott, Racine, and Shakespear [sic]," in *Complete Works*, 12:336–46.

say, but as a sign of debasement. Having announced that he will say just a "word" on the matter, Carlyle continues for several pages to discuss what he calls "the extempore style of writing" or "ready-writing." While granting that Scott's facility points in some sense to his "solid health," Carlyle reads it more fully and prominently as an index of the transformation of the organic into the mechanical that he everywhere deplores. Ready writing links up with ready reading as a mark of cultural decay, and it identifies the healthy Scott as diseased after all. The "infection" appears most markedly in Scott's obsession with building Abbotsford as family seat. It is not only that the goal is worldly and mean but that it compromises Scott's work as a writer, turning it into "manufacture" as opposed to "creation." Setting up a "Novel-manufactory," the novelist becomes a machine, "writing daily with the ardour of a steam-engine, that he might make 15,000*l.* a-year, and buy upholstery with it" (73). For Carlyle, Scott's career finally amounts simply to "writing impromptu novels to buy farms with" (83).

Scott himself encouraged such a reading, claiming in various Waverley frames and prefaces to be engaged in nothing more than making a living, exploiting the market, doing business, and so forth. So the introductory epistle to *The Fortunes of Nigel* (1822) argues that authorship is just as productive (pace Adam Smith) as "any other manufacture" (*Wav. Nov.*, 14:20); and the comic introduction to *The Betrothed* (1825) presents itself as the minutes of a shareholders' meeting of various Waverley characters and narrators, who plan to form a joint-stock company to write the novels. As Kathryn Sutherland has noted, Scott's prefaces as a whole form "an economics of the imagination," and their deliberate puncturing of the literary sphere and flaunting of the servile sphere of commerce have various and intriguing implications for the constitution of such an "economics" in early nineteenth-century Europe.[35] But Carlyle vehemently refuses to allow any such mingling of spheres and insists on keeping "Lit-

---

35. "Fictional Economies: Adam Smith, Walter Scott and the Nineteenth-Century Novel," *ELH* 54 (1987): 106. One of Sutherland's most interesting points is that Scott's fictional storytellers represent a peculiar combination of "an earlier, oral culture" and "the new fiction industry" (104), and her observation recalls Harry Levin's pithy remark on Scott: "His was a dual role: the last minstrel and the first best-seller" (*The Gates of Horn: A Study of Five French Realists* [New York: Oxford University Press, 1963], 45).

erature" firmly apart from "Book-publishing and Book-selling." Conjuring up a bizarre comic apocalypse ("the genius of Extempore . . . advancing on us like ocean-tides, like Noah's deluges—of ditchwater!"), Carlyle assures his reader that there is really no need to fear, for "it is not Literature they are swimming away; it is only Book-publishing and Book-selling" (82).

Carlyle reaccentuates (to use Bakhtin's term) the inherited sign of the Author of Waverley. His criticisms of Scott and the novels had been made before—the charge of commercialism in particular—but Carlyle's essay redefined the entire sign, splitting it into a secondary positive value (health) and a primary negative value (manufacture). Dislodging Scott from his position as Genius and Great Author, Carlyle moved him into the category of unserious writing, dismissing his narratives as in effect a form of female reading. What they were not, for all their lack of depth, was a form of feminine writing. Scott may not have risen "high" for Carlyle, but he was always *"broad"* (35). This is a point worth stressing, for the manliness of Scott's fiction depended centrally on its difference from the proper novel.

In a peculiar way, it was not so much blowsy female romance that threatened the masculinity—and hence literariness—of early nineteenth-century fiction as the contained feminine novel of domestic virtue. In the triangulation of the novelistic field effected by the Waverley Novels (female romance, feminine novel, manly historical fiction), it was the rational form of the proper novel with its valorization of the space of domesticity and "modern civilization" that was placed in definitive opposition to Scott's historical mode, even as his historical mode (in its healthy manliness) performed much of the same work as that of prudent feminine novelists. Certainly, Scott's first critics were eager to separate him from the proper novel, and his failure in the representation of domestic and genteel life ("well-bred" men and women) rapidly became a critical commonplace. Jeffrey, we recall, identified as Scott's chief weakness "his descriptions of virtuous young ladies—and his representations of the ordinary business of courtship and conversation in polished life."[36] Scott himself agreed, as in his often-quoted distinction

---

36. Review of *Tales of My Landlord*, ER 28 (1817): 197.

between himself and Jane Austen: "The big Bow-wow strain I can do myself like any now going, but the exquisite touch which renders ordinary commonplace things and characters interesting from the truth of the description and sentiment is denied to me."[37]

The province of "the exquisite touch" was a feminine province, and the novel's historical alliance as a genre with the details of everyday language and ordinary time placed it (in contrast to a genre like epic) within the feminine sphere. So when Scott embarked on his one attempt at the contemporary novel of manners in *St. Ronan's Well* (1824), he was highly conscious of entering a field shaped by women. His 1832 introduction to the novel calls off an honor roll of those who had "distinguished" themselves in this branch of novel writing: Burney, Edgeworth, Austen, Charlotte Smith, and Susan Ferrier (the writer to whom Scott had handed over his task in the postscript to *A Legend of Montrose* when he had prematurely announced his retirement). The point is not that Walter Scott was a proto-feminist—he was very much a benevolent tory patriarch—but that as a novelist he recognized and acknowledged the femininity of the field he entered. He also, of course, set his "Bow-wow strain" (no matter how self-deprecatingly) carefully apart from it.

What all this underscores is that in the early decades of the nineteenth century, the anxiety of influence for a male novelist was inevitably shaped by gender. Scott observes in his essay on Charlotte Smith that "within our time of novel-reading," a large number of talented women had marked the field, and once again (in the fashion of canon makers and bardic singers) he records names: Burney, Edgeworth, Opie, Austen, Radcliffe, Clara Reeves, Inchbald, and Mary Shelley.[38] It would be impossible, he adds, to find the same number of "masculine competitors" who arose "within the same space of time," and he concludes by speculating (inconclusively) about the causes for this imbalance of gender in the genre. It might be "mere chance" or

37. *Journal of Sir Walter Scott*, ed. W. E. K. Anderson (Oxford: Clarendon, 1972), 114.

38. *Sir Walter Scott on Novelists and Fiction*, ed. Ioan Williams (New York: Barnes and Noble, 1968), 190. The essay on Smith was written for *Ballantyne's Library* but did not in fact appear in it. It was first published in 1827 in Scott's *Miscellaneous Prose Works*.

perhaps the fact that "the less marked and more evanescent shades of modern society are more happily painted by the finer pencil of a woman." Then again it could be that "our modern delicacy, having excluded the bold and sometimes coarse delineations permitted to ancient novelists, has rendered competition more easy to female novelists." Whatever the case, Scott decides, this is "a subject which would lead us far, and which, therefore, it is not our present purpose to enter into."[39]

Enabled by "modern society" and "modern delicacy," the novel seems peculiarly hospitable to femininity and inhospitable to "masculine competitors." Underlying Scott's comment, as it underlies critical discourse in general in the early decades of the century (see Chapter 1), is a fundamental anxiety about modernity. The contemporary feminine novel sharpened apprehension of an attenuation of energy and imagination and of an absorption into mere temporality, and it gave to such apprehensions the particular edge of gender by placing in the foreground the increasing power of femininity vis-à-vis culture.[40] In different ways, Scott's historical novel spoke to that anxiety, and its success and authority for its first readers hinged on a certain refusal of (as well as complicity with) modernity. Hazlitt saw in *St. Ronan's Well* evidence of the diminishment suffered by Scott when he left "his fastnesses in traditional barbarism and native rusticity." Once out of his "fastnesses," Scott becomes vulnerable to the disease of modernity: "the level, the littleness, the frippery of modern civilization will undo him as it has undone us!"[41] Rooted in the "barbarism" and "rusticity" of romance, the Waverley Novels may risk dismissal from the literary sphere, but their narrative remains outside the contamination of the "littleness" and "frippery" of the modern civilization that supports the proper novel.

When he assessed Walter Scott for the English Men of Letters series in 1878, Richard H. Hutton returned to the motif of Scott's

---

39. *Scott on Novelists and Fiction*, 190.

40. There has been a great deal of recent interest in the question of culture and feminization in this period. See, for example, Nancy Armstrong's *Desire and Domestic Fiction: A Political History of the Novel* (New York: Oxford University Press, 1987) and the essays collected by Mellor in *Romanticism and Feminism*.

41. Hazlitt, "Sir Walter Scott," in *Complete Works*, 11:62.

unfitness for the domestic novel. He too drew on *St. Ronan's Well* to make his point, deploying the now standard line that its failure was the result of Scott's discomfort in "the narrower region" of the domestic novel and that Scott needed "a certain largeness of type, a strongly-marked class-life, and . . . a free, out-of-doors life, for his delineations."[42] As he makes his case for the superiority of Scott's type of novel, Hutton usefully recapitulates the debate that had established the authority of the Author of Waverley earlier in the century: "The domestic novel, when really of the highest kind, is no doubt a perfect work of art, and an unfailing source of amusement; but it has nothing of the tonic influence, the large instructiveness, the stimulating intellectual air, of Scott's historic tales. Even when Scott is farthest from reality . . . he makes you open your eyes to all sorts of historical conditions to which you would otherwise be blind. The domestic novel, even when its art is perfect, gives little but pleasure at the best; at the worst it is simply scandal idealized."[43] As was the case for Scott's first official readers, the value of the Waverley Novels for Hutton stands in direct opposition to that of the domestic novel, and his rhetoric of evaluation remains the same: "tonic," "large," "stimulating," "intellectual." The domestic novel is now less didactic and more artful (Austen, not Edgeworth, is its sign here), but Hutton admits it to art as technique ("no doubt a perfect work of art") only to exclude it from art as truth ("gives little but pleasure at the best").[44] And he keeps for Scott's historical fiction, as did the early critics, the power to "open" for readers "all sorts of historical conditions." That power to "open" not simply the fictional but the historical field stood strangely allied to the female genre of romance and in opposition to the rational, modern genre of the feminine novel.

At a crucial period in the formation of the modern literary

42. *Sir Walter Scott* (New York, 1878), 103.
43. Ibid., 104.
44. In her analysis of American response to the domestic novel later in the century, Nina Baym observes that the domestic novel was "both advanced as better than, and patronized as feebler than, other sorts of fiction—precisely as women were better and yet weaker than the other sort of human being: men" (*Novels, Readers, and Reviewers* [Ithaca: Cornell University Press, 1984], 207).

field, the Waverley Novels effected a remarkable synthesis of marginal and mainstream narrative forms that helped move the the novel as a genre into the literary field. At the heart of that synthesis stood an alliance with romance from which derived Scott's impact on the nineteenth-century discourses of both history and the novel. But the synthesis soon collapsed, and the proper novel and the domestic sphere, as Nancy Armstrong has been reminding us, achieved generic dominance after all.[45] Standing in peripheral relationship to the strong realist tradition of English fiction, the Waverley Novels are at once central to its history and anomalous within it. In their own day, their transformation of romance propelled them into the literary circle, but that transformation was also precisely what, in a later day, expelled them from it.

45. See Armstrong, *Desire and Domestic Fiction*.

Index

Library of Congress Cataloging-in-Publication Data

Ferris, Ina.
    The achievement of literary authority: gender, history, and the
Waverley novels / Ina Ferris.
        p.   cm.
    Includes bibliographical references and index.
    ISBN 0-8014-2630-8
    1. Scott, Walter, Sir, 1771–1832.   Waverley novels.   2. Scott,
Walter, Sir, 1771–1832—Criticism and interpretation—History.
3. Historical fiction—History and criticism—Theory,
etc.   4. Authorship—Sex differences.   5. Authority in
literature.   6. Scotland in literature.   I. Title.
    PR5341.F47   1991
823'.7—dc20   91-55076